BCS24K

AN AMERICAN
CRUSADE

AN AMERICAN
CRUSADE

The Life of Charles Waddell Chesnutt

Frances Richardson Keller

Brigham Young University Press

Library of Congress Cataloging in Publication Data

Keller, Frances Richardson, 1917–
　An American crusade.

　Includes bibliographical references and index.
　1. Chesnutt, Charles Waddell, 1858–1932–Biography. 2.
Novelists, American–19th century–Biography. I. Title.
PS1292.C6Z75　　813'.4 [B]　　77–14608
ISBN 0–8424–0837–6

o my husband
William P. Rhetta

For who knows yet whether our civilization has yet more than cut its milk teeth, or humanity has even really begun to walk erect?"

—Charles Waddell Chesnutt

CONTENTS

PREFACE
AND
ACKNOWLEDGMENTS

*I*n the year 1858—a little more than a hundred years ago and about three years before the Civil War—a light-skinned child was born to free Negro parents who had migrated north to Cleveland. His name was Charles Waddell Chesnutt; he lived through seventy-four years of American experience.

Certain choices were possible to him: whether to live as a white person, for he appeared white; whether to remain in North Carolina where at twenty he found himself married and teaching school; whether to chance a novel-writing career; how to engage his strength with problems of racial caste.

Chesnutt related these choices to his desire to champion black people. He saw a fault at the core of the American Republic: the Constitution guaranteed equal rights, but the culture had held many black people in slavery; from blacks and from others it still withheld equal opportunities. Yet Chesnutt knew there were those of all races and of all conditions who thought society ought to be open.

He knew that from the beginning American black people had differed on how to achieve equality. The young, irrepressible David Walker appealed to blacks to resist oppression to the death. Martin Delany, a physician, a writer, and a military officer, thought black people should return to Africa. The prosperous merchant James Forten wanted to employ pressure-group methods of the democratic state. Booker T. Washington thought Negroes should stay apart and build for the future, even though they must accept an inferior position for the present. W. E. B. DuBois thought Negroes should demand higher education and should insist at all times on all rights.

Charles Waddell Chesnutt first thought of achieving through literature a climate in which equality could exist. Though he failed, he dedicated his life to finding the way to succeed. He opposed some ideas of the black leaders; he supported others. He came to think, however, that none of their proposals would solve black problems or white problems, and that none of them would solve the color conflicts of American culture. Chesnutt discovered a distant resolution.

I cannot measure my appreciation of the generosity of Professor John Hope Franklin, Professor Joan M. Todd, and Professor Arthur Mann. They encouraged me by reading my manuscript and giving me the benefits of their scholarship, their literary judgment, and their experience. Whatever merits the book has are due to my efforts to meet the standards they set.

Other colleagues and friends read parts of the work. I am especially grateful for the suggestions of Professor Irma Eichhorn, William Walton Keller II, Julia Powell Keller, and C. Reynolds Keller, Jr.

Many people assisted me in gathering information. I am indebted to Ellen Holland Keller, whose persistence and insights enriched the Cleveland sections. James Garcia provided important New York information; W. L. Andrews supplied many genealogical materials. In his inimitable fashion Stephen B. R. Keller provided valuable leads. M. Sauzedde, Mayor of Thiers, France, provided an important source book. Rowena and Russell Jelliffe supplied recollections that broadened the study, as did Russell W. Davis. Charles L. Blockson and Helen G. Cornwell shared letters and memorabilia I could have seen in no other way.

The efforts of many librarians are represented in this book; I sincerely appreciate their letters in answer to my questions and the other help they gave me. I appreciate also the assistance and the hospitality of the staff of Fisk University. I am especially grateful for the skillful guidance of Virginia Hawley, Curator of Collections of the Western Reserve Historical Society.

I was fortunate that I was able to persuade Grace O'Connell, expert grammarian and authority on documentation, to work with me. Twice she typed my manuscript, contributing each time most generously of her expertise.

For the assistance of all these people I extend my thanks.

AN AMERICAN
CRUSADE

PHOTOGRAPHS

Charles Chesnutt and his brother Lewis in 1865. (Charles is at the left.)
Taken in Cleveland before the family moved to North Carolina.

Charles Chesnutt at sixteen, just beginning his teaching career.

Charles Waddell Chesnutt at twenty-five, principal of the training school for teachers in Fayetteville, North Carolina.

5

The Howard School in Fayetteville, North Carolina, a training school for Negro teachers, was started on the second floor of this building in about 1879. Charles Chesnutt was a pupil-teacher; later he became principal.

Charles Chesnutt's children in 1888: Ethel, Edwin, and Helen.

Charles Chesnutt in his early middle years.

9719 Lamont Avenue, Cleveland, where Charles Chesnutt lived the last twenty-eight years of his life. The house had fourteen rooms and was situated on a lot 300 feet deep by 70 feet wide. The family moved out in 1936, and the house was torn down when Charles Orr School was built.

Chesnutt's library in the house at 9719 Lamont Avenue. The family moved to this address in May, 1904. Chesnutt died there in 1932.

12

Charles Waddell Chesnutt in his later years.

Chesnutt's wife, Susan—after Chesnutt's death.

AN AMERICAN
CRUSADE

PROLOGUE: AS IT MAY HAVE HAPPENED

So orderly and of such import were the exercises in the clapboard school building on the twenty-fifth day of June, 1883, that parents and friends could scarcely forbear whispering to one another. Dr. T. D. Haigh, chairman of the board of trustees of the Fayetteville Colored Normal School; J. D. Williams, board member and president of the Fayetteville National Bank; and board member W. C. Troy took places at the front of the room beside the perpendicular American flag with the yellow cord and tassels. The Negro preacher Elder Davis joined them, seating himself on the other side of the room at the end of a table where stood a pitcher of water, a Bible, a basket of fresh-cut red roses, and diplomas neatly rolled and tied with ribbons of blue and gold. The young principal, Charles Waddell Chesnutt, took the seat nearest the speaker's stand.

In a long-sleeved, high-necked blouse of cotton-lawn and a rustling black skirt, the pianist entered. She placed her music on the rack and settled herself. At a nod from the principal she began to strike the opening chords of "Pomp and Circumstance." Walking by twos, cleanly dressed and solemn, the ten graduates came down the aisle.

Charles Chesnutt surveyed them. Some members of this class were his relatives. He felt a sharp awareness of the differences in the color of their skin. Glancing about the room, he saw his pregnant wife Susan, with their small daughters Ethel and Helen. There at the end of one of the front rows, partially hidden behind another basket of flowers, his little sister Lilly sat, with Lewis and Andrew, his brothers. Chesnutt's father Andrew folded his arms. His father's second wife, "Cousin Mary," smiled a small, resigned smile. Chesnutt saw some of the family of his predecessor Robert Harris and some of the Bryants. He noticed that William Cade had come. There was his Uncle Dallas Chesnutt, and

19

there was the white bookseller George Haigh, who stood at the back with his hands in his pockets. There was Chesnutt's darker-skinned cousin, John P. Green, a Cleveland lawyer paying a visit home. There was Professor Neufelt, the conscionable teacher of ancient and modern languages, the only good teacher in Fayetteville who "would teach a nigger." And as Elder Davis rose and lifted his arms to deliver the Invocation, Chesnutt caught sight of two white friends, A. H. Slocomb and E. J. Lilly, who had stopped at the Normal School for this occasion. It was the last time Charles Chesnutt would preside over the graduation ceremonies.

Chesnutt knew that he must go. But when the singers began their selection, he felt a surge of intense loyalty toward the school. It had become the foundation of an educational future for the Negroes of North Carolina. For this he had done yeoman service as teacher and principal. He wanted the school to progress, to endure. Who knew better than he the difference an educational institution could make? And who had felt more poignantly the stings of racial prohibitions? Though he appeared white, the customs of the South increasingly forbade interracial association, especially among people of similar tastes and accomplishments. The whole community seemed to be sinking to the level of John McLaughlin, a poor white clerk in Williams' store. Chesnutt bitterly remembered McLaughlin's words: "With me, a nigger is a nigger, and nothing in the world can make him anything else but a nigger."

Yes, Chesnutt knew that he must go, whatever the objections of his family and his friends. Though he had achieved as prestigious a position as a person of Afro-American descent could occupy in Fayetteville, things would "never, never, never" change. So it was up to him. He would go to the North, to a great city. He would ask no favors. He would expect no help. As Chesnutt listened to the graduation speakers, he grew firmer in purpose. He must go. He would "work, work, work!" He would live somehow by the skills he had mastered. He would achieve such excellence as to shatter the barriers of color and caste. He would do all this for himself and for his children; but most importantly, he would do it for his Negro people.

It was time to present the diplomas. Chesnutt called the name of each graduate. Just before the program closed, a student stepped again to the speaker's stand. Hesitantly she offered Chesnutt an album in which every member of the class had written some lines of appreciation. As he took the album from her hands, Chesnutt experienced a fulness of devotion to his people "at the South." Among them he had lived and learned and grown. He knew their needs. He understood their ruling passions. He felt a sharp sadness of parting, for he knew he could never come back to Fayetteville to live. As he bade the graduates godspeed and farewell, Chesnutt knew he would carry to the North an abiding concern for their welfare. He would carry the determination to harness his talents in their behalf.

Through the rest of his life, Charles Chesnutt would muse on the dim origins of the racial perplexities of his native land. He would think of Fayetteville, of his parents, his grandparents, his great-grandparents. He would think about the conditions that shaped the possibilities of their lives.

AN AMERICAN CRUSADE

1

FAYETTEVILLE: A POINT OF VIEW

From "Freedom" to 1856

Slowly the Cape Fear River wound its ancient way. It flowed from the hills, through the fields, the swamps, the forests, some sixty miles to the south-southeast, past Lillington, and on to a town at the head of the steamboat navigation.[1] Like other North Carolina towns, Fayetteville stood in corn and cotton-growing lands; but from the woods and the river arose as well a trade in turpentine and lumber. The town was small. Still, long before Charles Waddell Chesnutt presided over a final graduation ceremony in 1883, Fayetteville was a leading center of North Carolina. Among the inhabitants in 1850 were a few less than 3,000 white people, a few more than 1,500 slaves, and 465 free Negroes.[2] Among those 465 free Negroes were two young adults so discontented that they were planning to leave. Anne Maria Sampson intended to move with her mother to Cleveland; Andrew Jackson Chesnutt was heading north toward Indiana.

Their son Charles Waddell Chesnutt was born in the city of Cleveland in 1858. He became a writer—a story teller, a novelist, an essayist, a social historian, and an observer of his times. He became a champion of his race, a prophet of the twentieth century, a pioneer of a brilliant school of American letters, an advocate of militant, even radical solutions to the race problems of the United States. He spent most of that active life in Cleveland, the city of his birth. But he endeavored "to de-

---

1. Leon E. Seltzer, ed., *The Columbia Lippincott Gazetteer of the World* (Morningside Heights, N.Y.: Columbia University Press, by arrangement with J. B. Lippincott Co., 1952), pp. 327, 1054.

2. U.S. Census, *Population of North Carolina for 1860*, pp. 350-59.

scribe faithfully" Fayetteville and the North Carolina countryside, where he returned with his parents to live after the Civil War. He was then nine years old. There, in his words, he spent "the most impressionable years" of his life.

Fayetteville was not unusual as southern towns went in the 1850s. It was, in fact, profoundly human: it was a microcosm of other societies in which the strong took advantage of the less favored.[3] Over the years they assigned places. They made laws, they enlisted religion, they invented myths. Sometimes they used proscription; sometimes they misused knowledge; they regulated marriage. They installed these controls— if not by decree, then gradually, by practice. Though few could recall how the walls arose, most residents lived with restrictions on opportunities, on education, on labor, on social intercourse, and finally on thought.

The people of Fayetteville had thus lived together in long and profound disquietude, though most of the white people defended the slave society, and most of the darker people endured servitude. In these respects Fayetteville reflected the immemorial realities of American life.

To some white citizens life was orderly: they lived in respectable houses, somewhat set back, perhaps, from a pavement of brick, and they earned a way. To other white people, who might have served in a warehouse, a shop, a barrel or candle factory—or bored the trees for turpentine—Fayetteville offered an occupation and a wage of a sort. To those few residents who lived in houses on "The Hill," life was comfortable, the future assured. But to many more white people, who lived nearby on the land, poverty was paramount, and hunger was common. Still, to all the white residents, Negro slavery appeared to be, as one supporter characterized it, the "modus vivendi through which social life was possible."[4]

To slaves who lived in the quarters and who knew what it was "ter hab a oberseah dribin'... fum one day's een' ter de udder," life was hard. To other slaves who lived in the master's house, life was somewhat more bearable, though nightly "paterolles" kept them in line.[5] To all slaves a cruel fate might one day be mitigated, if only in another life.

---

3. Charles Waddell Chesnutt, "Temple Course Reading" (unpublished MS, n.d.), Charles Waddell Chesnutt Collection, Erastus Milo Cravath Memorial Library, Fisk University, Nashville, Tennessee, MS 10 (hereinafter cited as CC, Fisk).

4. William A. Dunning, "The Undoing of Reconstruction," *Atlantic Monthly* 88 (1901), 449.

5. Charles Waddell Chesnutt, "Hot Foot Hannibal," in *The Conjure Woman* (Boston: Houghton Mifflin, 1899), pp. 109, 221.

But to the few free Negroes, to Indians, and to "others," life was almost unendurable.[6] Denied most rights that white people enjoyed, free Negroes were held in disfavor. Slaves looked down upon them. White people found them a slippery, vexing problem. What if the slaves should be scheming revolt and the free Negroes should help them? To white people that possibility was more disturbing than the embarrassment they caused. Many white residents had concluded it was wise to supervise free Negroes carefully, though some were almost white. By a series of laws the North Carolina Assembly constructed a code to control them.[7] In the 1850s Anne Maria Sampson and Andrew Jackson Chesnutt dreamed of escape.

Half a century later, in 1908, their novelist-son Charles Chesnutt wrote to a correspondent. He said that he knew his "pedigree" for a hundred and fifty years: "It would make, I suspect, a somewhat ragged family tree in spots." He wrote this because he was among those Negroes who appeared white, the result of a mixed racial ancestry. He described them—and himself—in his writings; once in an unpublished novel manuscript he noted that "free people of color were often more white than black, and in many of them a constant infusion of white blood had almost wiped out the darker strain."[8] "But at any rate," he continued in the letter of 1908, "in the legal line of descent it [his ancestry] ... was always free in both sides as far as my knowledge goes."[9]

Yet, in the 1850s neither of Chesnutt's future parents felt free. In the gathering holocaust, the white people of Fayetteville had grown more anxious about the Negro population. The free Negroes of North Carolina had become a "caste within a caste." In Fayetteville they must walk an earthly purgatory. Many white people held them in contempt, though some, like the editor of the Carolina Observer, sympathized with them. In the 1830s he had regretted their disfranchisement.[10] But most white people and many slaves despised free Negroes. Though slaves were exploited, they knew that they were needed; their place was secure. But

---

6. John Hope Franklin, *The Free Negro in North Carolina, 1790-1860* (Chapel Hill: University of North Carolina Press, 1943), pp. 192-225.

7. Walter Clark, ed., *The State Records of North Carolina* (Winston, 1905).

8. Charles Waddell Chesnutt, unpublished MS for *Mandy Oxendine*. CC, Fisk, MSS. 5, 71. A date, page 19, is "Aug. 3, 188?."

9. Chesnutt to Dr. Park, Dec. 19, 1908, Charles Waddell Chesnutt Collection, Western Reserve Historical Society, Cleveland, Ohio (hereinafter cited as CC, WRHS).

10. Fayetteville *Carolina Observer*, Jan. 13, 1831.

there was a question whether white people needed free Negroes. They had reason to feel unwanted.

In the manuscript for a novel, Charles Chesnutt later described their situation: "Despised and of no account socially among white people, they in turn looked down upon the slaves and thus constituted a class apart."[11] His character Mandy is a free Negro girl who appears white and who wants to pass as a white person. From her point of view hers is the most difficult of all situations:

"I'd ruther die than to be a nigger again," she said fiercely, "to be hated by black folks because I'm too white, and despised by white folks because I'm not white enough."[12]

Yet the climate had been less hostile for some time prior to the 1850s. If, as he seemed to suggest, some of Chesnutt's ancestors were free Negro men living near Fayetteville before the American Revolution, they might have enjoyed some privileges of white people.[13] But that changed in 1785, when the General Assembly of North Carolina passed "An act to Restrain the conduct of slaves and others"—in Wilmington, Washington, Edenton, and Fayetteville. Free Negroes, mulattoes, and others of mixed blood who were not slaves must register and pay two shillings to the town clerk and eight shillings to other officials. For this, they would receive a badge of cloth, bearing the word "free." Thenceforth within those towns they were to wear that badge on the left shoulder.[14]

Ten years later in 1795[15] another law provided that if there were some reason to believe that a free Negro might be "dangerous to the peace," a jury could be "empanuled," a trial held, and "bond and security" required. If the free Negro could not provide "security," "he, she or they shall be sold." If "free people of colour" should "collect together in arms," three Justices of the Peace could call forth a "sufficient number to suppress such depredations and insurrections." If a free Negro should assist the slaves in an act of rebellion, or even promise to help,

---

11. Luther P. Jackson, *Free Negro Labor and Propertyholding in Virginia* (New York: Atheneum, 1969).

12. Chesnutt, *Mandy Oxendine,* CC, Fisk, p. 33, 41.

13. *United States First Census, 1790;* 31 free persons—not listed as whites or as slaves—lived in Fayetteville.

14. Franklin, *The Free Negro in North Carolina,* p. 60, from Clark, *State Records,* pp. 727-28.

15. During this period the Assembly met three times in Fayetteville.

the penalty was "death without benefit of clergy." Such was the climate in North Carolina in the early years of the republic.[16]

The North Carolina Assembly passed other measures of restriction before the birth of Chesnutt's father in 1833.[17] They passed an act to prevent "All persons from teaching slaves to read and write, the use of figures excepted." A free Negro who disobeyed would be "fined, imprisoned or whipped, at the discretion of the court, not exceeding thirty-nine lashes, nor less than twenty lashes." Free Negroes could not "Game" with slaves; if they did, they would be whipped, "not to exceed thirty-nine lashes on his or her bare back." They could not peddle wares outside their county of residence, unless seven justices acting together were willing to grant a license; the charge was eighty cents. A fine of fifty dollars for each offense or imprisonment for six months was the penalty for each infraction. For leaving the state and remaining ninety days away, the free "person of colour" could never return.[18] In North Carolina the free Negro was expected to carry a certificate of freedom to prevent being taken for a slave.[19] He could not serve on juries, nor could he testify against a white person. His evening activities must cease at curfew (in Fayetteville a bell rang out from the Market House at nine o'clock).[20] A free Negro could not own a gun or dog without a license, nor could he drink liquor. By the time Chesnutt's father was born in 1833, these measures so circumscribed the liberty of free Negroes that they were scarcely better off than slaves. It must have seemed to some of Chesnutt's grandparents that their lives were more precarious.

In 1835, two years after Charles Chesnutt's father was born, free Negroes lost the right to vote in North Carolina,[21] but they could still own property. Transactions were difficult; yet Chesnutt's father, Andrew Jackson Chesnutt, was fortunate to inherit a farm near Fayetteville, down the road from Person and Cook Streets.[22]

---

16. Franklin, *The Free Negro in North Carolina*, pp. 61-62.

17. Chesnutt to Mr. M. [sic] C. Newbold, May 24, 1922. CC, WRHS.

18. *Acts of the General Assembly of the State of North Carolina at its Session Commencing on the 25th of December, 1826* (Raleigh: Lawrence & Lemay, 1827), 1830, 1831, 6, Secs. 1, 2 (hereinafter cited as *Laws of North Carolina*.); 1830, 1831, 4, Secs. 1, 2; 7, Secs. 1, 2.

19. John A. Oates, *The Story of Fayetteville* (Raleigh, N.C.; The Dowd Press, 1957), p. 696.

20. Chesnutt, *The Conjure Woman* (1969), p. 3; and *The House Behind the Cedars*, p. 3.

21. *Laws of North Carolina*, 1860, 1861, p. 68; 1834, 1835, 7.

22. John W. Parker, "Chesnutt as a Southern Town Remembers Him," *The Crisis*, July, 1949, p. 206. *Records of Deeds of Cumberland County, North Carolina*, Archives of the State of North Carolina, Raleigh, N.C., 25 April, 1871, Deed No. 2; Deed No. 3.

Chesnutt's parents secured some education as they were growing up in the late 1840s and early 1850s. While no state law prohibited teaching free Negroes, Fayetteville made no provision for schools for them; the quasi-private white schools, for which North Carolinians provided sporadically, offered no welcome, though occasionally they tolerated a free Negro pupil.[23] White people disapproved of public education; they particularly disapproved of education for Negroes beyond that needed by apprentices.[24] Indeed, the Seventh Census of the United States shows that free Negro families of Cumberland County, where Fayetteville is the county seat, reported not a single child in school in 1850. In spite of this indication of community disapproval, and even though the census-taker suggested that Chesnutt's mother was illiterate at eighteen, she gave a high priority to education.[25] How Anne Maria Sampson and Andrew Jackson Chesnutt managed to get the rudiments of literacy is mysterious.[26] There was a Presbyterian day school for colored children;[27] perhaps Chesnutt's parents attended classes.[28] But whatever the means, whatever the dangers, Chesnutt's parents transmitted a thirst for knowledge to their son Charles. It stayed with him all his life.

Chesnutt's parents and other "free" Negroes had been given to understand that they were unwanted in Fayetteville. Beyond the studied indifference, beyond the neglect, the rejection, and the suspicion, they sensed a rising hostility.[29] As white people felt themselves attacked, as the system of caste accordingly hardened, life for free Negroes grew more dangerous. Each of Chesnutt's future parents felt disheartened with prospects in Fayetteville. Each felt fearful. Separately, they made arrangements. Anne Maria and her mother, Chloe, gathered their possessions and and planned with other free Negroes to go to Cleveland. Andrew Chesnutt intended to live with his uncle in Indiana; he hoped to improve his prospects. In 1856 when Andrew was twenty-three, they

---

23. Oates, Story of Fayetteville, p. 699.

24. The Weekly State Journal (Raleigh), July 24, 1861. The law excluded Negroes from public schools.

25. Seventh Census of the United States, Cumberland County, Fayetteville District, Aug. 3, 1850, Entry No. 218.

26. Groups sometimes engaged a teacher. "Subscription schools" were private.

27. Perry, "The Negro in Fayetteville," in Oates, The Story of Fayetteville, p. 699.

28. A. J. Chesnutt to John P. Green, April 18, 1871. John P. Green Collection, WRHS, Cleveland. If authentic, this unpolished letter is evidence of Andrew Chesnutt's literacy.

29. Chesnutt, "The Gray Wolf's Ha'nt," in The Conjure Woman (1899), p. 172. Chesnutt catches the studied indifference of the white community toward free Negroes.

joined an exodus; they set out from Fayetteville in a train of covered wagons.[30] As the present was barren and the future looked bleak, they felt they had little to lose.

Fayetteville and the American War

The prelude to the story of Charles Chesnutt ends as his parents-to-be left Fayetteville by wagon train. Probably they had met, but they could not foresee that they would marry, that their son Charles would be born in two more years, that a Civil War would be fought, or that they would return to Fayetteville within the decade. To those who stayed, Fayetteville remained a bastion of ancient arrangements by which some held advantage and others depended on their dominance. The little town on the Cape Fear River remained unchanged until the conflict came.

But Fayetteville felt the ravages of war. Long a center of military activities, Fayetteville boasted several soldierly organizations and an armory that had stood before the Revolution.[31] The town was also the site of a large but less historic government arsenal; now this plant had been enlarged to house machinery captured from Harper's Ferry.[32] Because Fayetteville was a stronghold of Southern loyalties, where people ardently supported the Southern cause,[33] the town became a center for Confederate activities, and the arsenal became a supply station for Confederate armies. The factories of Fayetteville labored to furnish it.[34]

But their labor was lost. In the spring of 1865 General William Tecumseh Sherman's Savannah veterans advanced through the Carolinas. In Fayetteville General Hardee's Confederate regulars and General Wade Hampton's cavalry soldiers waited to do what they could.[35] Outside the town gathered a crowd of refugees, stragglers, free Negroes,

---

30. Helen M. Chesnutt, *Charles Waddell Chesnutt, Pioneer of the Color Line.* (Chapel Hill: University of North Carolina Press, 1952), p. 2.

31. Oates, *Story of Fayetteville,* p. 243, "Why the Fayetteville Light Infantry?" Branson's *North Carolina Directory,* L. Branson, ed. (Raleigh, 1884), p. 253.

32. William T. Sherman, *Sherman's Civil War* (New York: Collier Books, 1962), p. 446. See also H. V. Boynton, *Sherman's Historical Raid: The Memoirs in the Light of the Record* (Cincinnati: Wilstach, Baldwin Co., 1875), p. 208.

33. John G. Barrett, *Sherman's March through the Carolinas* (Chapel Hill: University of North Carolina Press, 1956), p. 139; R. Yates, "Vance and the End of the War," *North Carolina Historical Review* 18 (October, 1941): 320.

34. Branson's *North Carolina Directory,* pp. 249-50. Several "Manufactories" listed in Fayetteville could have contributed supplies of war materials.

35. Sherman, *Sherman's Civil War,* pp. 445: 46.

and whole families of slaves, some in frightened disarray and some in expectant excitement.[36]

To the south of Fayetteville the rains had swollen the streams and flooded the lowlands so that Sherman's armies could advance only by laying and relaying roads of logs and brush. Henry Hitchcock of Sherman's staff wrote his wife that Sherman's armies crossed eight or nine rivers and "impassable" swamps, although strong earthworks and artillery had been thrown up. But no ardent spirit could have matched the know-how, equipment, and numbers of Sherman's forces.[37] On the eleventh of March Sherman reached Fayetteville, even though on the night of the tenth he had taken refuge in "a little church called Bethel, in the woods...from a terrible storm of rain, which poured all nights [sic], making the roads awful."

It is difficult to determine what occurred in the confusion of retreat and occupation. General Sherman did issue orders for the destruction of the arsenal.[38] Even though a former army friend of Sherman stayed to plead, Union Colonel Poe's men carried out the order. When rams had sufficiently weakened the walls so that the roof fell in, the soldiers started fires by using the ornamental woodwork. Poe's men protected the neighborhood, however; only one nearby residence suffered damage. As the firing progressed, Confederate shells that had been stored underground began to explode, so that a great din arose in the holocaust.[39] It appears that earlier in the morning the Confederates had shipped machinery and stores out of Fayetteville by rail and had managed to distribute to Hardee's fleeing soldiers a few Enfield rifles snatched from the arsenal.[40] From other accounts, pillaging and lawlessness prevailed before General Baird took command by Sherman's direction, although "very little personal violence was inflicted upon the people of Fayetteville."[41]

According to Union General O. O. Howard's account, he found a

---

36. Barrett, *Sherman's March*, p. 142; Anderson, *Confederate Arsenal*.

37. Henry Hitchcock, *Marching with Sherman: Passages from the Letters and Campaign Diaries*, M. A. DeWolfe Howe, ed. (New Haven: Yale University Press, 1927), p. 264; Boynton, *Sherman's Historical Raid*, p. 208.

38. Orders cited by Samuel Hawkins, Marshall Byers, *With Fire and Sword*: "Or. 47, Pt. 2, Ser. 1."

39. Barrett, *Sherman's March*, p. 141. Sherman turned his back on his army friend, Edward Monagan; p. 142.

40. Anderson, *Confederate Arsenal*, p. 238.

41. Barrett, *Sherman's March*, p. 142.

large quantity of cotton consumed by fires the townsmen had started.[42] When Hardee's soldiers burned the Clarendon bridge, as Sherman anticipated, they left a few men to complete the destruction. So, upon his arrival, Sherman issued Special Field Order Number 28 for the laying of pontoons for crossing the river. By other accounts, he ordered that all railroad property, all shops, factories, tanneries, and grist mills—except one water mill for the people of Fayetteville—be demolished. In spite of the burning, and regardless of who did it, Sherman wrote that Sunday, March 12, was "a day of Sabbath stillness in Fayetteville," that "the people generally attended their churches, for they were a very pious people," who "too were resting from the toils and labors of six weeks of as hard marching as ever fell to the lot of soldiers." Aside from the carrying out of his instructions about the arsenal, Sherman reported little destruction. In three days he moved along so as to allow "as little time as possible" for organization to General Joseph Johnston's army, then regrouping at Raleigh.[43]

Already Appomattox Court House, some ninety miles to the west of Richmond, Virginia, was near. Fayetteville shared the desolation of the South when Lee surrendered there. And Fayetteville lived the last despair when General Joseph Johnston gave up to Sherman just sixty miles to the north at Durham station.

Interlude

Separately, as they had laid their plans when they left town ten years before, the Chesnutts now made plans to return. But now they were married and were parents of three small sons.[44] Andrew Chesnutt had served the Union Army as a teamster.[45] Like other Negroes he hoped that the Civil War would bring the "Promised Land." But because he had experienced caste discrimination and hardship in the North, he decided to return to Fayetteville. He would take his chances there, where he could be near his ill, elderly father.

But Anne Maria thought of her girlhood in North Carolina. She remembered the cruel shrugs, the disappointments, the shattered hopes. She never believed that the iron bars would melt, even though Sherman

---

42. Oates, *Story of Fayetteville*, p. 412. In anticipation of the arrival of the Union Army, on February 28, 1865, the town council of Fayetteville passed an order for the destruction of all cotton (p. 271).

43. Sherman, *Sherman's Civil War*, p. 446.

44. The marriage license is dated July 25, 1857. CC, Fisk.

45. H. Chesnutt, *Pioneer*, p. 4. There is, however, no U.S. government record of this service.

had marched from Savannah and stopped in Fayetteville, dismantling the physical walls. She thought her children would have a better chance in Cleveland. But she had to accept her husband's decision.

Fayetteville and the Aftermath of Freedom

"Who has not seen somewhere an old town that, having long since ceased to grow, yet held its own without perceptible decline?" So Charles Chesnutt wrote of "Patesville" as he described the thoughts of a character returning after the Civil War. Some years after his novel was published, Chesnutt wrote to a childhood friend that "Patesville" was indeed Fayetteville.[46] He described the physical features. There had been "some changes, it is true, some melancholy changes, but scarcely anything by way of addition or improvement to counterbalance them." Where once handsome buildings had stood, a few blackened fragments of walls remained. Yet the red brick Market House, with its tall tower and its four-faced clock, "rose as majestically and uncompromisingly as though the land had never been subjugated." The returning visitor saw the same small weather-beaten buildings, the same shops, and a warehouse or two, the same brick pavements, the same leafy arcade of oaks and elms. He walked in a staid residential part of the town and on until, as he walked, the residences deteriorated to a row of "mean houses flush with the street." He saw garden paths, "bordered by long rows of jonquiles, pinks, and carnations, inclosing clumps of fragrant shrubs, lilies, and roses already in bloom." On "The Hill" still stood the few fine houses.[47]

The Chesnutt family was deeply concerned as problems arose and adjustments were tried. At first most white people lived in dread of anarchy. They thought that Negroes would refuse to work. They feared revenge and a great black insurrection.[48] Casting about, and frantically hoping to resurrect the controls of the slavery system, the Provisional Legislature of North Carolina wrote a Black Code: many white citizens of Fayetteville hoped that these strict laws would deal with the menace of an uprooted slave population.[49] It is true that in Fayetteville many newly freed Negroes were destitute, for they had depended on others.[50]

---

46. Chesnutt to E. J. Lilly, Oct. 16, 1916. CC, Fisk.

47. Chesnutt, *The House Behind the Cedars*, pp. 1-13; 132.

48. C. Vann Woodward, *The Strange Career of Jim Crow* (New York: Oxford University Press, 1966), p. 23.

49. Chesnutt, *The Conjure Woman* (1899), p. 85.

50. Ibid., p. 65. Chesnutt, *The Colonel's Dream* (Garden City: Doubleday, Page Co., 1905), p. 24.

34

And some may have grown desperate, for no one assisted them. But other Negroes were ready to assume responsibilities.[51] To those who had been free Negroes before the war, as indeed to many white people, the struggle to get along was an old exigency. Some, like the Chesnutts, had long studied how to make the best of troubling circumstances. Now they hoped that fairer arrangements could be made. In the first "critical year" of their return they despaired when the state Legislature enacted the Black Code; they hoped anew when the Republican Congress in Washington, acting against President Andrew Johnson, repudiated the Black Code and passed the Reconstruction Act of 1867.

Upon Andrew Jackson Chesnutt's return to Fayetteville in 1866, his father—Charles Chesnutt's grandfather—furnished money for a grocery store on Gillespie Street, between the Market House and Russell Square.[52] Probably because Jack Chesnutt (Andrew Jackson Chesnutt) extended credit too generously thereafter, the store failed.[53] Subsequently, Jack operated the farm on the Wilmington Road, and then he operated a "transfer" business.[54]

In the shifting fortunes of Reconstruction, Andrew became for the two years of Republican rule in Fayetteville (1868-1870) a Justice of the Peace of Cumberland County and a Town Commissioner.[55]

Though no law forbade it, it was difficult for free Negroes to acquire capital through their own efforts before the Civil War, and it was difficult for Negroes to do it after the War. Considering the obstacles, Charles Chesnutt's father managed adequately. And some of Chesnutt's free Negro forebears, like some others of his ancestors, felt they had a stake in the future of Fayetteville. Others sought their fortunes elsewhere.

Before the Chesnutts returned to Fayetteville, Congress had established the Freedmen's Bureau. That year, 1866, Congress broadened the Bureau's powers so that it could distribute relief, lease lands, provide medical care, and establish schools.[56] Starting many operations just as North Carolina enacted the Black Code, the Bureau came into con-

---

51. Joel Williamson, *After Slavery: The Negro in South Carolina During Reconstruction* (Chapel Hill: University of North Carolina Press, 1965), pp. 32-63.

52. H. Chesnutt, *Pioneer*, p. 4. See discussion chapter 6.

53. Probably 1872.

54. Oates, *Story of Fayetteville*, p. 711. Parker, "Chesnutt as a Southern Town Remembers Him," p. 206.

55. Oates, *Story of Fayetteville*, pp. 241-42; and H. Chesnutt, *Pioneer*, p. 5.

56. W. E. B. DuBois, "Reconstruction and Its Benefits," *American Historical Review*, 15 (July, 1910): 781-99.

flict with every accepted way of doing things in Fayetteville. Yet many Negroes and some poor white people looked to the Bureau for salvation. Others hoped it would show the way to improved conditions.

For a time Jack Chesnutt believed Fayetteville would benefit from the Bureau's influence. He understood that lack of education kept his people powerless. He wanted schools for his sons; he wanted them to escape the poverty to which ignorance would condemn them. So when he returned to Fayetteville, he was "largely instrumental" in the establishment of the first public school for Negroes; it became the Howard School.[57]

Later, in the spring of 1868, he joined three Negro ministers of Fayetteville—Robert Simmons, Thomas Lomax, and George Granger—and David Bryant, a farmer, in the purchase of a piece of property;[58] on behalf of the Negro community they bought the land for about $140.[59] They had intended to work through the American Missionary Society,[60] but they decided to transfer the property to the Freedman's Bureau Perhaps this was the only way they could induce North Carolina to sponsor a normal school for colored teachers at Fayetteville.[61] Accepting the gift, the Bureau erected a building for $3,800 and furnished it for $400. The Negro citizens of Fayetteville then raised and donated another $200.[62] After this, North Carolina appropriated $2,000 for the expenses of the first year.[63] The sum was small, so small that appeals to the northern Peabody Fund soon had to be made.[64] Still, this enterprise was a milestone in the reconstruction of North Carolina, a crucial step

---

57. Bishop James W. Hood to S. S. Ashley, Nov. 2, 1869, North Carolina Department of Archives and History, Doc. No. 6; Oates, *The Story of Fayetteville,* pp. 698-99; Parker, "Chesnutt as a Southern Town Remembers Him," p. 205.

58. J. W. Hood to S. S. Ashley, Superintendent of Public Instruction and Secretary of the Board of Education, State of North Carolina, Nov. 2, 1860, North Carolina Department of Archives and History, Doc. No. 6; Oates, *Story of Fayetteville,* p. 711.

59. James W. Hood to S. S. Ashley, Nov. 2, 1860, North Carolina Department of Archives and History, Doc. No. 6. See Oates, *Story of Fayetteville;* an article, by-line "By the College," gives a slightly different version.

60. Oates, *Story of Fayetteville,* p. 711.

61. Frenise A. Logan, *The Negro in North Carolina, 1876-1894* (Chapel Hill: University of North Carolina Press, 1964), p. 143.

62. James W. Hood to S. S. Ashley, Nov. 2, 1869.

63. Logan, *The Negro in North Carolina,* p. 143.

64. School Committee, Chairman of the Board of Examiners, and County Board of Education to Reverend B. Sears, D.D., Agent Peabody Education Fund, Aug. 19, 1875, North Carolina Department of Archives and History.

toward an educational future for Negroes. James W. Hood, a resident of Fayetteville, soon to become a bishop of the African Methodist Episcopal Zion Church,[65] noted the small appropriation, but he urged support.[66] Unlike most enterprises of Reconstruction, this school survived Bourbon "redemption"; today it stands as Fayetteville State University.

For the last three years of his residence in Fayetteville (1880-1883), Charles Waddell Chesnutt served as principal of this Normal School;[67] it was a natural succession. He and the other Chesnutt children had attended the Howard school; before the Chesnutts returned, that school had been organized by a group of Negroes—A. W. Shitvield, Hettie McNeil, M. E. Pearce, Susan Cain, and the man who became the first principal, Robert Harris.[68] Harris noticed the abilities of a boy in his classes. The encouragement and direction he gave that boy—Charles Waddell Chesnutt—proved a powerful influence in Chesnutt's life.

In the complex shifting social arrangements tried out in Fayetteville after the war, more and more people began to realize that education was far behind the needs of the new situation. Illiteracy was high in the towns and the countryside. It was by no means likely that every white child would get a common school education.[69] For the children of the former slaves and the children of the former free Negroes the prospects were slight. Charles Chesnutt experienced these conditions; except for his short four-year attendance at the Howard School, he educated himself. By the age of sixteen he was teaching in country schools. The novel he wrote about a young teacher is still unpublished, but it contains detailed descriptions. The teacher "set out for the scene of his labors during the next two months, the length of the school term provided by law for free public instruction." The character Lowery experienced the frustrations of trying to do a year's teaching in two months. The school house was:

---

65. Oates, Story of Fayetteville, p. 711; Elizabeth Balanoff, "Negro Legislators in the North Carolina General Assembly, July, 1868-February, 1872," North Carolina Historical Review, 69 (January, 1972): 36, 37.

66. Logan, The Negro in North Carolina, p. 143. Chesnutt, "Appreciation of Joseph C. Price, Orator and Educator" (unpublished MS, n.d.). CC, WRHS, p. 5.

67. Biennial Reports of the State Colored Normal School at Fayetteville, North Carolina, 1879-1880, 1880-1881, 1881-1882, 1882-1883, North Carolina Department of Archives and History, Doc. Nos. 6 and 8.

68. Logan, The Negro in North Carolina, p. 142.

69. Claude A. Nolen, The Negro's Image in the South (Lexington: University of Kentucky Press, 1968), p. 133; James H. Boykin, The Negro in North Carolina Prior to 1861 (New York: Pageant Press, 1958), pp. 67-76.

a rude log structure with a clapboarded roof, [which] stood on the ridge of a sand hill, in a little clearing in the pines. Every tree whose shade might have mitigated the summer heat or softened the glare of the sunlight had been cut down for a distance of fifty or sixty feet on either side of the schoolhouse. The windows of the hut were unglazed, and provided with wooden shutters. There were cracks in the wall, where the mud that had filled the interstices between the unhewn logs had fallen out. There was a weather-beaten aspect about this rude temple of learning, in keeping with the character and fortune of the community.[70]

Chesnutt wrote that the law of the state provided for free schools, but public opinion—"the opinion of the governing class"—still "regarded free schools as a burden upon a community not yet recovered from the impoverishment and industrial paralysis resulting from Civil War." Webster's blue-backed spelling book—"the palladium of Southern education since the days of Noah Webster"—was in the schoolhouse. As the teacher talked to his pupils, he noted the several degrees of difference in their skin color. Only two or three "could read simple English taken at random, though most had learned some part of the spelling book by rote." The pupils had done this much to the accompaniment of the hickory stick in other summers. One of the pupils explained that the white school "is kep' in Snow Hill Baptis' Chu'ch 'bout two mile from yere on de Lumberton Plankroad."[71]

The experiences of the teacher reflect Chesnutt's experiences when he was seventeen in 1875. For six years the laws had provided a system of free public education.[72] Still, the schools were indifferently managed and the financing was grudgingly arranged. Sometimes the law provided for segregation and sometimes it did not; but segregation always occurred.

Yet these were years in which Northern white teachers had poured into the South—to teach the former slaves.[73] The teachers had an effect, though they often became victims of an ostracism so complete that they left.[74] Sometimes needy Southern white women took their places; this

70. Chesnutt, *Mandy Oxendine*. CC, Fisk, p. 18.

71. Logan, *The Negro in North Carolina*, pp. 9, 142, 412.

72. Woodward, *The Strange Career of Jim Crow*, p. 24.

73. Henry Lee Swint, *The Northern Teacher in the South* (Nashville: Vanderbilt University Press, 1941); Willie Lee Rose, *Rehearsal for Reconstruction: The Port Royal Experiment* (Indianapolis: Bobbs-Merrill, 1964).

74. Chesnutt, "Cicely's Dream," *The Wife of His Youth*, p. 154.

was a change white people desired so long as contacts were limited to the schoolhouse.[75] One way and another in those unpredictable times many Negroes learned to read and write.

Like the residents of other southern communities, the residents of Fayetteville lived through times of change and chance. Congress disallowed the hastily enacted new Black Code by 1867, and it established a military command-district. The Negroes of Fayetteville, like those of other towns, could vote—under military protection. No Negro had been allowed to do that since Charles Chesnutt's father was a child in 1835.[76] The 1867 Constitution of North Carolina provided universal manhood suffrage, white and Negro, and it eliminated most property and religious qualifications. But by that year, 1867, the Freedman's Bureau closed its doors because Congress refused to fund it. The next year, 1868, United States military rule also came to an end in North Carolina. Republicans took over. Many white people resented this; they registered their feelings by voting for Democrats so that Republicans lost control of both houses of the Legislature at the next elections of 1870.[77] Although the Republican Party was thenceforth doomed in North Carolina, Charles Chesnutt voted for Republicans from the time he first could vote in 1879 until and after he left the state. Even into the early 1880s the Chesnutts hoped that the Republican Party might revive, that schools and franchise might open the way to a more open community.[78] But their hopes were vain. After their brief ascendancy, Republicans never returned to power.

The Democrats attained power by alarming enough voters; they proclaimed the falsehood that "The Negro dominates the Republican party!"[79] Fayetteville heard its share of demagogues delivering such charges during the years of Chesnutt's young manhood, from 1875 to 1883; many white citizens were anxious to prevent Negro political activity in

75. Chesnutt, "The Bouquet," *The Wife of His Youth*, pp. 269-90.

76. *Laws of North Carolina*, 1834, 1835, 7.

77. Oates, *Story of Fayetteville*, pp. 241-42. Oates describes the time 1868-1870 as a "time of trouble." He conveys the feeling many white people experienced upon being ordered to turn the town over to a Reconstruction group, and the relief felt after the elections of 1870.

An entry in Branson's *North Carolina Business Directory*, 1867-1868, p. 35, shows: "Mayor and Commissioners appointed by Gen. Sickles, in place of those elected by the people, removed."

78. Oates, *Story of Fayetteville*, p. 580, furnishes names of Republican leaders.

79. Logan, *The Negro in North Carolina*, p. 14.

the whole of eastern North Carolina. They feared that the large black population might become a political force.[80]

Perhaps because of frequent changes and insecurities, white people and black people turned toward the churches of Fayetteville. Almost without exception they turned to Protestant churches; the Methodist and Baptist denominations soared to a new strength.[81] Religion had long been a part of life in Fayetteville.[82] From dimmest childhood, residents had listened to sweet-toned bells sounding the hours of services. Like other Southern communities, Fayetteville had depended upon preachers to maintain the status quo and to comfort the disadvantaged. After the war the need became acute. But those Protestant churches that had Negro members could hold them no longer; great numbers preferred their own Methodist and Baptist churches.[83] By 1880 the Evans Chapel of the African Methodist Episcopal Zion Church of Fayetteville had a membership nearly equal to the town's entire slave population of 1860.[84] A great revivalism arose. Many felt uneasy about the arrangements of daily living in Fayetteville, as others had felt unsettled about the slave situation. The tensions of change and resistance, combined with the needs, hopes, desires, and despairs of the moment, produced a heightened anxiety.

White and black people could tolerate uncertainties until they became too great. Then many felt a compulsion to release their feelings. Larger numbers than ever attended camp meetings, evangelical revivals, every kind of religious gathering.[85] Like those of other communities and like many white ministers, the Negro ministers of Fayetteville were often uneducated. Sometimes religious sincerity and oratorical talent were combined; some ministers preached as earnestly as they preached eloquently. But others began with a cunning gravity, then roused their hearers to fervid outpourings. Preaching as vividly as ever the Puritan John-

---

80. Chesnutt, "The Race Problem," pp. 9-10; 49-59, passim. CC, Fisk.

81. Woodward, *Origins of the New South,* pp. 170-73.

82. Chesnutt, *The House Behind the Cedars,* p. 132. Chesnutt mentions "the slender spires of half a dozen churches," suggesting they are symbols of the society.

83. August Meier, *Negro Thought in America 1880-1915: Racial Ideologies in the Age of Booker T. Washington* (Ann Arbor: University of Michigan Press, 1968), pp. 130-33; Chesnutt, *Mandy Oxendine,* p. 75.

84. Logan, *The Negro in North Carolina,* p. 165, gives the membership of the African Methodist Episcopal Zion Church of Fayetteville in 1880 as 1,459. Cf. *Eighth Census of the United States, Population of North Carolina,* 1860; the slave population of Fayetteville in 1860 was 1,519.

85. Woodward, *Origins of the New South,* pp. 170-72.

athan Edwards depicted damnation, they excited their gatherings to near hysteria.[86] On such occasions conversions increased. But some saw the need for a better prepared ministry.

In searching for the causes of social maladies, many people attended temperance meetings; not a few joined in an effort to institute prohibition. There were those in Fayetteville who were glad to find a plausible explanation for whatever failing was at hand. There were some, like Chesnutt, who may have hoped that temperance zeal would spill over to other areas of reform.[87]

For a time it appeared that there were changes in the public aspects of life in Fayetteville. The governor ordered the mayor and the commissioners to turn over the authority to new officers. But no one thought that most white people were ready to see any changes in social relations between the races.[88]

In 1875 in the town of Raleigh, R. B. Glenn, a Republican, made a speech. "You may call it foolish pride, you may call it groundless prejudice," he said. "But the God who made us both placed it there . . ., implanted in us the principle that it is not right, proper or just that the Anglo-Saxon and African races should mingle together on terms of social equality."[89] Glenn distilled the understanding among white people of all classes: Social equality was unthinkable.

The concept of the open society frightened them.[90] White people in Fayetteville believed that if whites and blacks went to school together, if they worked together, if they voted and held office on equal terms, if they received the same service in public conveyances, if they commanded the same consideration in hotels and restaurants, any other distinctions would become superficial.[91]

Yet some white men in North Carolina disagreed. The turpentine merchant A. H. Slocomb regretted that a man of Charles Chesnutt's ability should conclude he must leave Fayetteville.[92] Men like Slocomb

86. Logan, The Negro in North Carolina, p. 169; Chesnutt, unpublished manuscript of an address (no title, n.d.). CC, Fisk. Chesnutt discusses preachers.

87. Chesnutt. Journals 2 and 3, passim.

88. Logan, The Negro in North Carolina, p. 171; E. Franklin Frazier, Race and Culture Contacts in the Modern World (New York: Alfred A. Knopf, 1957), pp. 253-68.

89. Quoted in Logan, The Negro in North Carolina, p. 174.

90. W. E. B. DuBois, quoted in Staughton Lynd, ed., Reconstruction (New York: Harper & Row, 1967), p. 46.

91. Nolen, The Negro's Image in the South, p. 29.

92. A. H. Slocomb to Chesnutt, March 9, 1889. CC, Fisk.

hoped that the Civil Rights Act of 1875 would improve practices. On the other hand, a North Carolina Negro told a traveler that "social equality is humbug. We do not expect it, we do not want it. It does not exist among blacks themselves. . . . We simply want the ordinary civil rights."[93] Still it appears that many white people remained preoccupied with the fear that social equality was what Negroes most desired.

And so the area of civil rights became a testing ground. For years it was a field where skirmishes took place; finally it became the field where the battles were fought. White people disagreed with one another;[94] yet to many the question was simply how far civil rights could be extended to Negroes without according them social equality.[95] Often the two overlapped. The crucial question for many Negroes was how to secure the daily civil rights necessary to self-respect. Some soon despaired. But others in North Carolina were hopeful in the early years and even up to the early 1880s that a resolution could be achieved.

Fearing that the differences of color would become negligible, white people in control had used color to establish inferiority and to deny privilege. They had constructed a rationale that God, not men, had arranged a social hierarchy. They had foisted the idea on disadvantaged white people as well as on black people. Otherwise, poor white people might have found common cause with Negroes.[96] Subconsciously sometimes, and sometimes knowingly, white leaders began to plan how the races could be physically separated to a greater extent than had appeared necessary under the slave system.[97] But this was forbidden by the Civil Rights Act of March 1, 1875, which required that Negroes be accorded services and civilities in public places. So the people of Fayetteville gradually became victims of a general cultural instability. For a long time many were unsure how to behave.

New contacts took place between the races, as black men appeared at the town hall, at the polls, in the jury box, and on the witness stand. White people experienced new feelings as they saw Negroes in first-class railroad coaches, in restaurants, and in hotels, or as they noticed in-

---

93. Quoted in Logan, The Negro in North Carolina, p. 175. See Perry's article on the Negro community in Fayetteville in Oates, Story of Fayetteville, p. 701.

94. Woodward, The Strange Career of Jim Crow, pp. 31-65, passim; C. Chesnutt, Journal 3. CC, Fisk.

95. Chesnutt, The Colonel's Dream, p. 166.

96. Chesnutt, Evelyn's Husband, p. 54. CC, Fisk.

97. Woodward, The Strange Career of Jim Crow, p. 354; James Russell Lowell, Political Essays (Cambridge, 1871), p. 260.

creasing numbers of black children and older black people going to school. Yet arrangements between white owners and black servants and laborers still had to be made.[98] For a time in North Carolina some social invitations were tried here and there. Many were uncomfortable about this. Probably an editorial in a Democratic newspaper expressed how most white citizens felt. It labeled the Civil Rights Act of 1875 "The Civil Social-Levelling Rights Bill."[99]

There is an old, unhappy, communal way of meeting a challenge to custom. The South knew it, for the slavocracy had depended on it: to employ "the triumvirate of force, violence and terror" when black-white conflicts arose.[100] Long before the War, Fayetteville had seen its terrors. There had always been the dread of insurrections.[101] After the Civil Rights Bill of 1875 became law, an urgent fear settled upon the white community, a fear that a greater horror than slave revolts—the social equality of the races—would come to pass.[102] The level of violence rose on the back of this fear. There were lynchings and near-lynchings, incidents of murder, and episodes of violence. Chesnutt witnessed some of these happenings.[103]

He realized that the thought of marriage between the races epitomized the other fears of the white society; white people believed social equality would follow. Forbidding intermarriage was the strongest hold of the caste society.[104] Chesnutt considered the feelings that produced this stand and the misinformation that sustained it. There were reasons why he should have thought about the long consequences of this prohibition.

Currents and cross-currents surged through the air. Often Chesnutt hoped that white people were learning a measure of accommodation, that the old order was giving place to new arrangements, and that justice would one day prevail.

---

98. Woodward, *The Strange Career of Jim Crow*, pp. 31-65, passim.

99. Quoted in Logan, *The Negro in North Carolina*, p. 175, from the *Greensboro Patriot*, March 3, 1875.

100. George B. Tindall, *South Carolina Negroes, 1877-1900* (Columbia: University of South Carolina Press, 1952), p. 253.

101. Chesnutt, *The Marrow of Tradition*, p. 278.

102. Logan, *The Negro in North Carolina*, p. 185.

103. E. J. Lilly to Charles Waddell Chesnutt, July 7, 1916. CC, Fisk.

104. Nolen, *The Negro's Image in the South*, pp. 29-39; Logan, *The Negro in North Carolina*, pp. 183-84; W. J. Cash, *The Mind of the South* (New York: Alfred A. Knopf, 1941), pp. 117-120.

In the years from 1866 to 1883 Charles Chesnutt lived through an attempt to lower the bars of the caste society. That effort failed in Fayetteville and in the South; yet Chesnutt still believed that the open society could become a reality. In a series of journals he began to put down his thoughts as he worked and tried to educate himself. He recorded the directions of his mental, emotional, and social growth. He recorded his efforts to understand the life about him and his attempts to shape the style of his life. He wrote of the persons who influenced his thinking, of the pressures he felt, and the problems he met. He recorded a growing frustration and the death of a dream. His journals trace a search for an identity, revealing the development of a plan for a lifework. In these journals, which provide the subject matter of the next chapter, the inner experiences of the young man play a counterpoint over the life of the little, profoundly human, discordant North Carolina community on the bank of the Cape Fear River.

AN AMERICAN CRUSADE

2

A JOURNEY WITH
A YOUNG MAN'S
JOURNALS

To Be or Not to Be—in North Carolina

Chesnutt wrote the words: "I believe I'll leave here and pass...."[1]
He could have passed; his skin was fair. At seventeen he considered it. On that last-of-July morning in 1875, when he went swimming at the pond in the early air of the Carolina countryside, someone mistook him for a white person. But then the man found out. "I'll be damned if there's any nigger blood in you!" the fellow said.

"I believe I'll leave here and pass, for I am as white as any of them." Charles was thinking of the problems he faced. He needed money. It was risky to depend on teaching. He knew the pitfalls. He had experienced them. A year ago at sixteen he had begun his "Journal and Notebook."[2] He had traveled the countryside, carrying his teacher's certificate, for it allowed him $40 a month. But when Charles returned to Charlotte he wrote in his journal, "I don't know what to do, I shall continue trying. I ought to make 'Nil Desperendum' my motto."

He never altogether despaired although he experienced every difficulty. Before leaving Charlotte he tried again. He walked twenty-three

---

1. Charles Waddell Chesnutt, Journals and Notebook, 1 July 1874 to August 20, 1875, CC, Fisk. Chesnutt kept a series of journals between 1874 and 1883. They are the major sources for chapter 2. They are hereinafter cited as Journal 1, Journal 2, or Journal 3. The quotation is from Journal 1, p. 130. This journal contains 160 pp.; some are numbered; some carry only a date or have no notation; some are both numbered and dated.

2. Chesnutt was born June 20, 1858. He started his journals at sixteen, in 1874. For his views on racial terminology as he uses it in the journals and in later writings see "The Term *Negro* (unpublished MS, n. d.). CC, Fisk. He outlined a "lively controversy," concluding that a term should take in all "to whom it is applied." The writer has used all the racial designations—*black, colored, Negro, Afro-American*—generally selecting the term that gained greatest acceptance at the period considered.

miles out in Gaston County to find that there was no school there. Somewhere along that excursion he found Cicero Harris, brother of Robert Harris and Principal of the Howard School in Charlotte. That very evening they packed and started for Raleigh together. There an educational convention was in session, and Charles attended two sessions. Then, in exhaustion, he fell asleep on an old sofa: "When I awoke the meeting had adjourned," he remembered later. "I blundered downstairs, and wandered about a good while, but reached Mr. Alston's at last. The next day I started for home."[3]

The summer of 1874 was well along. He was surprised to hear how plainly his littlest sister, Lilly, could talk. His young cousin Mary Ochiltree, now married to his father, was taking care of the children.[4] Charles visited, "bummed around," and finally got a break. He became the teacher at the "public" school at Mt. Zion, a district near the farm. As he began to teach the scholars—forty-four of them—he found "a few... hard cases, but I manage to manage them." He hoped not to have to manage them long but to return to Charlotte on more favorable terms that winter. By August 17 a letter from Cicero Harris seemed to settle that. Harris's niece, Victoria Richardson, would get that position.[5]

Charles had been allowed to read the journal that Cicero Harris kept, and he began to keep his own journal. He started copying a few paragraphs from a "Handbook for Home Improvement." The passage concerned the value of keeping clean: Mohammed "made frequent ablutions a religious duty," Charles wrote, "and in that he was right. The rank and fetid odors which exhale from a foul skin can hardly be neutralized by the sweetest incense of devotion." More to the point, he remarked that not everyone could "wear fine and elegant clothes, but we can all... afford clean shirts, drawers and stockings."[6]

He began to learn to play the organ at Robert Harris's house. He began to write bits of fiction in his journal, imagining himself lost in a swamp, wandering, and finally arriving at Farmer Bright's.[7]

---

3. Journal 1, entries written between and including July 3, 1874 and August 10, 1874. CC, Fisk.

4. H. Chesnutt, *Pioneer*, p. 7. See autograph album given Charles by pupils, of whom this cousin was one. An entry of June 25, 1883 is "Your loving cousin, Mattie Ochiltree." CC, Fisk.

5. But Chesnutt did teach in the Howard School under Cicero Harris in the fall.

6. Journal 1, July 3, July 5, July 26, August 10, and August 17, 1874. CC, Fisk.

7. Chesnutt later used the cypress swamps of the Cape Fear River country as the setting for short stories and for his novel *The House Behind the Cedars*. Journal 1, pp. 20-24. CC, Fisk. The simple description is written with artistry.

Following the little story he wrote that "the above is my first real attempt at literature." He felt the artist's need of the audience: "The reader will please pardon all faults and errors and I will try and do better the next time. (If anyone reads it beside myself)." He was learning to write. He used his first journal for other reasons as well—to unburden himself of troublesome feelings, to express alternatives, to explore the possibilities for a life style.

He read Barnes's *History* "of our country," and he studied algebra. He wrote more stories depicting the life around him. One was a story of a fight that happened when Mrs. Revels's cow strayed into Joe Adkins's field; another centered on a boy with an ungovernable temper who threw himself into a stream; and a third was a story about a dog and a country doctor. He commented on his reading: *Uncle Tom's Cabin* "was no ways old to me, although I have read it before." He read a book on teaching, another on South America. He reread *Pickwick Papers,* "A splendid book," and he studied Quackenbas's *Composition and Rhetoric,* after which he tried writing an essay and some religious poems. Seizing a topic much preached upon at revival meetings, he wrote a temperance play, *The First Glass.* He studied German, and he tried a fable, "simply to practice writing it." By himself and without guidance, he lived the equivalent of a small college session. Charles was the only person among the people he knew who was doing this; he seemed to think it natural to teach himself Latin, Greek, German, French, algebra, history, and music. He rose at six, read till breakfast, ate, studied until school time, taught until three in the afternoon, then left for home and read again until dusk. And then he could "think over what I have read."

So it had been until the early fall of 1874. It was a summer of hope and disappointments, of efforts and frustrations, of loneliness, and of agonizing appraisals. He saw the country people, black and white and in-between—saw them close, that summer and the next. He lived their lives. He felt the reaches of their poverty, and in the fervor of his youth he searched the reasons for it. He felt the innuendoes of the color line, from every angle, as only he could feel them, being black and white. Later he would write the complex haunting fiction of the people; he would write it as an artist, revealing what he heard, saw, and felt. Later still, he would search, find, and champion an answer to the problem of racial caste in America. He believed he had found the only answer.

He struggled to make a living, to help his father, to get an education. In June of 1875 he went to see about a school at Jonesville (or "Jonahsville," he ruefully wrote). The railroad fare was high at fifty cents for ten miles, "just double the fare on the other roads." He had to stop and inquire at houses, climb fences, and cross over many cotton fields until finally he found the "Church" appointed as a place of meeting. It was a dilapidated, windowless structure made of chinky logs. It had a rough interior and a dismal air. For seats there were ten or a dozen "slabs" with legs made of oak saplings. It had an "awful-looking" pulpit at the side of the room, and one lamp suspended by a string. Part of a chimney, made of logs and clay, was intended to allow smoke to rise from a fireplace, but Charles pitied "the deluded being who imagines that a fire would burn in it." At seventeen he could convey the weight of ignorance and poverty pervading a place, and he could create a feeling of foreboding.

Here he met the men who came to look him over. It was a painful occasion. They began by criticizing the former teacher for favoring one pupil, a little "yellow" eight-year-old girl. The teacher had treated her better than the others. Charles thought that these men were prejudiced against the little girl because she was "yellow" (they meant light-skinned). He thought this because they mentioned no other reasons and because they were "the blackest colored people . . . that I ever saw."[8]

His feelings were intense, and important to him. Later Charles used themes centering about an identity crisis of a mulatto person, and he satirized black people for adopting white values in relations with one another. Now such experiences aroused him. He saw, learned, realized, felt, criticized, questioned, wondered, censored, and deplored, as young men do, the styles and values of the times.

The day did not end at the "Church." He was taken to meet Mr. Ayler, a German immigrant to Jonesville some five years back, who seemed to be a spokesman. Charles could speak a little German. But what this man said displeased Charles. Partly in German he told Charles that the white people would never respect him if he taught a colored school; the colored people ought to have colored teachers, and the whites white teachers. And then he offered Charles the white public school.

It had happened again. Mr. Ayler either thought that Charles was white or he was willing to encourage Charles to pass for white. "I respectfully declined," Chesnutt wrote. Charles gave the matter a good deal of thought, for it was thrust upon him: "The upshot was that there was not enough money for me." No one knows whether they offered him so little that having no job would have been as good, or whether they offered less than they would pay someone else, or whether they could not have offered him enough. But in the early years, when he was poor and striving to learn, Charles Waddell Chesnutt often confronted

8. Journal 1, pp. 24, 31, 49-54, 55-65, 71, 72, 74. CC, Fisk.

the American dilemma of color caste in the cruel alternatives it presented to him. Should he pass himself off as a white person and move to a
new place? Should he take this way to get an education? Should he do
this if it meant denying his family, his friends, his people? Later, he
would explore and deal with these problems in stories; now at firsthand,
he learned the subtleties.

That night he stopped with a black family, who gave him a "good
supper, much better than I expected." They also gave him food for
thought. In his anger and bitterness he was sharp with them. Why, he
demanded, wasn't it possible to pay more for teachers and preachers?

The father answered, "Well, but we haven't got any chances. We all of
[us] work on other people's, white people's, land, and sometimes get
cheated out of all we make; we can't get the money."

"Well, you certainly make something?"

"Yes." A pause, in which the father seemed to say "We live, we are
here."

"Now, I'll tell you...," so Charles recorded the conversation, "You
say you are all sinless and get cheated out of your labor. Why don't you
send your children to school, and qualify them to look out for themselves, to own property, to figure and think about what they are doing,
so that they may do better than you?"

"We can't do it was all [I] could get out of them." Charles wrote in a
mood of finding fault, although at seventeen he knew about being hun-
gry, burdened, and poor. He lashed out: "I learn from Mr. Davidson
[one of his inquisitors in the Church] and from what I have seen myself
that they [are] a very trifling, shiftless set of people up there. Their children are following in their footsteps."

Charles scarcely knew that he expressed his frustration in finding his
people trapped in a syndrome of color and caste and suffering the perils of poverty and inequality. Nor did he realize that he was beginning to
outline the framework within which his life's endeavor would be posed,
that he was forming the questions he would seek to answer.

There were four beds in the main room, and Charles feared that he
would have to share one of them. Instead, he and Alex, who had
brought him there, rolled up in featherbeds and slept in a shed. In the
morning they got the same meal again. Charles had the impression that
these country people lived in great narrowness of mind. At that time he
blamed them for it. Still, he felt their despair, as he could feel their bit-
tersweet will to live. He also saw their strength and humor. Alex said a
prayer that night and sang a hymn. Charles described the censure he
brought on himself when he cleaned his shoes on Sunday morning. An
old lady who had been listening the night before told him that he

couldn't fault the country people, and [you] right from town, cleaning [your] shoes on Sunday."

"I told her that I couldn't do it on Saturday for I wasn't there."

"Why not Saturday night?"

"I told her I was too tired. And that I had been living with a preacher, as true a Christian as there is, and that he cleaned his boots on Sunday."

But the old lady only said she hoped the Lord would forgive him.

Back in Charlotte he took an examination and got a new teaching certificate. The next day he set off for Spartanburg, an old town in the South Carolina mountains. Charles liked Spartanburg. He saw no homely people: "Nearly everybody is handsome, especially the more refined."

Perhaps because Spartanburg had seemed inviting, he was more lonely during the eight weeks of the school session. He began to miss Josie, a girl in Charlotte; he wondered if she loved him and would remain faithful. He found his pupils slow and the possibilities for excitement slight. He felt many pulls. He wanted to be superior to the country people, and he wanted to slip back to those who knew him. He realized that his family needed help on the farm and that his father would be angry unless he sent money home. "I suppose I am considered a prodigal, a reprobate, a spendthrift," he wrote. So out of the $37 he got on August 7 he sent $15 to his father and $2 to Lewis.[9]

If only he could write to Josie without her mother's reading the letters—he felt sure Josie's mother would read his letters: "It is a shame for a fellow to be obliged to confine himself to such cold sentences as a mother will hold discreet." This was his journal: "Here is a lock of her hair. I kiss the lock of hair and press it to my bosom. Would it were she!" He was troubled by thoughts about how he ought to behave: "I never will, God help me, act in any way but that in which every gentleman should act toward a lady." He certainly had his notions about how a gentleman should act. He mooned and pined his share; he wished that he were twenty-five; then, if he had a thousand dollars, he could marry Josie. He loved a girl "not anyways good looking." But her faults were nothing. He sighed, and then he had a good laugh: "Cripes. What a fool I am, sitting here ... I thought I was more of a show than that!"[10]

This was his seventeenth summer. One day he took a disastrous walk to Spartanburg. He ate a big meal there, too big, and immediately set

---

9. Journal 1, pp. 17, 77, 78, 80, 83, July 1, 1875, 99-103.

10. Ibid., p. 141. Chesnutt appears to have made a mistake in numbering pages. The next number after 131 is 140.

out to walk the ten miles back. He sweated. The wind blew hard, but he got soaking wet. The result was a case of something like the grippe or influenza. Caster oil was no help. Feeling put upon and lonely, he began to hope that he would not remain forever "dyspeptic." He wondered if he would live the school term out. In a triumphant understatement, considering how lonely and discouraged he felt, he wrote that "teaching school in the country is pretty rough for those who are not used to it."

He could scarcely have realized how much he was learning about the people and the lives they lived. He tried to straighten himself out on matters of sex and religion. He tried writing a little of everything. At one point he wrote that it is not good to be too religious, too modest, or too virtuous; this would be fanaticism, or prudery, which is nearly as disagreeable as immodesty. He decided to get religion, for he felt the need: "Lord, help me to pray and make a man, a Christian of me. I never have been happy since I quit that first attempt I made to seek the Lord." But if he found the Lord, and the Lord guarded him from Sin's advances, he wanted the Lord to protect Josie too: "Guard her from Sin's advances. Keep her virtuous and pure!"

There were twenty-six "scholars" in his school, mostly girls. Those who went to school and those who did not go were ignorant. Some of the twenty-six could "come no more right now till we finish layin' by." The people of Charles's family knew the necessity of "layin' by" as well as the country pupils knew it. They lived close to poverty. But what the country people did not know amazed Charles.

He found it tiresome to teach his classes. In desperation he asked the pupils to sing the lesson; one of them, Louisa Peak, relieved his boredom by whining through her nose in an astoundingly "droll" manner. Charles reflected that he was well paid and that he was getting over the grippe. He half-congratulated himself when he did not feel lonesome.

He got back to his reading. Cowper had become an old friend. But Byron's *Don Juan* seemed "unchaste," the language "none too pure," and the sentiments "decidedly impure." Despite these Victorian reservations Charles liked Byron. He struggled to teach his pupils the rudiments of literacy; he shared their lives. He went to revival meetings. He helped with the work: he plowed, cut wood, carried water, milked cows. He listened to the tales the people told. At seventeen he had been away from home two years.

While Charles was sorting out these matters of religion, morals, sex, and a life's work, he was thinking about problems of color and day-to-day options. Never free of these problems wherever he went, whatever he did, he tried suppressing the matter—to forget it—but often he either had to explain that he had Negro blood or go along with those who

53

thought him white, who otherwise would have treated him differently. He felt better when he confronted the matter.

Charles Chesnutt liked his teaching less and less. Being homesick and feeling guilty about having failed to send more money back to Fayetteville contributed to this. He would confess that his "daddy" had "some little cause to be displeased with me, for seventeen dollars a month sounds pretty big." Charles spent this amount for his needs and for books. "But I will explain all to him," he added, "And may the Lord soften his heart!" He wrote that schoolteaching had ruined his health. In a touching sentence he communicated his pain in feeling part man and part boy: "I don't feel at all like a boy of seventeen should." He would go home after school was out "if I live and nothing happens." Teachers were underpaid; he wondered whether medicine would be better. The best doctors advised him to go to a medical college: "I can't follow this advice as there is business which prevents me. That business is to make money to pay my way. Then perhaps I will go."

But he could continue his education by himself. That seemed the only available positive action. He felt newly certain that "uneducated people are the most bigoted, superstitious, hardest-headed people in the world!" All those around him believed in "ghosts, luck, horseshoes, cloud signs, witches and all other kinds of nonsense, and all the argument in the world couldn't get it out of them." Being ignorant also had ugly effects on character, he thought. He wrote that country people "accuse you indirectly of lying, almost of stealing, eavesdrop you, retail every word you say, eavesdrop you when you're talking to yourself, twist up your words into all sorts of ambiguous meanings, refuse to lend you their mules... good-sized liars, hypocrites, inquisitive little wenches. "I wouldn't," he exploded, "teach here another year for $50 a month!" And then he applied himself to do a Latin lesson in the journal.[11]

Chesnutt was indignant. He felt that he treated people fairly. He felt outraged that poverty made people hard, tricky, and immoral. The country people thought Charles put on airs. Perhaps they thought him foolish. At times he was outspoken, but his *Conjure* stories show that he learned a wisdom.

He dwelt little on the past, but he knew it was there; it was rich, painful, pregnant with questions. He cherished the half-actual, half-fanciful pictures that would come to his mind: Why had his mother persuaded her mother to leave their North Carolina village and go in a wagon train to Cleveland five years before the Civil War? Why had they left the

---

11. Ibid., pp. 105, 90-103 passim, 108, 113-17, Friday, August 13, 1875, Aug. 11, 1875, 152.

world they knew? It was because they were persecuted. They could find no security and no hope of improvement in the hardening climate of North Carolina. They made easy scapegoats and dangerous examples. Their rights were gone, they had no vote, they were forbidden to marry white people, and they could scarcely find work or education. They were little better off than slaves.[12]

But his mother had defied all that! She had secretly taught slave children to read and write.[13] At times he remembered the tales of the wagon train bound for Cleveland and of the free colored people, one of whom was his grandmother. His father had taken his chances too; he had joined the wagon train and headed north to live with his uncle in Indiana. It must have been on this journey that Andrew Jackson Chesnutt—Jack—fell in love with Anne Maria. Some months after he got to Indiana he came back to Cleveland to marry her.[14]

Their sons Charles and Lewis heard these stories. Charles remembered hearing about Oberlin, a station of the underground railroad. His parents had moved there from Cleveland. He and Lewis remembered tales about when two slave catchers and a United States Marshall arrived and arrested John Price, a fugitive slave who had long lived in Oberlin. Students, professors, Andrew Chesnutt, and others got buggies and saddle horses and chased the slave catchers. They rescued the slave in Wellington, but Andrew Chesnutt found himself detained for violation of the Fugitive Slave Law. Because the Oberlin judge sympathized with the rescuers, he nullified the warrant against Charles's father, whose name had been misspelled, with a 't' put in the middle—*Chestnut!*[15]

Charles may not have remembered when the babies came, another boy soon after Lewis, and then a little girl who died. They had moved back to Cleveland when he was still small, for there was no work in Oberlin that would provide a living. His father got his old job driving a horse car on the Cleveland line;[16] they had gone to live with Anne

---

12. Chesnutt's daughter, Helen Chesnutt, provided a brief outline of this background. I have treated the material, like most family remembrances, as part fact, part legend. See chapter 6.

13. Chesnutt to M. [sic] C. Newbold, May 24, 1922. CC, WRHS.

14. Marriage Certificate, CC, Fisk. Anne Maria Sampson and Andrew Jackson Chesnutt married in Cleveland, July 26, 1857.

15. This story is variously told. Helen Chesnutt, *Pioneer*, p. 3, gives a version similar to that used in the text. See John Selby, *Beyond Civil Rights* (Cleveland and New York: World Publishing Co., 1966), p. 15.

16. William Ganson Rose, *Cleveland, The Making of a City* (Cleveland: World Publishing Co., 1950), p. 473.

Maria's mother in a small house on Hudson Street. But his father soon went away. Believing in the cause of the North, Andrew Chesnutt had enlisted as a teamster in the Union Army, and he had served until the end of the war.[17]

One thing seemed sure. The North won a military victory. Slavery was illegal. Negroes who had been slaves were free—and former slaves were to become citizens. It ought to have meant a new day. At the moment the war ended, Andrew Chesnutt found himself in North Carolina near Fayetteville. He went to the town to seek his father; finding him ill and infirm, Andrew sent for his wife and their sons.

Charles thought about his mother, who had talent and a taste for the life of the mind. She was able, ambitious, knowledgeable, and proud. She resented injustices, and she wanted to live where problems of color would be minimized. In moving to a friendlier city she had hoped to be done with the place of iron bars. She and her husband had moved to Oberlin, where there was an open atmosphere, and she hoped her first son could get an education at the college.

But life became difficult. Babies came fast; she needed help. Then the war came, overriding everybody's struggles. She and her children had to remain with her mother in Cleveland. Anne Maria believed it was her war; she hoped that it would reorder the world. Still she wanted never again to live in North Carolina. She doubted that life would be better in Fayetteville, or that, even if it were improved, it would be good. She yearned to use her powers. Probably she exerted an influence in setting the directions for her son's life.

Charles knew that his mother felt reluctant to return to Fayetteville. But her husband decided that. His father backed him in a small grocery business on Gillespie Street, and Anne Maria had to choose between living with her mother or with her husband.[18] With her three little boys she started for Fayetteville. Charles could have had no illusions about how hard a time his mother had. Three more babies came after they returned to Fayetteville, all girls. His mother needed Charles all the time he was not attending school or helping in the grocery store. Life was too hard, the demands were too great, and she was unable to find the strength to meet them.

---

17. Elmer O. Parker to the writer, Nov. 30, 1971 states no record appears in General Services Administration Archives. See H. Chesnutt, Pioneer, p. 4.

18. H. Chesnutt, Pioneer, p. 3. See List of Taxable Persons, Fayetteville, Cumberland County, in Raleigh, North Carolina. Chesnutt's paternal grandparent listed an "old Thames store," "lower Fayetteville," at $300. This was probably the grocery store turned over to Andrew Jackson Chesnutt.

Physically worn out, she grew discouraged; she died in Fayetteville in 1871 shortly after Lillian was born. So Charles remembered grief as well as the struggle to get along, and he remembered his promise that he would care for all the children.[19]

Charles's father felt less concern about his son's education, for he was pressed; there were six young children. Charles's grandmother was the closest female relative, so it was incumbent on her to take charge. Soon she had sent for her eighteen-year-old niece, Mary Ochiltree. She offered "Cousin Mary" a chance to go to the Howard School if she would help the Chesnutt family. Cousin Mary accepted; within the year Andrew Chesnutt married her.[20]

In time these memories merged in Charles's mind, as the sweet fragrance of the lilacs blends with the heavy odor of the magnolias. He knew that he was lucky to have started in the Cleveland schools, then to have gone to the Howard School. He had worked in the grocery store, sweeping floors, moving cracker barrels, and listening to folk from the countryside. He learned the measures of their talk, listened to their superstitions, and heard the wild, poetic conjure stories that they sometimes slyly told for fact. And he heard the Negroes of the town when they stopped to talk about the tides of the Reconstruction. He must have shared these thoughts with his mother.[21]

Perhaps he sometimes heard the secretly spoken thoughts, the suspicions and the certainties that were seldom mentioned in Fayetteville. They were perplexing thoughts of color, lineage, caste, and relationships. They were hushed realities. He must have questioned who he was, and who his ancestors had been.[22] Discussing his qualifications for producing a novel of the color line, he noted that he "possessed such opportunities for observation and conversation with the better class of white men in the South as to understand their modes of thinking."[23] Probably he learned exactly how he came to be the color he was.

In the journal he recorded a few flash pictures: He was in the store. Suddenly, there were people shouting in the street; he heard loud voices and screams. He left the store and followed the crowd. At the corner of

---

19. H. Chesnutt, *Pioneer*, pp. 4-6. See also A. J. Chesnutt to J. P. Green, April 18, 1871, John P. Green Papers. WRHS, Cleveland.

20. Probate Records, Fayetteville District, Cumberland County, North Carolina Archives, Raleigh, North Carolina; will of Andrew Jackson Chesnutt, June 21, 1920.

21. H. Chesnutt, *Pioneer*, p. 5.

22. Chesnutt to Dr. Park, Dec. 19, 1908, p. 3. CC, WRHS.

23. Chesnutt, Journal 2, p. 164. CC, Fisk; see also chapter 6.

the Market House a white man shot and killed a Negro. Charles witnessed it. Though the white man was tried and convicted of the murder, he was later excused from finishing the sentence.[24]

Life was hard and puzzling, yet Charles had some reasons to feel that he was fortunate. He made two friends who encouraged him. They were the brothers Robert and Cicero Harris, mulatto Negroes whose families had also migrated to Cleveland before the war. Both had attended the Cleveland High School. After the war both returned to Fayetteville. Robert Harris became principal of the Fayetteville Howard School, of which he was a founder, and Cicero Harris became principal of a similar school in Charlotte.[25] They knew the South. Robert Harris took things where they seemed to be and accepted what he could get from whatever source he could get it; he applied for and received money from the northern Peabody Fund. He knew how to work through established institutions. He even tried to get an appointment for his pupil Charles Chesnutt to the United States Naval Academy. Though Harris often succeeded, this effort failed. Charles made high scores on the entrance tests, but the examiners rejected him when they learned of his race.[26]

Charles remembered a day in his fourteenth year when his father decided he should have a job; since the family needed money, Charles should leave school. He found Charles a job keeping books and doing odd work for the saloonkeeper. That day Robert Harris sent his other pupils home and talked to Charles's father. They struck a bargain: Charles would stay in school as pupil-teacher and he would earn a small salary.[27]

All these memories mingled. Charles hardly paused to sort out what happened when. Young as he was, he could have suffered anxieties; happily, he was too much occupied with plans for the future.

Before long Andrew Chesnutt had to close the grocery store, and the family moved to the farm two miles out on the Wilmington road, where many free Negroes had lived before the war. There was more work to be done. Charles did chores and worked in the fields. He got hold of a small stock of dry goods; on Saturdays he peddled door-to-door, selling

---

24. H. Chesnutt, *Pioneer*, pp. 5 and 6; E. J. Lilly to Charles W. Chesnutt, July 7, 1917. CC, Fisk.

25. Chesnutt to M. [sic] C. Newbold, May 24, 1922, CC, WRHS. Cicero Harris later became a bishop of the African Methodist Episcopal Zion Church.

26. G. W. Jewett to Prof. Robert Harris, May 29, 1873, The Schomburg Collection, John Bruce Manuscripts, Collection No. 919, New York Public Library, New York City.

27. H. Chesnutt, *Pioneer*, p. 8.

pins, buttons, needles, and thread.[28] It was discouraging because the neighbors had little more money to buy than the Chesnutt family. It was a difficult struggle to keep things going. Charles talked to Robert Harris. At the age of fifteen, he realized that he must confront his poverty, though it meant leaving home and striking out. He knew that teaching in a colored school would provide a precarious income. He knew he would be expected to send money home. But it was time to try. He was fortunate that Robert Harris sent him to Charlotte as assistant to Cicero Harris.

Charles felt the blight of color discrimination through his early years though he was almost white. He understood what this meant in terms of opportunities. Already feeling the weight of the situation of the black man in the American Republic, feeling his powers, and angry, he wrote the words in his seventeenth summer: "I believe I'll leave here and pass, for I am as white as any of them." He seemed to realize that he was approaching a key decision in his life.

Beginning Not to Be—in North Carolina

"A man may spring from a race of slaves!"[29]

Yes. He would show to the world that a man could spring from a race of slaves.

"A man may spring from a race of slaves...yet far excel...."

He made the decision: "I will live down the prejudice, I will crush it out!" He wrote the words in the silent, friendly journal. He had seen that first-class teachers would not "teach a nigger." He had learned that the hard way, though he looked like a white person. He had found it impossible to persuade first-class teachers to work with him. He would not settle for other teachers.

At eighteen he left the country school and went to Charlotte to become principal of the school where he had taught through two winters.[30] Society had made up its mind about Charles Chesnutt: It would have him teach in "colored" schools the rest of his life, teach only what he knew right then, and do it in North Carolina. But Chesnutt realized he had scarcely begun to learn. And he had made no decision about what to do with his life.

Charlotte was better than the hills near Spartanburg, but Charles began to understand that he could be lonely anywhere. His journal became more important. He started a second journal and he set down several good reasons for doing so. But the real reason was "to improve

---

28. Parker, "Chesnutt as a Southern Town Remembers Him," p. 205.

29. Chesnutt, Journal 2, p. 84.

30. H. Chesnutt, *Pioneer*, p. 15.

myself in the art of composition... If I write trash, no one will be the worse for it. If I write anything that is worth reading, I perhaps shall be the better for it."[31]

The days were short as Charles explored an outward-expanding mass of experience, taught himself how to get around, and acquired tools. He liked languages; he wanted to understand algebra; he grasped for all that had happened in the short past of his country and the long past of the world. He felt a bitter yearning for a good school. He let himself imagine what a professor or an obliging classmate could do "to help construe the hard passages."

He began to read *The Iliad* in Latin and found the story compelling, the people fascinating, their problems real, live, and unsettled. The *Iliad* transcended the distance and the difficulty Charles experienced. He began to write comments: "It's presumptuous and yet maybe something's left to say!"[32]

Achilles could call a council even though Agamemnon's power was absolute and divine! And that council could dare to accuse Agamemnon of greed! Charles thought of the meaning of this idea for democratic government: How far is every person responsible for the acts of the society's agents? The *Iliad* gave Charles a chance to isolate and grapple with problems in social-political relations. He concluded that the Greeks were *aristocratic* democrats; they would check a "clamorous, vile plebeian"—with blows.

The gods were constructed like the Greeks, but larger. The gods would sleep, drink, laugh, visit, feast, quarrel, lie, and cheat. How could the Greeks worship such deities! He concluded they did it from fear, not love. Occasionally, he would moralize, though he generally offered an apology: "I hope my readers will pardon this digression"; then he would reach a conclusion, such as "The oldest man is not always the wisest."

From the *Iliad* he got some exalted ideas about Greek geography. The Greeks were lucky because they lived in "pleasant valleys, surrounded by lofty mountains, and watered by winding streams and perennial fountains—perpetual summer."[33] He never saw the thin soil, the rocks, the arid mountains, the desperate poverty.[34]

The *Iliad* led him to think about wars. When men realize that war is

---

31. Journal 2, p. 1, 1877, p. 84.

32. Ibid., November 1877. As in Journal 1, the pages are sometimes numbered, sometimes partly or completely dated; when there is no notation it is sometimes impossible to determine when an entry was made.

33. Ibid., pp. 24, 33, 12, 33.

34. See William H. McNeill, *Greece: American Aid in Action 1947-1956* (New York:

anything but romantic they will be less willing to undertake it; "when it is resorted to, the modern inventions and the voice of the world all tend to terminate it as speedily as possible."[35] He added a note: "Last sentence is bad." Whatever else he was doing, Charles Chesnutt was mindful that he was writing.

He got a sense of the merging origins of men. This was related to his involvement with racial problems. He knew the Bible stories. He had heard them sung, told, glorified, and applied to sinners.[36] Now he noticed that the *Iliad* stories resembled Bible stories. This showed that "all men come from a common stock." Their similar, often mutual, origins provided the "improbable legends in classical literature."[37] At eighteen he had uncovered an idea that would persist in his life and in his work. He almost passed it by.

In 1877, Charles left the school in Charlotte to become assistant to Robert Harris in the new Normal School in Fayetteville. He was to teach reading, writing, spelling, composition, and other subjects.[38]

He tried to plan to get free time. He rose at 6:00 a.m., took a walk to join the people around the Market House, listened to the cries of the peddlers, smelled the fried fish and the fresh gingerbread, and watched the people going to the dry goods store and the butcher shop. Then he went home, built up his fire, and began his algebra. It was nearly impossible to get everything in. He would have to find some other time than ten o'clock at night to practice writing. By then he was too tired and his thoughts were unclear.

He grew more intense about his studying. "I seem to be working in the dark," he wrote. "I have to feel my way along." But he sustained himself with the thought, "I manage to make better headway than many who have the light," and he reflected that he had learned to be self-reliant.

He felt a desperation about gaining knowledge. It was related to his anger about being obstructed because he had African blood. He considered alternatives. Slowly, he had realized that to pass would solve no

---

Twentieth Century Fund, 1957) and *The Greek Dilemma: War and Aftermath* (Philadelphia and New York: J. B. Lippincott Co., 1947). These studies appraise the geography and the poverty of Greece.

35. Journal 2, p. 36.

36. Ibid., p. 151. This page also carries a date of March 11, 1880.

37. Ibid., p. 39. See Charles Waddell Chesnutt, "The Origins of the Hatchet Story," *Puck*, 15, No. 633, April 24, 1889, p. 134.

38. H. Chesnutt, *Pioneer*, p. 15.

problems. It never crossed his mind that he could be inferior. But no good teacher would teach him. He was "a nigger" to those teachers who knew Latin, German, French, and music. The Latin rhetoric he had been studying spilled over: even in the North, "prejudice sticks, like a foul blot on the fair 'scutcheon of American liberty.' "

He was angry; but he had made the decision not to pass, and he never changed his mind. At the same time he decided that he would go North. There he would enjoy privileges if he could pay. He felt confident that by sheer excellence of performance he could show the world the foolishness of prejudice. He would exalt his race. He would compel admiration on society's terms. If anyone was so conceited, so blinded, and so ignorant as to disregard the difference between merit and incompetence, he would ignore that person. He would neither pass nor struggle against impossible odds. He would succeed, and he would improve the position of the Negro race; "I will show to the world that a man may spring from a race of slaves, yet far excel many of the boasted ruling race!"[39]

He wrote these plans at eighteen, though there were levels on which race loomed as a massive obstacle to the hopes of the young and gifted. There were many reasons why he arrived so soon at the decision to make his confrontation with racial dilemmas the project for his life: his pride, his love for his relatives, his sense of justice, his awareness of his powers, and his anger over the exploitation of his people. Perhaps the most important reason was his need to find a purpose for his life.

In the never-published *Mandy Oxendine* (c. 1897), Chesnutt's character Lowery considered the matter. Lowery reflected that

in spite of [the] disagreeable features of his position, he had never felt the inclination to give up his people and cast in his lot with the ruling caste.[40]

Judging from Chesnutt's life, Lowery was stating the conclusions from which Chesnutt never swerved. On November 11, 1905, he answered a lady who asked who he was: "I share the blood of the race. I lived in North Carolina from the age of 9 to that of 25. I taught school there, and many of my relations, including some of the nearest and dearest, are living there still. I could never be so placed in life that I should not have an abiding interest in the welfare of our people in the South."[41]

---

39. Journal 2, Nov. 30, 1877, p. 84; June 28, 1880, pp. 204, 84.

40. Chesnutt, *Mandy Oxendine*. CC, Fisk, 5, 41.

41. Chesnutt to Mrs. W. E. Henderson, Nov. 11, 1905. CC, Fisk.

Education and Identity

Charles cast about to learn about writing. He got the idea of conceiving a plan. He thought about Aristotle's ideas. He discussed "great ideas" in his journal, comparing them to the Trojan Horse. A "great thought" would be an insight about how people could understand one another. If only great thoughts could be got past the barriers in people's minds as the wooden horse was got past the gates of Troy! Charles made a bitter observation that had little to do with writing: "There's one way that will show us soonest the folly of prejudice—that's being subjected to it."[42]

At the Howard School there was an attractive, light-brown-skinned young woman teacher, a daughter of the proprietor of the barber shop in the Fayetteville Hotel. Her name was Susan Perry.[43] Charles spent time with her at the school, then courted her at her family's home, an "ample, old house, with white columns, and magnolia trees by the door."[44] On June 6, 1878, fourteen days before his twentieth birthday, Charles married her.[45] They began a life together in two rooms in the Perry house. Ten months later, their first child was born.[46]

Occasionally Charles paused to reassure himself about his journal writing. He would like to recall the date of a conversation with Professor Ladd, who visited at the Fayetteville Hotel last fall (1878). But he could recall only the conversation. Professor Ladd had encouraged him, and Charles had written: "I have worked with increased ardor, and with a greater confidence in my own powers." "I do not place too high a value upon the Professor's opinions," he added. But he did place a high value on them, for he was already thinking that he wanted to pass examinations at "a higher tribunal." He wanted to be published, to make a reputation, to influence people. He wanted to write. He was letting himself know about it through his journal.[47]

Professor Ladd had mentioned a job in the North. Charles had once started to study stenography; now he would learn in earnest. Nobody in

---

42. Journal 2, pp. 87, 93, 94.

43. *Ninth Census of the United States, Census of 1870,* Cumberland County, Fayetteville District, North Carolina, June 28, 1870, Entry No. 82.

44. H. Chesnutt, *Pioneer,* p. 16.

45. See Document, CC, WRHS. Alex McNeill certified that the Marriage Register shows this marriage on June 6, 1878.

46. Journal 2, p. 94.

47. Journal 2, April 23, 1879, p. 111, 124.

Fayetteville, white or black, knew anything about stenography.[48] But after eight months Charles could take a sermon down "nearly if not quite verbatim."

He had a long talk with Dr. T. D. Haigh, the white physician who attended his wife when the baby came. He told Dr. Haigh that he intended to obtain his "proper standing in society" and that he wanted "to be judged on merit." Dr. Haigh said it was possible that Charles could succeed in the North; there were more opportunities and fewer prejudices.

Charles became definite: "I will go to the Metropolis," he wrote after this. He would go and stay, as Franklin, Greeley, and others had stayed. And he would expect no help or favors. He knew he would receive no help. "I will live somehow, but live I will, and work." He would seek employment in some literary occupation. He would depend on stenography. Then he would "work, work, work! . . . Trust in God and work." He would "test the social problem." He found himself face to face with deep aspirations as well as with ordinary needs. He also at this time confronted the implication of these plans: "This work I shall undertake not for myself alone but for my children, for the people with whom I am connected, for humanity."

It was a frightening commitment. He would achieve such excellence as to shatter the barriers of color and caste. Charles had by now lived for some time with these thoughts. He seemed comfortable when he had written them down. He went on with a reminder, a platitude: "He who would master others should first learn to master himself."

At twenty he took stock. He was a teacher and a father; he was ambitious and he wanted to be famous. He was given to "aerial architecture." He imagined himself as a lawyer, a physician, an architect, a farmer, a minister, a teacher, a poet, a musician, a reporter, an editor, an author, a politician. He imagined himself as rising to the top. For the present, teaching limited his development, and his discontent made him irritable. He needed greater self-control, but that would be his last attainment. He added that he had greater experience of books and life than most men at twenty and that he was generally respected, for he tried to appear in a good light.

Much of the time Charles was absorbed in the challenge of mastering new material, but there was a level at which he was thinking about racial questions. Sometimes he commented on incidents involving race relations. In 1879 the *Christian Union,* a newspaper, had taken alarm over

---

48. H. Chesnutt, *Pioneer,* p. 16.

the intimidation of voters. A correspondent disapproved: "Let the colored people protect themselves," the letter said. An "intense white light of criticism" would protect them anyway. Though Charles was skeptical about the "intense white light of criticism," he admitted that for ten or twelve years after the war Negroes in North Carolina had "little or no trouble in the exercise of their political rights." Chesnutt thought in 1879 that other Southern states might look to North Carolina. He hoped that full human recognition might come in time: "In this country of rapid changes the time of that recognition is not very far off."

Charles thought that the North had found it against their interest long before the war "to oppress the colored people." It had not crossed his mind that racial prejudice could be strong in states that had abolished slavery. There were shifting currents, but Charles then thought they were residual waves from slavery, not rising caste constructions. He hoped in 1870 that "the unreasonable prejudice against Negroes would finally disappear."

It was a period of tremendous industrial growth. Black people were the majority of the laboring class in the South. Some were menial workers, but others knew mechanical trades. One day there could be a middle class, and it would have to be recruited from the colored people. Charles did not underestimate the disadvantages Negroes faced. But he felt young, strong, full of hope. The American people would "recognize worth, ability or talent wherever it shows itself." Like young Americans everywhere he believed in "The American Dream" and he applied it to the situation closest to him: If "the colored people as a class, show themselves worthy of respect... the old prejudice will vanish." Negroes encountered more obstacles to overcome, but at twenty-one in 1879, he wrote, "They will overcome them."

He prepared a reply to the letter in the *Christian Union,* ending with passionate words: "The Colored Man in America will become a strong pillar in the Temple of American Liberty and be 'bone of one bone, flesh of one flesh' with the New American Nation!" But, "This letter was not published," he wrote. "I am glad of it. It was not worth publishing." All the same, he had expressed an idea. Despite the complexities of cultural values that affected Charles, the idea was then and always his deepest dream.

Charles intended to go to the metropolis. He practiced stenography; finally he got a job reporting lectures for Professor Todd at the white Normal School. Soon that seemed a small matter. He counted his chickens. He would go to Washington; he would send his brothers to college, resign his position, build a fine house, edit a great journal, and acquire a world-wide reputation! The Normal School job was little more

65

than a living. But Charles could laugh. "I had just sufficient sense left to engage myself for the next session"—at the Normal School.[49] But the week after the Normal School closed, he said good-bye to Susan and the baby and set out toward Washington.[50]

On a second-class ticket, he got "the full benefit" of the dirt and the smoke from the engine. The train was provokingly slow. The route lay through Raleigh to Norfolk, where he would connect with a steamer for Washington. This was an "accommodation freight train." Charles described the coach: "A small, badly furnished box, with dirty floors, dirty windows, and ... an empty water can, with a battered tin cup to tantalize the thirsty traveller." The "victim" could read, smoke, or count rails in fences. He could get out at stations for a drink, and walk a few miles down the track, then sit down to wait for the train. "The Captain, as he is called in the South—such is the mania for titles!"—allowed Charles to ride first class as far as Franklin, where he changed for Norfolk.

That was a change for the worse. Charles rode in the second-class car. Another traveler was in the same fix, so it was fairly bearable until they took on about fifty black workers going to work on a truck farm. They filled the seats and the standing room and had to sit in each other's laps. The day was warm and the laborers dirty; Chesnutt wrote that "the odor may better be imagined than described." Charles sympathized with the man from Weldon who stuck his head out of the window. Soon one of the black men began singing hymns, as if he were at a camp meeting. The same man took his "sister" on his lap. Such was the fervor of the caresses he bestowed on the girl that Charles doubted she was his sister.

They arrived in Norfolk at 6:00 a.m. Charles bought a ticket for Washington on the *George Leary,* a roomy steamer. He noticed the handsome women. He heard piano-playing in the ladies' cabin; he heard a "string band for quadrilles" on a lower deck.

Charles had not thought about the smells and sounds and sights of the city. But when he arrived in Washington, they commanded attention. In the city he took a friend by surprise. "W------" lived six stories up in the business part of the city, in a comfortable but dirty room. One had to bring water from a hydrant next to the water closet on the fourth floor. The hydrant was so near the water closet that Charles could not drink the water. He was aware of the noise six stories down. It was "worse than a dozen grist mills." The sounds rose from a pavement of cobblestones; one could hear "the rattle of the cars and wagons, the

---

49. Journal 2, April 23, 1879, pp. 112, 121, 113, 171, 115, 116, 124.

50. H. Chesnutt, *Pioneer,* p. 18.

tramp of pedestrians, and discordant yells of the newsboys and fruit vendors"; all this made "a hideous noise."

Soon Charles started out. He described the capitol effusively: "From its lofty summit the Goddess of Liberty looks down upon the broad land which acknowledges her sway." Twice Charles visited the Senate. He heard Senator James G. Blaine and Senator Zebulon B. Vance. Once he went to the House. Suddenly, a flurry arose. The Speaker rapped so that Alexander H. Stephens, formerly Vice-President of the Confederacy, but now old and decrepit, could roll his invalid's chair down the aisle. Charles wanted to hear Senator Blanche Bruce, the colored Senator from Mississippi. He "did not have that pleasure as he was always absent when I visited the Senate Chamber."

He found the colored schools "well graded." They had efficient teachers, usually intelligent, good-looking young ladies. "There are eight colored school buildings in the city," he wrote. He visited Howard University and noted that it occupied "a very healthy location, removed from the noise and dust, and quite near enough for the conveniences of the city."

He was eager to get to the business that had brought him to the city. Everybody realized it was difficult to find government employment, for all positions were "gifts of political favoritism." Charles discovered that ability does not insure opportunity. He found himself confronting indifferent people hustling about. He saw that nobody would give him a job just because he could take down a message. He needed to do more maneuvering, and he needed further preparation.

Charles was conscious of class differences; he was coming to understand that they characterized all societies. As for Washington—it was beautiful, large, and systematically planned. The people had an easy bearing that set them apart from country people. But he disliked some things: there was too much noise, too little fresh air. Hydrant water was good, but not as good as water drawn from a well. There were too many people. As for city living, he would like to live just far enough away "to avoid the disagreeable things," just near enough to get "a taste of its pleasures."

He experienced an old failing—homesickness—and it overwhelmed him, though he knew he had gained more than he had lost. He had surveyed a beautiful city; visited Congress; heard great men speak; and visited art galleries, schools, and museums. He reflected that his new knowledge divested the city of glamorous stage effects. There were advantages for the present in the job he had. On Thursday a letter from Susan arrived.[51] Charles packed and started home.

---

51. Journal 2, pp. 130, 131, 132, 140, 145; H. Chesnutt, *Pioneer*, p. 18.

He reached Fayetteville on Sunday morning, and, finding everybody well, ate breakfast, took a warm bath, and gave himself up "to rest from the fatigue of travelling." Except that Charles was not prodigal, this homecoming was like that of the Prodigal Son. Charles was the only person who thought he should go out to conquer the world and attempt to change it. He had surveyed the possibilities and he had returned. His father and his brother came to see him at the Perry house. In his journal Charles exaggerated his reception. During the next week, "several thousand people, more or less, have come up to me with beaming eyes and extended hands and inquired 'how I liked my trip?'" Information traveled fast in Fayetteville! Charles thought that either "I am popular, or...these are inquisitive people."

Like the Prodigal, Charles had had telling lessons: He did not "understand phonography well enough"; more important, there would be other obstacles. One needs money. This was sobering. It is difficult to get a job; it takes knowledge and energy to look in the right places. He wrote that "The advantages of city life can only be fully enjoyed by the wealthy, while the poor feel the full weight of the discomforts."

But unlike the Prodigal, he intended to leave again. He made a plan for the summer of 1879—his twenty-first summer: one hour for Latin, one hour for German, one hour for French, one hour for literary composition, and one hour in the garden. Then he would practice shorthand. The rest of the time he would read and tend the baby. For a while he would give up daydreaming about future triumphs, the "dangerous profession of aerial architecture." By applying himself he could become somewhat independent. Writing these ideas helped him tolerate the unfulfilled present. Charles Chesnutt settled down to sustained study. He did not change his decision to "go to the metropolis." He merely postponed the move.[52]

The Protestant Ethic and the Hopes of the Heart

Charles stopped writing in the journal. For the next eight months (1879-80) he only copied poems and entered words from ballads. When he returned he made an explanation, as if to a neglected friend.[53] Actually, he had stretched his capacities; he had married, and he felt less need.

But he was returning. Frequently he had an idea about a story or a character; such a thought could blaze through one's mind like a meteor

---

52. Journal 2, pp. 143, 201, 143, 144, 147.

53. Ibid., p. 151.

and disappear. Perhaps he hoped that in the journal he could keep some of those thoughts from flashing away.

He wrote about a revival in Fayetteville.[54] He had been struck by the singing; perhaps the spirituals would interest literary people. They were original, though they were "crude," "unpolished"; but one feels natural ability and character. There are writers who rank higher for originality than "polish," writers like "Burns or Bunyan," for example. He thought of their simplicity, of the "force which accompanies simplicity."

Charles related his thoughts about other subjects to writing. He analyzed the ballads: they take figures of speech, such as "The Life Boat," "The Gospel Trains," "The Old Ship of Zion," and they carry out the metaphor. "The verse is generally the merest doggerel but the ideas are often good." The tunes are well adapted to congregational singing; the leader sings the verse alone, or sometimes with whoever knows the words. The best part is the chorus, when the congregation joins in. The words are distinct, the time is perfect. What an improvement over the "slow, tiresome drag with which the ordinary hymn tunes are sung!" The fine time resulted from the perfect, simple rhythm of the tunes and the habit of keeping time with the feet or upper part of the body.[55]

Charles had never been to a revival that lasted so long, or got such results: 104 persons joined the church; 400 professed religion.[56] "The bar-rooms have been nearly depopulated, for the revival has reached some of the most confirmed evil-doers." He wrote about financial aspects with quiet humor: the minister had raised a debt of $100 (for the parsonage), bought an organ for $130, bought a clock for $10, then raised his salary by $125 for the next three months. "He is an energetic man. He has a queer way of mixing up religion and money." The preacher could tell the Bible stories with such an appropriate touch of local color that listeners felt involved.

Charles felt a greater urgency about his studies and, also, greater confidence. By June 1880 he had made "considerable progress by my unassisted efforts heretofore, and feel that I can make greater now."

But in March, Robert Harris became ill. "I sincerely hope he will recover, but fear that he may not," Chesnutt wrote. Soon some were making calculations about who would succeed Harris as principal of the Normal School.

---

54. Revivals were frequent events.

55. Journal 2, March 11, 1880, p. 151.

56. Ibid., p. 157. The number who joined the church is almost illegible. The figure may be 104 or 704; probably it is 104.

About then Charles read an exciting novel, *A Fool's Errand* by Judge Albion Tourgee, who had come to live in the South after the War. How did Northerners feel about the former slaves? Charles guessed that "There is something romantic, to the Northern mind, about the Southern Negro." As a writer he realized that there is a romantic side. But Chesnutt thought Northerners understood that Southerners were blinded "by the hazy moral and social atmosphere which surrounded the average Negro." People in the North escaped too much familiarity, as well as an excessive veneration for "our institutions." They "see in the colored people a race but recently emancipated from a cruel bondage; struggling for education, for a higher social and moral life, against wealth, intelligence and race prejudice, which are all united to keep them down." Northerners were still ready to listen to what was wrong, ready to help, interested in "all that is spoken or written" about an oppressed race.[57] Perhaps Charles remembered the reception accorded the tale of Simon Legree and Little Eva.

Charles found *A Fool's Errand* provocative. He had heard that Judge Tourgee sold his book for $20,000.[58] Charles was excited by the possibilities of writing about the subject that interested him most deeply, and at the same time making a living:

If Judge Tourgee with his necessarily limited intercourse with colored people and with his limited stay in the South can write such interesting descriptions, with such vivid pictures of southern life and character as to make himself rich and famous, why could not a colored man who has lived among colored people all his life; who is familiar with their habits, their ruling passions, their prejudices, their condition, their public and private ambitions, their religious tendencies and habits, why could not a colored man who knew all this and who besides had possessed such opportunities for observation and conversation with the better class of white men in the South as to understand their modes of thinking; . . . why could not such a man . . . write a far better book about the South than Judge Tourgee or Mrs. Stowe has written?[59]

But Charles never commented about the implication of Judge Tourgee's title. The theme was that the Northerner had come to live in

57. Journal 2, June 25, 1880, pp. 203, 157, 158, 152.

58. The figure is unsubstantiated, but the possibility of making money by writing influenced Chesnutt, as did the subject.

59. Journal 2, p. 161.

the new South on a fool's errand; he met defeat and had to withdraw from the South.

Charles decided to record impressions as well as conversations among Negroes for stories. He would record only conversations between Negroes and conversations with white people about Negroes.

He began with a conversation with the prominent George Haigh about a lady who had a servant problem after the war:

"Well," [Charles told him], "that is one of the inconveniences that the rich have to suffer that the poor are not troubled with. . . ."

Mr. Haigh continued his complaints: "It's hard to get honest ones [servants]. . . . [It's a] pity their ministers don't preach to them [not to steal] as a fundamental doctrine approved by their religion."

"Well, they do," Charles answered, "And you—"

But the bookseller went on:

"It's hard work to get a servant that won't steal. . . . They carry off all the cold victuals, and you have to support their pigs and dogs if they have any. . . . And they are so extravagant. You've no idea what a quantity of good victuals they throw into the swill."

"You ought to superintend their work and see that they do it right," Charles said.

But Haigh had given up: "You can't superintend them. If you look into the kitchen or venture a mild remark . . . they get mad right away, and tell you by their looks. . . ."

Charles told Haigh that this was the result of slavery. Then Haigh said something that caused Charles to remark, "There is less drunkenness among the colored people of this town than might have been expected."

Haigh agreed: "Yes, there is."

Charles suggested that Robert Harris had trained his scholars in temperate ways. The bookseller agreed with this principle: "Well, that is the only way you can get at them. Begin when they are young and train them up to it."[60]

There were temperance meetings, there were country camp meetings, there were revival meetings, and there was church. Charles attended

---

60. Ibid., p. 162. This conversation is written in longhand. Chesnutt also occasionally uses shorthand, in margins.

them all. Always he looked for ways to change his situation. Once he spoke to the Negro preacher Elder Davis about Representative Daniel Russell, their Congressman. Elder Davis thought he could get a favor from Russell, but he saw a different future for Charles.

"Professor Harris is going to die," he said, "and you must take that school. We want it and we'll get it." Davis also had other plans; he hoped Fayetteville would become a port of entry. Then they would want Charles for Collector of Customs.

Each of these positions would have been an improvement, yet Charles wanted neither. "My tastes lie in a different direction," he wrote.[61] He would wait and search and study.

He often talked with Elder Davis, and he set down some insights that emerged from these conversations.[62] Elder Davis had concluded that he had three classes of people to preach to and that he had to preach to them all at one time; in fact, he had to preach to them all in one sermon. First were the educated people. They had gone to school, and they knew what preaching was. But they were a small minority. Second were those who were moderately intelligent, but who had very little learning. The lowest class were the "ignorant, unlettered, naturally stupid ones who can't be reached by anything but excitement and extravagance." They were the most numerous, by far.

Elder Davis understood his problem: he had to "please 'em all and keep the church together." That was the only way he could depend on his salary. So he had developed a plan. First, "go at it in a regular pulpit style." This meant "fling in a trifle of Latin and Greek," divide the sermon into headings, even read from a manuscript. That much for the intelligent class. Next, come down a little—throw in colloquialisms, make slips in grammar, forget to stick to the text, only throw in a big word here and there "as a sort of puzzle you know," to keep up dignity. This would take care of the second class.

But to please the third class—the most numerous—required a "tug of war!" For that he shut the Bible, rumpled his hair, shoved up his coat sleeves—"have taken my coat clean off in country churches." Now he left the text altogether. It was best first to go down to the depths of hell and depict all the horrors of damnation—to give them "the flames, the anguish, the shrieks and groans of tortured souls." Next, appeal to those sinners present to think about this that they would be coming to:

---

61. Ibid., p. 171.

62. Chesnutt, *Mandy Oxendine.* CC, Fisk, pp. 78-81. In this work, Chesnutt details another outdoor camp meeting as Lowery observed it.

"I forget all about grammar and come down to plain 'niggerisms.'" The last thing is to leave hell and take the "audience" to heaven, giving them every glory of that blessed place. Here he would use up the Revelations and all the older prophets; and after that fall back on his imagination—point to the long white robes for all the angels, the starry crowns, the golden slippers. When the audience was worked up to just the right pitch, he would achieve a smashing climax: he would bring his fist down on the Bible, knock the water pitcher off the pulpit, and launch into a final burst to bring the house down.

The preacher was effective. If anything, he understated the results of his antics. Charles saw Davis jump down from the pulpit and run across the altar. This precipitated a rare scene. "The whole house rose as if by magic." Everybody was seized with an impulse to make all the noise possible. The mourners writhed and shrieked. Two sisters hugged one another "with suffocating energy." Another sister threw herself violently about—Charles thought she would break her back on the benches. Another sister tried to shake hands with every person in the church. Some laughed hysterically, others cried. Some "amused themselves" by tearing off their clothes, while others, "less considerate but more economical," tore off the clothes of their neighbors. There was much crying of "Mercy" by the sinners, and much getting down on the floor as low as possible. Those other participants, Christians, shouted "Glory!" and they jumped up from the floor as high as they could. The preacher let it run; then instantly, as if by "animal magnetism," he stopped it. Charles thought the preacher's fortune would be made if such charisma could be projected through the telegraph![63]

Charles asked Elder Davis whether he thought this sort of performance had an elevating effect; did Elder Davis not think he should lift the people up as well as please them?

To this the preacher, never at a loss, pointed to a stick on the floor. "I can't pick it up," he answered, "without putting my hand down to it. And so it is with the more ignorant class of our people; you must go down to them before you can bring them up, which can only be done by excitement. Then you can work on them . . . like getting in new ground. You must first grub at the soil, break it up, and then you can cultivate it."

Charles laughed, but the preacher had made his point. Yet Charles wished never to witness such a scene again; Elder Davis and his calculations troubled him.

---

63. Journal 2, p. 171.

There were other conversations with the bookseller George Haigh, who was a repository for the town's opinions and concerns, its expectations and many confusions. Once they discussed those Negro families who left Fayetteville in the 1850s. Haigh thought they were the town's "best colored families," and that it was a loss when they left. Charles, whose parents had been among them, reminded Haigh of the circumstances: "You had taken away their suffrage, the laws were becoming more and more severe toward free colored people; and they felt that their only safety lay in emigration to a freer clime. They didn't know how soon they themselves would be made slaves. They had been deprived of every safeguard of liberty." Charles wondered why Haigh thought it was strange that they left. He expressed what he often implied in his journal: "I can't see how intelligent colored people can live in the South now." He stated the reasons: there was a prejudice; it was impossible to rise in the social scale.

The bookseller thought that the grades of society were the best preservations of the society. But Charles spoke of how the North was forging ahead in science, in art, in literature. He grew excited; he offended Haigh, who also grew excited. This fretting about one's condition was fighting against God! Charles should understand that God placed men as they are!

"Would you consider a slave as fighting against the will of God if he sought his freedom?" Charles flung back.

Haigh did not answer this embarrassing question. He hoped to soothe Charles by remarking that these thoughts were perfectly natural. But in spite of perfectly natural thoughts, things would "never be different, for the line must be drawn somewhere, and the best plan is to draw it where it is." Haigh dreaded the possibility that social barriers could break down; would there be any society left?

Charles was neither soothed nor appeased. If social barriers broke down, society would regulate itself. But Haigh rambled on. Things "never, never, never" would be changed. The only thing to do if a man didn't like it was to go away.[64]

Charles believed that Haigh was right. He felt impatient. Already he had witnessed so many changes in social use and custom that he knew things could be different. Even the climate of opinion was shifting. Sometimes he believed that a well-timed push would be enough.[65]

Meanwhile Charles was taking over Robert Harris's duties; for Harris

---

64. Ibid., pp. 182, 183, 184.

65. Logan, The Negro in North Carolina, passim.

had now nearly lost the use of his legs, and he suffered delusions. The delusion that he could get well was a last blessing.

Charles took part in every kind of activity in Fayetteville.[66] Once there was an enthusiastic gathering of Republicans at the Market House. In the warmth, someone nominated Charles Chesnutt for town commissioner. He accepted—only to regret that he had done so. Several white people "remonstrated." George Haigh spoke to him about the "indiscretion." "Captain Williams," "Powers," and "several others" had "contrived to put so many 'fleas in my ear' that I sent in my formal withdrawal to the Chairman of the Committee and backed off as gracefully as possible." Perhaps there had been an agreement as to who should have the nomination; perhaps people disagreed among themselves except on the understanding that a white person should be nominated. In any case they objected, as their predecessors had objected to his father's brief term as a town commissioner. Relations were strained. Everyone wanted to forget the matter.[67]

About a month before his twenty-second birthday in 1880, Charles made a long entry. He wrote about the directions his life could take. One was to pursue pleasure; the other was constantly to undertake mental activity. It seems that Charles was striving to confirm a pattern for his life. Neither taste nor habit would incline him to "mere animal enjoyment," but "The Devil is a skillful strategist," who throws darts "from within and without." Evil intrudes and cannot "easily be driven away." He would never become a drunkard or a rake. These were "the coarsest forms of vice."[68]

The second course, constant employment of the mind, would be salvation. His thoughts welled up like waves on a beach; they reached a threshold where he could swim with them; then receded, surged, and receded again. His mind had to be active, with good or evil thoughts. One needed "compulsory" occupation for the mind. One's profession took six hours, one slept about eight hours, and this left ten hours. Keeping busy can be as demanding as a city editor's daily task of supplying forty columns of newspaper material. Chesnutt expressed a concern of industrial man: How can a person find life bearable without meaningful work to do?

66. Charles W. Chesnutt to E. J. Lilly, Oct. 16, 1916. CC, Fisk.

67. Journal 2, May 8, 1880, p. 185. See Oates, Story of Fayetteville, pp. 241-42. Chesnutt's father was a town commissioner in 1868-1870, during the Governorship of William W. Holden in the brief Republican period. The author conveys the resentment over the appointment of three Negroes among the Commissioners.

68. Journal 2, p. 188.

Now Charles approached problems with greater maturity. It was necessary to endure frustration: "A child may cry for the moon," but a wise man should be "content to wait." If there was no good conversation he could read about a subject, then find another author who looked at it from a different perspective. After that he could refer to historical facts. A man should come to "opinions of his own"—not about such technical questions as whether the planets are inhabited, but about history and politics.[69]

How would he pass the summer? He would get regular exercise and study. He would try to find teachers "for my favorite studies." He would fish, and he would rent a piano. He would subscribe to papers and magazines. If Susan and the baby were gone he would have time. By all these activities he could "kill the time to advantage." Then he drew a line through those words and wrote "pass the time pleasantly and profitably."

Charles had hoped for lessons in French and German from E. M. Neufelt, and he had hoped to study Greek. Though some of Professor Neufelt's patrons objected to his teaching a Negro student, Professor Neufelt told Charles that he was sufficiently independent to lose twenty scholars, and that he would try to make arrangements.[70]

Charles suffered from loneliness. "I would like to have a friend my equal or superior in attainment, talents and ambition," he wrote. "Solitude is best for study, but one needs conversation and recitation and discussion to fix what he has learned upon his memory." He must cease to long for what was beyond his reach. "I must take my Journal for my confidant," he wrote. He could "write in it things that I cannot well tell to other people." It seemed that he got more encouragement from others than from his family. They could not understand his need for his studies nor could they understand his feelings. His journal would not condemn him for egotism. It was painful to reflect that the people dearest to him were in some respects farthest away.[71]

Charles wanted to write. He had made attempts to put down a story or a poem, and he had shyly tried to communicate with an audience he pretended was there. All that gave way to a matter-of-fact recognition.

One day an urgency came over him; he felt afraid to start, for he had little experience with composition. Nevertheless he felt pushed toward the idea. He made a list of accomplishments: a knowledge of the classics, a speaking acquaintance with modern languages, an "intimate

---

69. Ibid.

70. Ibid., June 25, 1880, p. 199.

71. Ibid., p. 201.

friendship" with literature; seven years of teaching, two years of marriage, and one year of fatherhood. All of this would contribute. He had lived fifteen years in the South "in one of the most eventful eras of its history." He had lived those years among a people whose life was rich in appeal to human sympathies, "under conditions calculated to stir one's soul to the very depths." A writer could use this experience with tremendous effect.

Why would one write aside from feeling that one must write? It would be "for a purpose, a high and holy purpose." The object of his writings would be "not so much the elevation of the colored people as the elevation of the whites." His reason for writing had changed. He would use whatever appealing story he could devise to touch the feelings of those who perpetuated a cruel custom. He would seek the elevation of the whites, "for I consider the unjust spirit of caste which is so insidious as to pervade a whole nation, and so powerful as to subject a whole race and all connected with it to scorn and social ostracism—I consider this a barrier to the moral progress of the American people."

As his ideas crystallized, he saw that it would be useless to begin "a fierce, indiscriminate onslaught," or to try "an appeal to force." There would have to be a moral revolution. Charles thought how the abolitionists had stirred people's feelings in behalf of the slave. They had appealed to principles of humanity lying dormant "in the northern heart." Charles never considered whether the Southern heart differed from the Northern heart. But he reflected that it had taken power to free the slave. Charles believed that "Education is fast freeing the Negro from the greater bondage of ignorance." It would be impossible to storm feelings: "The garrison will not capitulate," he wrote, "so their position must be mined."

Literature would mine the garrison. The Negro's part was to prepare for equality when literature had opened the way. Literature would "accustom the public mind to the idea; and while amusing people, lead them on, imperceptibly, unconsciously step-by-step to the desired state of feeling." He had expressed "the high and holy purpose." "I would gladly devote my life to the work," he wrote.

Then Professor Neufelt found he could give Charles lessons in French and German three times a week, for five dollars a month; Charles would gladly have paid ten. Charles wondered if Professor Neufelt felt sympathetic because, being a foreigner and a Jew, he had felt the sting of prejudice. Did "a fellow feeling make us wondrous kind?"

Though Charles found the French pronunciation difficult, he made rapid progress in German. Soon he could translate from English to both languages.

That summer he read of a book purporting to have been written by a "carpetbagger who was born and bred" in the South. This book confirmed Charles's belief that the former slaves remained interesting subjects to people in the North. He could probably safely wait to publish until he could do his subject justice.

Soon Charles was reading *Faust* in German. By August he was getting along in both languages. He wrote some verses in his journal, including a rhyme that George Haigh had recited:

Whigs
Feed on pigs
And ride in gigs.
Democrats
Eat dead rats
And ride on cats.

This rhyme had helped influence Haigh to become a Whig.

Charles paused to look over his journal at the end of that summer of 1880. He had written a great deal about himself. If a relative, or perhaps a friend, should write a biography of him—if he should distinguish himself, and someone should use the entries in his journal—he would seem to posterity "a most conceited fellow"—unless, by a happy chance, the writer should turn out to be a person "of excellent taste and literary judgment."

He made the last entry in the long second journal: on March 26 of the next year, 1881, he had finished Thackeray's *Vanity Fair*. Every time he read a good novel he wanted to write one. This seemed crucial to his dreams. "It is not altogether the money," he said. "It is a mixture of motives. I want fame, I want money, and I want to raise my children in a different rank of life from that I sprang from."[72]

To Be—in Cleveland

"His morality is high toned, and although colored he is a gentleman." Charles would never forget that recommendation. He carried it to Raleigh when the Board requested he apply for the appointment as principal of the Normal School.[73]

But now that Robert Harris was dead, Charles knew he did not want to become principal.[74] Believing in progress,[75] feeling the American

---

72. Ibid., pp. 194, 195, 196, 198, 205, 220, Sept. 8, 1880, 220, March 26, 1881.

73. H. Chesnutt, *Pioneer,* p. 25. This is one of many letters Helen Chesnutt quoted or cited but did not include in materials presented to Fisk University.

74. Journal 2, p. 181.

75. Ibid., p. 111.

Dream, expressing it,[76] he had wasted little time in mourning his circumstances or a fate that seemed to condemn him to live in them. He had educated himself, he had learned shorthand; he had even recently taken down a speech of Frederick Douglass for the *Raleigh Sentinel*.[77] He had built an image of the role he wanted to fill. It did not encompass becoming or remaining principal of the Normal School.

But he had gone to Raleigh to apply for the position.[78] He and Susan had moved to a house of their own, for they expected a second child in another month.[79] Because they considered Charles a good, stable Negro, the members of the Board recommended that the principal's salary be raised from $62.50 to $75 per month.[80] A letter to Governor Jarvis urged the Governor to "recognize the justice of increasing the salary."[81]

Charles got the appointment and the increase in pay. To all appearances the young Chesnutts were well enough off after that. They bought an organ. In December their second daughter was born, and Susan employed a woman to help with the housework and the care of the babies, Ethel and Helen.[82] It was expected that Charles would fill the shoes of Robert Harris.

But Charles was discontented. At twenty-two he was married, twice a father, and established as a school principal. But he intended to pursue another course. He read and studied as he slept and ate. He practiced shorthand. He took down sermons and all the lectures he could attend.[83] He joined in community activities; he acted as organist at the Methodist Church where his father was secretary-treasurer, and he became superintendent of the Sunday School.[84] He began to offer Latin

---

76. Journal 3, March 7, 1882. Chesnutt wrote "Can work produce success? Then success is mine!" Earlier, Journal 2, April 23, 1879, he wrote "Work, work, work! I will trust in God and work."

77. H. Chesnutt, *Pioneer*, p. 26. The date was October, 1880. Helen A. Whiting, Teaching Principal, Atlanta University Laboratory School, Paper 17, Moorland-Spingarn Collection, Howard University, Washington, D.C.

78. Journal 2, p. 161.

79. H. Chesnutt, *Pioneer*, pp. 25-26.

80. Dr. T. D. Haigh, Chairman, J. D. Williams, President of the Fayetteville Bank, and W. C. Troy were white Board members of the State Colored Normal School; letters, CC, Fisk, Nov. 18, 1880, June 24, 1882. Journal 2, April 23, 1879.

81. Journal 2, p. 183. An editorial, *Fayetteville Observer*, June 21, 1883, mentions Chesnutt's "acceptability to the patrons of the school and the citizens generally."

82. H. Chesnutt, *Pioneer*, p. 25.

83. Journals 2 and 3, passim; H. Chesnutt, *Pioneer*, p. 26.

84. Parker, "Chesnutt as a Southern Town Remembers Him."

lessons to young colored people for one dollar a month, as well as voice and organ lessons for twenty-five cents a lesson.[85] He could use the money; although he was better off, his expenses had increased disproportionately. Two years earlier, in 1877, he had kept an account of "outlays," and had finished by scrawling "Failure!" on the page.[86] He terminated his lessons in French and German because he could not afford them, but also because he had learned about all he could from his teacher.

He wrote in the third and last of his Fayetteville journals sporadically, taking up his pen only when there was something out of the ordinary. His life was full; he had come to terms with many needs. He no longer felt pressed to discover directions. At twenty-two, an age when many still search, he knew.

But he still recorded conversations as well as insights, and he still put down observations about his reading. He read Goldsmith's *Rome,* and Merivale's *Rome.* A scholar should strive to be "accurate in all he knows," but it is difficult to be accurate. He began to wrestle with problems of how to find information: what information is trustworthy, and whose interpretations are meaningful in terms of the questions? Historians differed; inherent in their presentations were distinct points of view. Depending on their interests they told different stories about the same events.

A few days later (on January 21, 1881), he noted that he was reading part of a "thorough course in history and poetry." But between comments he would record a conversation.

He talked with Robert Hill, a former slave. Robert told Charles that a white man tried to persuade him to vote for the Democrats, because it would be best to "let them damn Yankees alone." But Robert Hill told the man that "Them damn Yankees" had made the only laws favorable to colored people. Charles and he thought that it would be best for property owners to administer local affairs in the South and so prevent the Democrats from dictating everything, even office-holding; and they thought that they should support only Republicans in national affairs.

Then Robert Hill told Charles that he, Charles, had been the subject of another discussion. Charles felt the fascination of hearing himself talked about. Robert had been speaking to John McLaughlin, a poor white clerk in Williams' store. McLaughlin had asked about Charles: "What kind of a fellow was he?"

---

85. H. Chesnutt, *Pioneer,* p. 26.

86. Journal 2, Oct. 27, 1877, p. 206.

"Well, sir," was the answer, "He's a perfect gentleman in every respect; I don't know his superior."

"Why," said McLaughlin, "he's a nigger, ain't he?"

"Yes, but—"

"Well, what kind of an education has he?"

"He's not a college-bred man, but he has been a hard student all his life. You can't ask him a question he cannot answer," said Hill.

McLaughlin continued his questions:

"He's this shorthand writer?"

"Yes, sir."

"Does he think he's as good as a white man?"

"Every bit of it, sir," and Robert Hill supplied more information about Chesnutt's accomplishments.

But McLaughlin was unimpressed. He delivered what Charles called "the opinion of the South on the Negro question":

"Well, he's a nigger; and with me a nigger is a nigger, and nothing in the world can make him anything else but a nigger."[87]

By then Charles believed that McLaughlin had expressed the hard Southern view of race relations; the report buttressed his determination to alter the conditions of his life.

By March 1881 Charles had also read a play by Moliere, probably in French,[88] and he had "skimmed" a book by William Wells Brown. Books were events. Many were provocative, absorbing; but this book, *The Negro in the American Rebellion*, excited him because it lacked those qualities. "Dr. Brown's books are mere compilations," he wrote, "And if they were not written by a colored man, they would not sell for enough to pay for the printing." The book strengthened his opinion that the American Negro who could write a good book was yet to become known.[89] He grew more hopeful and determined that he might be the first Negro to write a good novel.

That would have to wait. At twenty-three, he was still seeking a way to get to the city. He found examination periods irksome, and other problems more irksome. One spring day he had to keep his "men" in to lecture them on "wenching."[90] Then the girls got into a fight. "The young

---

87. Journal 3, Jan. 15, 1881; Jan. 21, 1881. Some entries extend over several pages, with or without numbers.

88. Chesnutt gives the title in French—*Le Mari Confondu;* and in English—*The Cuckold.* By this time he occasionally wrote in French in the Journal; he read French competently. Journal 3, March 17, 1881.

89. Journal 2, March 16, 1879, p. 161; Journal 3, March 17, 1881.

90. Journal 3, April 10, 1881.

folks seem to have spring fever," wrote this twenty-three-year-old Normal School principal, who was himself young in the springtime of 1881. "I suppose the weather affects them somewhat like the other young animals. I am afraid they are told very little at home about correct principles."[91]

Despite the malaise he felt, despite the ominous conversations, Charles was sometimes still hopeful for the Negro in North Carolina. In May of 1881 he wrote that the colored man was "moving upward" very fast. He thought perhaps the Prohibition Movement could partly break down the color line. He hoped that it would bring white and colored people nearer together, "to their mutual benefit."

For this reason he went on August 3, 1881, to a Prohibition meeting at the Market House. There was an anti-Prohibition meeting the same evening at Liberty Point. But he did not even record how the people voted the following day. He seemed more interested in going to Carthage to see his wife and babies, for they had been away for a month. But he took along his Shakespeare, a "Mental Philosophy," a "Logic," and a few other books. He wrote no more till the end of the year, on the last night, December 31, 1881. He had been reading *King Henry the Sixth* and thinking about Falstaff, Pistol, and Fluellen, the amusing characters he had met while reading *Henry the Fifth*.[92]

Charles had always hoped that the Reconstruction years would finally set the South on the road to achieving equality of the races; but he was not unaware of the changing winds. He had measured the obstacles the former slaves would encounter; he had surmounted many of them. He knew they were formidable. To reveal them would indict those who sustained them and exonerate those who suffered from them. In January of 1882 he wrote some bitter, satirical verses. They were never published, and he did not copy them into the journal. But he did preserve them with the title "A perplexed Nigger" written in his hand across the first page:

I'm "quite an intelligent nigger"
As words in our section go.
I live in the land where the rice
And the cane and the cotton grow.
I'm quite an ambitious nigger,
But, the Democrats now being in,

---

91. Chesnutt's Ms, "A Teacher Should Be a Christian Gentleman," unpublished. CC, Fisk.

92. Journal 3, May 4, 1881; Aug. 4, 1881.

I'm afraid I can't get elected,
To the Legislature again.
. . . .
And it's right good American logic—
Indeed, it's the general belief,
When a nigger can't prove himself honest,
He certainly must be a thief—
A white man's regarded as honest,
Until his rascality's shown;
But a nigger, you know, is *different*
As the white folks have always known.
. . . .
Down here, if a crime is committed,
And the criminal cannot be found,
Suspicion will rest on a nigger,
If there's one in a mile around.
And then, if the nigger's imprisoned,
Whether guilty they don't wait to see,
They take him away from the gaoler,
And swing him right up to a tree.
. . . .
Perhaps some wise man of the white folks,
Will make the mystery plain,
Why justice and Christian charity,
Are different for different men;
Why they set us aside in the churches
And even in the common schools,
And in the insane asylums,
They separate even the fools![93]

Sometimes he still had hope, but without doubt he deplored the direction opinion was taking by the spring of 1882. He knew that for many people the institutions of caste, now reappearing, would always be God's way. He had heard people say that conditions would never change; now, in spite of the war and the changes it had brought, he had frequent forebodings. He had heard Negroes speak of "white friends." He wrote in his journal that, for himself, he had no white friends. A man who felt himself too good to sit at a table with him or to sleep in the same hotel was no friend. Friendship exists between men who have

---

93. Excerpts from Chesnutt, "A Perplexed Nigger" (unpublished MS), January, 1882. CC, Fisk.

common interests, "who are equals in something, if not everything." He felt that old sharp longing for a friend: "I hope yet to have a friend," he wrote. "If not in this world, then in some distant future eon."[94]

He grew more impatient with the daily irritations. He felt some hesitation about leaving the school, but weightier reasons for going. The most important was to "serve my race better in some more congenial occupation." Second, he could protect his children from "the social and intellectual proscription" of which he had been a victim. He visited New York and Cleveland in the summer of 1882, and the trip confirmed his impressions. After he took the thirty-six-hour return journey from Cleveland to Salisbury, North Carolina, he found his family—who had been spending the summer there—"in good health and spirits." He wrote a letter to his Cleveland cousin, John P. Green: "[Salisbury] is a dirty, slow looking place after a couple of months in your pretty towns and beautiful cities of the North." He believed he could "endure the South three or four years longer."[95] But he stayed at the Normal School only one more year.

He concentrated on the shorthand so intensively that by the end of 1883 he could write 200 words a minute.[96] This was a high skill compared to what he could do in 1879 when he had gone "to the North"—to conquer the world. He would be twenty-five on June 20, 1883. He announced his decision: He would go, and he would never come back to the South to live. He had made no change in the goals he had worked out before his first trip. He had shifted no commitments; he had altered himself.

Charles knew that his family would try to dissuade him. They were satisfied to have him remain principal of the Colored Normal School.[97] Susan expected another baby in September; there would be three children, and she wanted him to stay. Charles also confronted a deep reluctance that families sometimes convey when one of their number strikes out. They cannot approve his choice of adventure or his hope of distant achievement. Chesnutt's father told him how glad he had been to return from Cleveland where he had gone in his youth. Sisters, pupils, friends, associates—all begged Charles to stay. Had he listened, Charles might have imperiled his sense of direction and diminished the energies of his

94. Journal 3, March 7, 1882.

95. Chesnutt to Hon. J. P. Green, Aug. 30, 1882, John P. Green Papers, WRHS.

96. H. Chesnutt, Pioneer, p. 31.

97. Fayetteville Observer, June 21, 1883.

personality. He might have dribbled away his talent. He might have written no novels; he might have taken no memorable stands.

He wrote his letter of resignation on May 12, 1883.[98] It carried his "earnest wish that the school may long continue to prosper." The Board accepted his resignation regretfully, for Charles had been an excellent principal. Dr. T. D. Haigh, the chairman, wrote that "his conduct as a citizen has been such as to merit and receive the approval of all" and that "He carries with him the good wishes & commendations of our best people."[99] J. D. Williams, board member, and president of the Fayetteville National Bank, wrote that he considered Charles "reliable," of "unusual acquirements," and "natural gifts." He commended Charles to the "confidence and respect of those with whom he may hereafter be associated."[100] A. H. Slocomb, the leading turpentine merchant of Fayetteville, offered to arrange a credit for Charles with his New York factor.[101] The *Fayetteville Observer* even carried a commendatory—if condescending—editorial,[102] and the students at the Normal School gave him an autograph album in which each had written some lines.[103] Whatever their motives, people regretted his departure. But Charles was on his way. He never came back to Fayetteville to live.

98. Chesnutt to the Board of Managers of the State Colored Normal School, May 12, 1883. Quoted in H. Chesnutt, *Pioneer*, p. 32.

99. T. D. Haigh, no addressee, June 27, 1883. CC, Fisk.

100. J. D. Williams to Whom It May Concern, June 27, 1883. CC, Fisk.

101. H. Chesnutt, *Pioneer*, p. 33.

102. *Fayetteville Observer*, June 21, 1883.

103. Album. CC, Fisk.

AN AMERICAN CRUSADE

3

A REHEARSAL FOR ACHIEVEMENT: SIX MONTHS IN NEW YORK (JUNE TO NOVEMBER, 1883)

eaving his pregnant wife and the rest of his family in Fayetteville, Charles Chesnutt departed for New York.

"There was a charm about the 'Old Town,'" said the critic-historian Hamilton Wright Mabie, who understood Chesnutt's work and the sociological changes taking place in New York City.[1] In 1912 Mabie wrote a book about an earlier literary New York, noting that it "depended largely on neighborliness and the narrower interests which thrive in a small and homogeneous community." By 1890, however, New York had become "A metropolitan city with a population of four million souls and the old city had shrunk politically into the borough of Manhattan." It had "shrunk till it was hard to recall the obliterated outlines." New York, wrote Mabie, "had grown by the process of destruction"; it had "become metropolitan through successive stages of self-effacement." The streets presented "no traces of the old lanes and highways save an occasional name."

It was true. From the ends of the earth all kinds of people had converged upon New York City, and they had obliterated the old outlines. They had come from the countrysides—from the North, from the South. Some had walked. Some had come in wagons. Others had come on horseback—alone, and traveling in groups. After the 1840s some had come by train. For years many had been coming by boatloads from over the seas, from English or Irish or German lands. They had come seeking places and ways to live. By the 1880s many were coming as

---

1. Hamilton Wright Mabie, *The Writers of Knickerbocker New York* (New York: The Grolier Club of the City of New York, 1912), pp. 3, 120-121; "Two New Novelists," *Outlook*, Feb. 24, 1900.

well from Austria, Russia, Poland, Italy, and Serbia; some of these "new" immigrants were people of darker complexions. Most had experienced poverty. Most faced struggles. Most came to know slums, sweatshops, sickness, days of toil, nights of hunger. They huddled together in dense colonies, taking refuge in one another.[2]

Yet Charles Chesnutt and the other newcomers had arrived in the foremost city of an incredibly rich land at a time when the production of goods was soaring. Quick communication was becoming routine, quick transportation dependable. Inventions were revolutionizing life. A conspicuous few, whose holdings had recently risen from seizure or connivance, could sponsor an ideology of equal opportunity. To certain critics it began to appear, however, that opportunity was unequal, that it might be possible to banish want, that it might be conceivable to lift the poor above subsistence. They expressed their insights. But instead of improvements the New York City of 1883 presented to Charles Chesnutt and to other light and dark newcomers the enigma of civilizations: where wealth is greatest, the struggle to exist can be most desperate. While riches had been accumulating in New York City, a festering poverty had spread. The lords of industry and finance, as greedy and quarrelsome a lot as any old-world predecessors, exercised over the fortunes of millions a power almost divine.

Well before he left Fayetteville, Charles Chesnutt realized he would face a merciless competition. After his explorations in Washington, Cleveland, and New York he returned to Fayetteville to perfect his shorthand. He found himself presenting his skill and his letters of recommendation in the heart of the Wall Street district.

Chesnutt walked through Battery Park and Washington Park and down Broadway and up the shop-lined avenues. He saw the skyscrapers of lower Manhattan, and he saw the amusement places and a dazzling glitter of white night lights. But living in New York was different from visiting. There were new throngs in the streets; there were new landmarks rising over old places. For twenty years the great Cathedral of St. Patrick had been under construction at Fifth Avenue and 50th Street. Now it opened its doors. Chesnutt saw the imposing Fifth Avenue mansions and the high-stooped private dwellings that rose in the vicinity of Fifth Avenue and 34th Street.[3] From them the wealthy and the fashionable sallied forth on the business or pleasure of the day. Their mansions often figured in front-page stories of city newspapers.

---

2. Mabie, *The Writers of Knickerbocker New York,* pp. 3, 4, 120-121.

3. Susan E. Lyman, *The Face of New York City As It Was and as It Is (1848-1948)* (New York: Crown Publishers, 1954).

New York was a city of contrasts. It was apparent that the building industry had not begun to catch up with the housing needs of the multitudes. From the 1840s on newcomers were fortunate if they were able to do as well as the "converted" family structures to be seen at every turn. Most of the buildings, and most of the newer "Dumbell tenements," seemed to a country person to be conceived especially to shut out light and air. All over New York the once luxurious brownstones—those indices to the city—had become cheap boarding places. Where any lot was vacant, it had been peopled with squatters, the homeless, who had thrown up shacks of such materials as they could lay hands upon. Till someone claimed the property, they lived with goats and pigs in a squalor almost as debased as that of tenement dwellers.[4]

Charles Chesnutt had prepared himself to get along in this New York. He found immediate employment. His daughter tells us that he became a reporter for Dow, Jones, and Company, a Wall Street news agency.[5] Dow Jones, still a flourishing Wall Street concern, has preserved records only as far back as 1889, however. In that year the firm began to publish the *Wall Street Journal*. Prior to that date, and presumably in 1883 when Chesnutt was employed, it published *Dow & Jones*, a bulletin containing news of customers and their transactions on "The Street." This bulletin was written on "flimsy," and it was hand delivered daily by messengers in the Wall Street area. Unfortunately, no copies—and no personnel records for this period—have been preserved.[6]

Helen Chesnutt tells us that in addition to his work at Dow, Jones, and Company, her father supplied a column of "Wall Street News and Gossip" for the *New York Mail & Express*,[7] then a great daily paper of New York. The column appears in each issue during this period. Though there is no by-line, and though the tone differs little if at all from that of the same column printed in the paper before and after Chesnutt's stay in New York, it is possible that he wrote it. This was one way to edge into the publishing world. Miss Chesnutt quotes a later essay in which her father recalled the Wall Street figures William Vanderbilt and Jay Gould and recalled interviewing Cyrus W. Field, the own-

4. Ibid. Lyman estimates 5,000 squatters lived east of Central Park.

5. H. Chesnutt, *Pioneer*, p. 34.

6. Richard Gillespie, Public Relations Officer, interview with James Garcia, analyst, International Business Machines Co., New York, at Dow, Jones, and Company, *The Wall Street Journal*, Jan. 17, 1971.

7. H. Chesnutt, *Pioneer*, p. 34; Chesnutt to Mrs. L. M. Barnett, July 7, 1924. CC, WRHS.

er of the paper, and Henry W. Clews, a prominent banker.[8] Perhaps the unidentified persons quoted from time to time in the Wall Street gossip column were these individuals. From these reporting experiences Chesnutt undoubtedly learned a good deal about American business, especially railroads, finance, and insurance. He also learned from reading the *Mail & Express* and other New York papers; often he clipped and preserved interesting items.

Certainly the New York experience was broadening. Chesnutt used much of what he learned in stories; some of the life he observed provided material for his last published novel, *The Colonel's Dream*. Chesnutt could scarcely have failed to notice items like the one the *New York Mail & Express* carried on June 12, 1883, on the front page—where the Wall Street gossip column appeared. It covered eight inches of space. The headline was "The Vanderbilts Return." The article described the arrival of William H. Vanderbilt, then in control of a $100 million railroad fortune, his son George, and Colonel Jacob H. Vanderbilt; all were returning from Europe on the *Britannic* which had docked a little before midnight. Some of the passengers, among whom were J. Pierpont Morgan, the Very Reverend Roger Berbeist, Baron de Ropp, and others, preferred to remain aboard till morning, but the Vanderbilts disembarked and were driven at once to their Fifth Avenue mansion:

At an early hour this morning [the paper said] the house was astir and seemingly alive to some important event. Carriages in great number came and went. The busy hum of voices was heard all over the house; children of all sizes and ages ran frolicking through the halls and up and down the broad staircases, and [sic] the walls reechoing their merry laughter. Servants flitted to and fro and ever and anon were heard the report and fizz of the champagne corks as they flew from the long pent-up bottles.

In the same issue on the same page Chesnutt could have read about an instance of the high railroad accident rate of the time. The item covered an inch of space: a freight train locomotive left the track and rolled "down a forty-feet embankment, fatally injuring a brakeman named Vernox. The engineer and fireman were also severely injured."

Indeed, Chesnutt could have noticed such contrasts in all the New York papers during his six months' stay. On Sunday, July 1, 1883, for example, the *New York Times* chronicled zestfully in two columns the

---

8. Ibid. The essay cited does not appear in the Freeney-Henry list of Chesnutt material at Fisk University.

fighting of a pistol duel between two Southern editors, F. J. Beirne and William C. Elam. It described the principals in detail:

In all these [editorials at issue], [Mr. Beirne] was open, frank and fearless. No attempt was ever made to take advantage of his opponents. . . . Beirne is one of the most companionable of men. He is openhearted, jolly and noted as one of the best story tellers in this section. As a mimic he has no equals. He wears a dark brown mustache and goatee.

On the same front page that Sunday morning in July, the *Times* found an inch and a quarter for an offhand article headed "Female Cashiers on the Warpath." This story bore a Chicago dateline:

Affairs at the Palmer House are in a critical condition. Miss Paine, the cashier, got married on Thursday and the five remaining female cashiers are on the warpath for husbands or revenge and are about to sever their connections with the hotel to the general regret of the male population of the caravanery. It is intimated that Potter Palmer will avail himself of the opportunity to substitute males in their places.

Again on November 1, 1883, the *Times* printed a long front-page article called "Why They Remain at Newport." The *Times* explained that "they" stayed there in order to get divorces under the liberal laws of Rhode Island; it gave details about several New Yorkers: Mrs. Henry Trumbull, was "a great favorite in social circles." She had just arrived at Newport with her children and twenty large trunks. A little earlier (September 1, 1883, and in many other issues), the *Times* briefly noted a railroad accident:

A defective switch threw the rear truck of a Cleveland and Pittsburgh Express from the track. The coach was dragged some distance, smashing the sides of several cars of a local freight train, which was standing on a side-track and killing John Raurbauge—a brakeman of the freight train, who was standing between the tracks.

During Chesnutt's stay in the city, the *New York World* also printed on October 18, 1883, a lengthy Vanderbilt story—a detailed consideration of William H. Vanderbilt's escape from a spill while watching the horse races. On the same page on the same day, the *World* printed a little accident story. There was "a terrible railroad wreck." The paper reported that the boiler of the engine exploded as a train was passing through central Iowa. Nineteen cars piled up four miles out of Oskaloosa. The engineer was instantly killed, and the fireman and another probably fatally injured.

Much of what Chesnutt observed and thought about at this time, whether from these newspapers or the life about him, provided material for stories. One story, "A Soulless Corporation," centers about a smash-up on a railroad and the claims growing out of the accident. It is a double-edged tale of a woman's attempted deceit about the value of her trunk.[9] Another, "A Cause Celebre," illustrated the uncertainties of trial by jury, and detailed complications like those which often come to the notice of railroad agents.[10]

Other stories—some certainly growing from experiences in New York—reflect Chesnutt's deepening perceptions about the institutions of the human past, especially slavery; they show a growing ability to deal with complexities. One such piece is a poignant allegory told in a New York setting. Chesnutt called this story "A Roman Antique." It is a sharp study of social relationships. "It was a warm day in Summer [it began] and I seated myself for a moment on one of the benches in Washington Square." An old Negro came hobbling along and sat at the other end of the bench, "lifting his battered hat to me deferentially as he did so." The writer of the story was "both surprised and flattered at such a manifestation of politeness in New York." The old Negro told a tale of having been Mars Julius Caesar's "fav'rite body-sarven' "; on re-flecting he reckoned that "I's 'bout nineteen hund'ed" years of age; he remembered that he had been with Caesar in Gaul. At the battle of Alesia he had grabbed a shield, rushed into the battle, and consequently had been laid up with an arrow wound for two or three months. When he got well, Mars Julius had given him a quarter, and had "lef' direc-tions in his will fer me ter be gradually 'mancipated, so I'ud be free w'en I wuz a hund'ed years old." But the old man had spent that quarter. He needed another. "Is yer got any small change 'bout yo' clos', boss?"

A vision of imperial Rome rose up before me, with all its glory and magnificence and power. In a fit of abstraction, I handed the old man a twenty-dollar gold piece, and when I started from my reverie, he had disappeared behind a clump of shrubbery in the direction of Sixth Ave-nue.[11]

In another story, a powerful indictment called "The Origin of the Hatchet Story," the narrator recalls how the anecdote of George Wash-

---

9. Chesnutt, "A Soulless Corporation," *Tid Bits*, April 16, 1887, New York Public Library.

10. Chesnutt, "A Cause Celebre," *Puck*, Jan. 14, 1891, New York Public Library.

11. Chesnutt, "A Roman Antique," *Puck*, July 17, 1889, p. 351.

ington and his hatchet had been drummed into his ears, and how the example of Washington's brave truthfulness had been "held up to [him] early and late and very frequently in a close and painful connection" so that he began "to hate the very name of Washington." That "fatal anecdote and its associations stood in the way" of the story-teller's "patriotic duty to place [Washington's] name first on my list of heroes." But the situation was to be remedied. Years later when the narrator of this story took a trip up the Nile, a speculator in mummies showed him a papyrus of the Nineteenth Dynasty that chronicled a legend about the childhood of Rameses IV. Rammy had received a small curved sword, or scimitar, of exquisite workmanship from his father, the reigning monarch, Rameses III. In joyous excitement little Rammy ran about the palace, "trying the temper of his new blade." First he nearly cut off the ear of a Nubian eunuch; then, "toddling" to the apartment of his mama he "deftly sliced off the head-dress of one of the ladies-in-waiting, taking quite a slice of the scalp along with it." He next amputated the little finger of one of the cooks, and then finished these experiments by playfully severing the head from the body of the old king's favorite slave, Abednego. In just the words that the early American writer Mason L. Weems used to tell the American cherry-tree story,[12] Chesnutt related the encounter between the monarch and his son. To his enraged father, little Prince Rammy made an answer:

"Sir," he said, "I can not tell a lie. I did it with my little scimitar."

For a moment Rameses III was speechless with conflicting emotions. Then the trembling bystanders saw the great monarch's face soften, and heard him exclaim in feeling tones:

"Come to my arms, my son! I would rather you had killed a thousand Hebrew slaves than to have told a lie. I thank Isis that she has given me such a son."

The narrator concluded:

The perusal of this interesting papyrus at once convinced me that the hated Hatchet Story was merely one of those myths which, floating down the stream of tradition, became attached in successive generations to popular heroes, and that consequently, no obstacle stood in the way of my complete veneration of the name of Washington.[13]

---

12. Marcus Cunliffe, ed., *The Life of Washington* by Mason L. Weems (Cambridge; Belknap Press of Harvard University Press, 1962), p. 12.

13. Chesnutt, "The Origin of the Hatchet Story," *Puck*, April 24, 1889, p. 134.

In still another eloquent story, "a tall, tolerably well-dressed and somewhat distinguished colored man" is able to sell a corn plaster for a quarter only after he has delivered an elaborate—and unorthodox—recital of the events of American racial history.[14] Most of these early stories, which span the time Chesnutt spent in New York and the first years he spent in Cleveland, illustrate Chesnutt's preoccupation with the unresolved racial conflicts of American life.

Chesnutt was lonely. He missed his wife; he felt concern for her welfare and that of the little girls and the expected baby.[15] It was difficult to find a suitable place for such a family to live. If he found a place, it would cost more money than Chesnutt could think about spending. Yet he never considered returning to Fayetteville. It was plain, as it had earlier seemed plain when he visited the cities of the North, that there were crucial advantages for those who could pay for them. Chesnutt loved the book-stores of the city, the libraries, the art galleries, the theaters. He realized how superior were the educational possibilities to those he had known in Fayetteville. He saw that to attain these advantages he needed to accumulate "a competence."[16] That would be difficult in New York. He also realized—through contacts there—what he later wrote in a novel: Within the new frameworks of industrial monopoly "competition would be crushed," and "labour must sweat and the public groan in order that a few captains or chevaliers of industry might double their dividends."[17]

Chesnutt estimated the compensation possible in New York for a drifting young reporter. He contrasted this with the amount required for the luxury he had seen in a New York office. He had seen "A handsome, broad-topped mahogany desk, equipped with telephone and push-buttons, and piled with papers, account books and letters filed in orderly array."[18] As Charles Chesnutt remembered his goals and mused on the limitations of his opportunities, he thought of the city of his birth. Cleveland, too, presented a complex and challenging situation, but Cleveland would be less impersonal; his objectives might be more easily attainable there. In his months in New York, Charles had realized that most employees—like himself—were alone and vulnerable; "for their skill, expe-

---

14. Chesnutt, "An Eloquent Appeal," *Puck,* June 6, 1888.

15. H. Chesnutt, *Pioneer,* p. 35.

16. Chesnutt, Journal 3, n.d.

17. Chesnutt, *The Colonel's Dream,* p. 5.

18. Ibid., p. 9.

96

rience and prospects of advancement," they might, at any change of masters, "receive their discharge."

Nearly six months had gone by. It was snowing, and the wind, blowing "straight up Broadway from the bay"—as often it blows in New York—"swept the white flakes northward in long, feathery swirls."[19] Charles Chesnutt presented his resignation to Dow, Jones, and Company, and he terminated his connection with the *New York Mail & Express*. He packed his valise and took the train for Cleveland.

---

19. Ibid., p. 5.

AN AMERICAN CRUSADE

4

THE EARLY
CLEVELAND YEARS,
1883-90

Chesnutt Comes to Cleveland

A train rolled toward northeastern Ohio in the late fall of 1883. It rolled toward the Flats of Cleveland, a half-mile-wide valley marking a separation of the city into sections, east and west. Once some Shaker men and women had chosen this "Valley of God's Pleasure"; there they had hoped to live, industriously and gently.[1] But now steel mills, oil refineries, and lumber yards loomed in the valley; from the Flats they sent their products along the banks of the Cuyahoga, which traced a crooked course to the lake. But most of Cleveland looked out from a plain that rose some sixty to eighty feet above the Flats and the river and stretched along the southern shore of Lake Erie.[2]

The young man scanned the tracks as his train drew into Union Depot.[3] He searched past clouds of coal smoke to see the chimney tops. At length when the train slowed to a halt, Charles Chesnutt lifted his valise and descended to the wooden platform. He felt "the raw winds" and "the chill rains." Soon he would feel "the violent changes of temperature that characterized the winters"; for in the late November of 1883, Charles Chesnutt had come to Cleveland to stay.[4] It became the

---

1. Cleveland Conference for Educational Cooperation, *Cleveland Student Life*, Preface by Newton D. Baker (Cleveland, 1930), pp. 121, 22. Eldress Molly Goodrich *et al.*, *Account of Early Shakers in Ohio*, Ohio Archaeological and Historical Society, Columbus (Union Village, Ohio, July, 1903).

2. Seltzer, ed., *The Columbia Lippincott Gazetteer of the World*, p. 419. Chesnutt, *The Wife of His Youth* (1899), pp. 228-30, 232, 233.

3. Chesnutt, *The Wife of His Youth*, p. 228.

4. Chesnutt, *The Conjure Woman* (1969), p. 1. Quotations from "The Goophered Grapevine."

"Groveland" of his stories.[5] He intended it to become the scene of a lifetime effort to dispel the blight of racial caste. Chesnutt believed that caste was racial, whatever class obstructions a man must face;[6] late in life he wrote that "Caste . . . has pretty well vanished among white Americans. . . . Between the whites and the Negroes it is acute, and is bound to develop an increasingly difficult complexity." "Let men rule or serve as their talents not their color, may dictate," he wrote.[7] He intended to benefit that "body of twelve million people, struggling upward slowly but surely from a lowly estate."[8]

He knew the condition of the Negroes of Fayetteville and the North Carolina countryside. Though Negroes would account for only 1 percent of the half-million people in Cleveland by 1910, he would come to know Negro life there.[9] In 1883 there were some 2,500 Negroes; he was to live through shifts in proportions: from 1910 to 1920 the Negroes of Cleveland would more than quadruple as the number rose from 8,500 to more than 34,000.[10] By 1930 it would more than double again, while the percentage of Negroes would rise to 5 percent of the population.[11] Chesnutt would also live through an upsurge of foreign-born persons in Cleveland. There had been Germans and Irish and English; as the numbers swelled there would be Italians, Czechs, and Poles. By 1910 those born in foreign lands would come to 35 percent of the people.[12]

His first concerns were a job and a place to stay. Chesnutt rode in a horse-drawn hack from Union Depot up a steep hill to the town.[13] Then

---

5. Chesnutt to Mr. William Dean Howells, April 31 [sic], 1900, Houghton Library, Harvard University.

6. Chesnutt, "Post-Bellum—Pre-Harlem," Colophon, A Book Collectors' Quarterly, Part 5, February, 1931.

7. Chesnutt to Professor Richards, Feb. 21, 1904. CC, Fisk.

8. Chesnutt, "Race Prejudice, Its Causes and Cures," Alexander's, July, 1905.

9. Chesnutt, "Post-Bellum—Pre-Harlem." Not paginated. Contributions printed by different presses, 1930-35.

10. U.S. Department of Commerce and Labor, Bureau of the Census, White and Negro Population (Washington, 1909), Table 11, p. 93. John Cummings, Negro Population: 1790-1915 (Washington: Bureau of the Census, 1934), Table 2, p. 25; Table 19, p. 74; Table 26, p. 424. U.S. Census, 1930, Negroes in the United States, Table 15, p. 32.

11. In 1930 there were 71,899 Negroes in a Cleveland population of 900,429.

12. U.S. Census 1930. For dimensions, Arthur Mann, Immigrants in American Life (Boston: Houghton Mifflin, 1968).

13. Chesnutt, "Uncle Wellington's Wives," pp. 228-29.

he walked around the corner past the new electric street car line.[14] Hitching posts were everywhere.[15] Sputtering arc lamps replaced the gas-flame jets that once had lighted the streets. Before long he took a horse coach to the square in the heart of the city. There in the chill November air he saw beds of frost-touched flowers; he saw statues and fountains standing still until winter should come and go.[16] He saw the courthouse; he saw lawyers, ladies in stiffened side-walk-sweeping dresses and high-topped button shoes;[17] clerks, politicians, policemen, businessmen hastening by; he saw the jail, the post office, and the four-story public buildings fronting on the square. Nearby he saw the market-place. From an elevated point he could look "down upon the lumber yard and the factories, which were the chief source of the wealth of the city." Beyond, he saw Lake Erie and the busy harbor of the St. Lawrence water route. He could look over "the fleet of ships that lined the coal and iron docks of the harbor."[18]

Owners of these enterprises lived in great houses on Euclid Avenue—handsome houses, "shaded by stately trees, and surrounded by wide-spreading lawns," lawns that in summer were "dotted with flower beds, statues, and fountains."[19] These were dramatic evidences of wealth. They evidenced, too, an inconclusive human triumph: Euclid Avenue followed the shoreline of a dried-up water[20] that once, in an age of melting ice, would have dwarfed the largest Great Lake.

Soon Chesnutt realized there were more degrees of social inequality in Cleveland than in the Southern town from which he had come. He saw, and soon, the shabby upper rooms for rent in houses in Irish and German neighborhoods. Already Negroes were unwelcome there.[21] He saw the bums, the beggars. He saw the immigrants, perplexed, search-

---

14. William Ganson Rose, *Cleveland, the Making of a City* (Cleveland and New York: World Publishing Co., 1950), p. 465. Samuel P. Orth, *History of Cleveland* (Chicago: Clarke Publishers, 1910), 2, 748. Elroy McKendree Avery, *A History of Cleveland and Its Environs* (Chicago: Lewis, 1818), 3, p. 462.

15. Rose, *Cleveland*, p. 437.

16. Chesnutt, "Uncle Wellington's Wives," pp. 228-29; and Rose, *Cleveland*, pp. 233, 437.

17. Rose, *Cleveland*, p. 432. H. Chesnutt, *Pioneer*, p. 79.

18. Chesnutt, "Uncle Wellington's Wives," p. 233.

19. Chesnutt gives the name "Oakwood" to Euclid Avenue; see "Uncle Wellington's Wives," p. 233.

20. Kane, "Cleveland," p. 510.

21. Chesnutt, "Uncle Wellington's Wives," p. 247.

ing such shelter as they could find. He saw the railroad workers, the dockers, the factory hands—the working women and children—the store-keepers, the odd-job whitewashers of basements and houses and fences, the servants, white and black—cooks, coachmen, houseworkers; the res-taurant-sweepers, and the tired women, "driven by stress of circum-stances, to the washtub, that last refuge of honest able-bodied pover-ty."[22]

At twenty-five Charles Chesnutt intended that this bristling, bustling, bursting Cleveland should be a land of opportunity. Here he could sup-port himself and his wife and raise their children; here he could be about the lifetime goals he had set in Fayetteville.

He thought that "the tendency of the present age is toward the aris-tocracy of merit—nature's aristocracy"; that Americans, especially, were producing "self-made men" because "our political system leaves the highest position within reach of the lowest." He expressed views like those of the Social-Darwinist William Graham Summer: a year before (in 1882) Chesnutt had written that "When wealth, office, fame are open to all, then the most worthy will grasp them."[23] But beyond having ab-sorbed this rationale for a rapacious age, Chesnutt was confident that he could write "stories" so true and so moving as to alleviate the evils of a caste society.

So Chesnutt settled himself; he found a place for room and board at 224 Garden Street.[24] His stenographic skills opened the way, and he found a job in the accounting department of William H. Vanderbilt's regretted purchase, the nearly bankrupt Nickel Plate Railroad Com-pany.[25] He was to write letters and total accounts. He could do this; Charles M. Williams, a student at the Fayetteville Normal School and later a faculty member, recalled his "special talent . . . for mathematics."[26] With characteristic energy he entered upon the adventures he had planned in Fayetteville.

In the next few years, Charles Chesnutt was to become lawyer, novel-ist, founder of a stenographic firm, spokesman for his race, pioneer of a third distinct approach to racial problems, and prophet of the twentieth

---

22. Ibid., p. 250.

23. Chesnutt, "The Self-Made Man" (unpublished MS), March 10, 1882, p. 11, CC, Fisk. This was probably for students at the Normal School.

24. Cleveland City Directory, 1884-85.

25. Josephson, The Robber Barons, pp. 186, 298.

26. Parker, "Chesnutt as a Southern Town Remembers Him."

century. He was also to become a social historian and an observer of his era.

Getting Established in Cleveland

Chesnutt brought a rich experience to Cleveland. But this twenty-five-year-old young man had first to decide where to live, where and how to buy food, how to manage transportation, how to establish himself. Arranging to live in a new place, dealing with cultural differences, and moving his family to Cleveland took time. Charles Chesnutt worked and planned. He walked the old boardwalks and the new Medina sandstone streets. Food was high in Cleveland; old potatoes were seventy-five cents a bushel, eggs were twenty cents a dozen, chicken was eighteen cents a pound. If you went as far as Erie Street, beautiful Euclid Avenue became another blighted section. The editor of the Cleveland *Plain Dealer* wrote on March 17, 1883, that Euclid past Erie was "a hogpen of filth and unsightliness."

Fires were taking a heavy toll. A theater was destroyed, and a lumber fire sprang up on the Flats. Fires in poorer districts left poignant testimonials. The new standard time had been adopted nationwide. A craze for bicycles and horse racing erupted. A rollerskating fervor resulted in the opening of a large new Casino Roller Rink on Forest Street, between Scoville and Garden where Chesnutt boarded, where for a quarter people skated and listened to the band in the evenings. A year later (1885) more than forty such rinks dotted Cleveland.[27] A thousand new sights and sounds accompanied an accelerated pace of life. Charles was aware of the contrast with the pace of life in North Carolina.[28]

In the mid-eighties everyone knew Marcus Alonzo Hanna, a "blunt and forthright businessman," a maker of industries and presidents. A person who had the money could buy "Hanna Hash" where cronies met.[29] The old industry had expanded: 87 refineries, worth some $27 million and employing 10,000 people, were operating.[30] One historian noted that in 1885 "John D. Rockefeller and generous Clevelanders made possible an extensive expansion of a haven for aged women"; but

---

27. Rose, *Cleveland*, pp. 432, 548, 467; James Harrison Kennedy, *A History of the City of Cleveland* (Cleveland: Imperial Press, 1896), p. 468; W. Scott Robison, ed., *History of the City of Cleveland* (Cleveland: Robison and Crockett, 1887), p. 214; Orth, *History of Cleveland*, pp. 600, 624.

28. Chesnutt, "The Goophered Grapevine," p. 7.

29. Rose, *Cleveland*, p. 471. The dish originated at the Hollander Hotel.

30. *Cleveland Board of Trade Annual Report*, 1885. The figure given for the number of employees in the oil industry in Cleveland in 1885 is 9,869 persons.

in the same year the "safety of the great [steel] mills in Newburgh was endangered during a strike of workers."

There was a national election in 1884; Chesnutt took an interest in electing Republicans. A torchlight parade was followed by a rousing drill corps presentation. A great revolving electric light played about the Public Square and the Forest City House; James G. Blaine and John A. Logan, Republican candidates for President and Vice-President, spoke at the Public Square. Not until the fifteenth of November did people know that a Democrat had been elected. Grover Cleveland, whose family could be traced to that of Moses Cleveland, founder of the city, would be the next President.[31]

Chesnutt was not without friends in this whirl of activities. Nor had he altogether forgotten his childhood. He remembered some people his family had known in an earlier Cleveland.[32] His darker-skinned cousin, John P. Green, had become a state senator. He remembered his father's struggles with new understanding: horse car drivers still worked from twelve to sixteen hours a day; they still received no more than $1.40 for a day's work. Their wages still were paid in tickets the drivers sold for cash.[33]

But Charles Chesnutt felt lonely. He missed his wife and the girls. He had never seen the baby, a boy named Edwin. Susan was restless, too; at twenty-two she missed her husband. She had disapproved his plans to leave Fayetteville; now she wrote:

How I long to be with you once more. I don't believe I ever looked forward to the coming of warm weather so eagerly before. I have found out since you left what you were to me. You were a companion, and you knew me better even than my father or mother, or at least you were more in sympathy with me than anybody else, and my failings were overlooked. No one can tell, my dearest husband, how I miss that companionship. God grant that we may not be separated much longer, for I cannot stand it, I am afraid.[34]

Susan had her hands full. But she took part in activities in Fayetteville—"a social entertainment for the benefit of the new school building."

31. Rose, Cleveland, pp. 465, 473; 467-70.

32. Russell H. Davis, Memorable Negroes in Cleveland's Past (Cleveland: Western Reserve Historical Society, 1969). Professor Richards resided near Cleveland. Chesnutt met other friends and acquaintances of Robert and Cicero Harris.

33. Chesnutt, "Jim's Romance" (unpublished MS). CC, WRHS. Jim, an elevator operator, says his job was "worse'n a street-car conductor's job." See Rose, Cleveland, p. 473.

34. Quoted by H. Chesnutt, Pioneer, p. 37, but not presented to Fisk.

for example. She needed "a black silk dress"; she wrote that she was "wearing the same dress I wore all last winter." But Charles sent no money for the dress. It was all he could do to pay the doctor and the other expenses for her and the children.[35]

By April in 1884 Charles rented a modest house on Wilcutt Avenue for $16 a month[36] and shopped for secondhand furniture. He hired a woman to clean the place and brought in groceries and coal and oil for a fire. Then he sent for Susan. In the spring of 1884, a Southern Negro family, a twenty-two-year-old mother with her little girls of three and four, and with an infant son in her arms, took the trip to the North to begin a new life.[37]

It was a hard trip. Once Susan had to postpone it, for she became ill; but on the thirteenth of May she and the children left. They went to Wilmington, and there took the mail train on which Charles's Uncle Dallas was a clerk.[38] Charles met them in Richmond, the end of the Southern line. Not surprisingly, he found his wife disheartened and his children exhausted and dirty. They rested in Richmond, then continued to Cleveland.

There were trying times ahead. The Wilcutt Avenue house was cold in the slowly advancing spring of 1884.[39] Life seemed hard and lonely. Susan had always lived among people she had known from childhood. Charles felt an urgency about the projects which brought him to Cleveland; weekends and late at night he wrote stories and essays and poems. He collected materials—descriptions, incidents of the day; he wrote observations about them, ideas, as he had always done; often he felt dissatisfied when he had explored an idea. Daytimes he worked at the Nickel Plate Railroad Company, striving to get ahead. Susan often found herself alone, faced with three demanding children who needed constant attention. In those days she was the only one to give it to them. At first she had few acquaintances. She felt lonely, distracted, trapped. Then she felt homesick, for the problems of adjustment were complex. Like other young mothers she longed to go back—to Fayetteville, where life at her family's home had been easier, responsibilities

---

35. Ibid., p. 37.

36. *Cleveland City Directory,* 1884-85; H. Chesnutt, *Pioneer,* p. 37.

37. H. Chesnutt, *Pioneer,* p. 37.

38. Oates, *Story of Fayetteville,* p. 711.

39. The Climatological Survey notes that the spring of 1884 and the spring of 1885 were extraordinarily cold. On March 21, 1885, the thermometer read -4 degrees. Rose, *Cleveland,* p. 471.

shared, the surroundings and daily routines familiar. She became ill. At length her doctor considered whether she should return to Fayetteville.[40]

Chesnutt may have remembered his own miserable homesickness when he had taught school near Spartanburg.[41] Already he had used situations of his life in his writing. Perhaps we get an inkling of his concern for Susan in his later "Conjure" stories.[42] The storyteller is the character John, who moved to the South to improve his wife's health. But Chesnutt could not have afforded to return. Nor would he have been willing to do so. His work lay ahead—in Cleveland.

Chesnutt did agree that Susan might go back to Fayetteville; but he insisted on getting a woman to help and on keeping the little girls.[43] So Susan had to choose between returning to a familiar, easier arrangement or staying with her husband and children. She stayed. Gradually she gathered strength to rise to the demands. It probably helped when in a few months they moved to a better house at 67 Ashland Avenue[44]—"a white one-story house in a wide, well-kept yard with a white picket fence around it."[45] The weather grew warmer. Susan's health and her confidence improved.

She needed both, for Charles was caught up in a spiral within the great whirl marking the industrial development of Cleveland. Midway through the decade, J. P. McIntosh of the Citizens Telegraph & Telephone Company first talked by telephone to persons in New York. That year, at thirty-seven, James Ford Rhodes retired from the Cleveland Iron and Steel Works, which his family owned in partnership with Marcus Hanna. He would devote the rest of his life to writing history.[46] But Chesnutt continued to take shorthand at the Railroad Company. He wrote on weekends and at night, saving stories and fragments. He practiced putting a plot together, delineating characters; he tried essays and articles. He read. He learned. Nearly always his stories centered about racial problems. He expressed many insights. He believed, as he wrote in the first of his published novels, that

---

40. H. Chesnutt, *Pioneer*, p. 39.

41. Chesnutt, Journal 1, p. 141.

42. Chesnutt, *The Conjure Woman*, p. 1.

43. H. Chesnutt, *Pioneer*, p. 39.

44. *Cleveland City Directory*, 1884-85.

45. H. Chesnutt, *Pioneer*, p. 39.

46. Rose, *Cleveland*, p. 469.

There are depths of fidelity and devotion in the negro heart that have never been fathomed or fully appreciated; ... in them, if wisely appealed to, lies the strongest hope of amity between the two races whose destiny seems bound up together in the Western world.[47]

But tragically for Charles Waddell Chesnutt, as for the United States, he was learning to write when attitudes toward the Negro were hardening. One by one the Southern states set about circumscribing the ingredients of equal citizenship, while the Northern states withdrew.

Chesnutt became aware of this ominous drift. He had hoped to appeal to people's feelings through "story" telling. The stories were true. and they touched immediate concerns; Chesnutt hoped they would influence readers and incline their hearts toward according opportunities to American black people. But he began to write articles and essays confronting racial issues and based on logic rather than on efforts to reorient feelings. Soon he found another involvement.

One day in 1885 when the need for counsel for the Railroad had become pressing,[48] the company transferred Charles to the legal department. Two years before, in 1883, a member of a Cleveland legal family had resigned as Judge of the Common Pleas Bench. His biographer suggests that Samuel Eladsit Williamson deserted the bench for the Nickel Plate Railroad because "the salary of the judge was not equal to the salary of the counsellor, and the duties of the latter are compatible with a larger degree of personal freedom and independence of action."[49] Whatever the reasons, Judge Williamson had built a reputation for "unswerving integrity," for "a power of analysis," and for an "intuitive ability to judge the character of men."[50] He had also built a reputation as a civic figure.

He discovered Charles, or Charles discovered him. The judge of men and the striving would-be writer found common ground. Soon the judge offered to sponsor Charles, and Charles decided to "read law" under Judge Williamson, while continuing as a stenographer. Judge Williamson could scarcely have failed to perceive Charles's talents; Charles could scarcely have bypassed this opportunity. Perhaps he sensed that a legal

---

47. Chesnutt, *The House Behind the Cedars*, p. 177.

48. Josephson, *The Robber Barons*, p. 186.

49. George Irving Reed, ed., *Bench & Bar of Ohio: A Compendium of History and Biography* (Chicago, 1887), 2, 219; No mention of John P. Green, Charles's cousin, a Negro attorney elected to the State Senate in 1882. This edition and the next fail to mention Chesnutt, who was admitted to the bar in 1887.

50. Avery, *A History of Cleveland*, 2, 488, 489.

background would strengthen arguments for articles and essays. At twenty-seven he plunged into the new discipline. In two years he took the Ohio bar examinations. "Mr. Charles W. Chesnutt, Cleveland...stood at the head of his class," reported the *Cleveland Leader* on March 4, 1887. He "made the highest per cent in the thorough examination, which was one of the hardest to which a class of students was ever subjected."[51]

Judge Williamson talked with Charles. They discussed racial prejudice in the United States and the difficulties a Negro attorney would encounter, however light his skin. In the course of their conversation Charles told the judge that he had thought of going to Europe—possibly to London. Perhaps he mentioned this at a time when no offers were forthcoming.

Though it is difficult to understand how Judge Williamson thought Charles could use American legal skills in London, the judge offered to supply Charles money to establish himself there.[52] Unfortunately, he felt it impossible to offer a place in his own well-favored office. It is interesting to speculate about the difference it might have made for Charles. Probably the judge felt it would jeopardize his standing if he sponsored a Negro, however talented, in his own firm. For Charles this must have been a disillusionment. He thanked the judge, but declined the money. He decided against a solution by escape. It was a typical decision, in harmony with the literary efforts he was making.

He decided to stay because he had formed a plan to mount an attack upon the "unjust spirit of [racial] caste." He wanted to bring about "the elevation of the whites,"[53] for this must be accomplished if ever there were to be improvements in race relations. He meant to write stories directed toward reorienting the feelings of white readers; he meant to write subtly, cleverly, so as to avoid defensive reactions, and so as to avert confrontations. He could follow this plan better in the United States. Success would be sweeter at home. He would try his way in the law, and he would write; he could fall back on shorthand.

But Chesnutt was realizing that racial prejudice was not as exclusively Southern as he had believed.[54] It was prevalent in the whole of the United States, and beyond. It was one way the powerful of the world could control the less advantaged and one way the less powerful could

---

51. Quoted in H. Chesnutt, *Pioneer*, p. 40.

52. Ibid., p. 41.

53. Journal 3, nearest date May 29, 1880.

54. A. H. Slocomb to Chesnutt, March 9, 1899, CC, Fisk.

retain some privilege. Gradually he changed his ideas about the location of racial prejudice.

He was aware of the stiffening Southern attitude in the unstable social climate, a climate now friendly, now hostile, constantly fluctuating. Chesnutt had still thought in the late 1870s that the Negro was making progress in education and that Negro suffrage was a dependable feature of North Carolina political life.[55] And in 1880-81 he had still hoped that a gradual, if painfully slow, process would bring improvements.

He then thought the Negro was fairly treated at the North Carolina polls. He knew the leaders of both races in Fayetteville.[56] He viewed their problems as a phase of struggles that could be expected in the wake of the war. But he grew irritated with limitations he had to face and tired of receiving small rewards, so that by 1882 he was out of patience.[57] Beyond doubt, he left Fayetteville in 1883 because he thought opportunities would be better in the North. He had believed that conditions in North Carolina were improving—but far too slowly for him.

Now in Cleveland the city and its population were expanding; transportation and communication were growing complex. Tom Johnson, later to be Mayor of Cleveland, bought the South Side Railway Company in 1887. By modernizing it, he became a power in the traction business.[58] The police inaugurated a patrol and communications system; they installed fifty alarm boxes at busy corners and connected them with signal instruments by twenty-one miles of wire. Two patrol wagons were to respond to any call for assistance. A Professional Society of Medicine organized in 1887.[59] The manufacture of Dr. E. E. Beeman's pepsin chewing gum was thriving. Chesnutt became involved with many of these developments through his stenographic business. Yet he watched the attitudes of North Carolinians.

He kept in touch with his North Carolina family. He corresponded with people of both races.[60] He read editorials in the *Fayetteville Ob-*

---

55. Journal 2, nearest date April 23, 1879, p. 114.

56. Oates, *Story of Fayetteville*, p. 508, names leaders of the Republican Party: "A. H. Slocomb, S. H. Cotton, Judge R. P. Buxton, A. C. McCaskill, Neil Waddell (a Negro)." The Negro physician, Perry, names Negro leaders, including Andrew and Dallas Chesnutt, father and uncle of Charles.

57. Journal 3, March 26, 1881.

58. Carl Lorenz, *Tom L. Johnson* (New York: A. S. Barnes, 1911), p. 159 and passim; also Rose, *Cleveland*, p. 473.

59. Rose, *Cleveland*, p. 484, 485.

60. John S. Leary to Chesnutt, Sept. 7, 1888; A. H. Slocomb to Chesnutt, Mar. 9, 1889; Charles N. Hunter to Chesnutt, Sept. 13, 1889. CC, Fisk.

server, and other papers. He wrote to institutions for information.[61] It became clear that several Southern states were enacting severe anti-Negro laws. Another desperate power struggle was taking place in North Carolina; Chesnutt asked about an editorial by George Haigh in the *Fayetteville Observer* of August 23, 1888. It castigated two Negroes, Broadfoot and Sudler. Their Negro attorney, John S. Leary, answered that the editorial was

not only false but bloodthirsty and intentionally so.... The whole thing was for political effect. And had this not... been an election year, what Broadfoot and Sudler did would not have been noticed.... Broadfoot and Sudler are not guilty of any crime. They were arrested and tried under the charge of being engaged in an "unlawful Assembly."[62]

Chesnutt investigated before forming opinions; in this spirit he had asked about Broadfoot and Sudler.

On another occasion in 1889 he inquired about a projected North Carolina election law. He wrote to Charles N. Hunter, editor of the *Progressive Educator,* a monthly journal published in Raleigh and devoted to "The Elevation and Culture of the Colored Race in America." In a handwritten reply Hunter promised to send a copy of the law; he commented on it:

This law, while a modification of the South Carolina iniquity, is designed and can be made to work the same result. As you will see, each applicant for registration is required to give the date and place of his birth, his last voting precinct, and his present residence. In these he must satisfy the Registrar, and in case he should fail to do this, his name shall not be entered. The Registrar is constituted sole judge of the qualification of the applicant. How many Negroes in North Carolina can give date and place of birth? ...

I am sorry that I cannot say that the relations between the races in our state are improving. I am sorry that I cannot say that they have grown no worse ... since you were here. The contrary is too true. There has not been such bitterness in North Carolina since emancipation barring the year immediately succeeding Reconstruction, the Ku Klux Era. Nor is this feeling confined to the Democrats. White Republicans are showing a bitter proscription of Negro citizens. Thinking colored citizens now have under advisement plans by which the race may be placed in an attitude that will command the just judgment of just

---

61. See information on Texas schools sent to Chesnutt. CC, Fisk.

62. John S. Leary to Chesnutt, Sept. 7, 1888.

112

men and women everywhere regardless of party. . . . I am not hopeless. This may be that dark hour just before the break of day.[63]

From such information Chesnutt reassessed the attitudes of North Carolinians. "I see from the papers," he noted in a letter to George W. Cable, "that the chapter of Southern outrages is not yet complete, but the work of intimidating voters and killing prominent Negroes on trumped-up charges (the true character of which is not discovered until after the killing) still goes merrily on."[64] Chesnutt grew much less hopeful than when he had lived in North Carolina.

He began to scrutinize opinions in the North. He tried every avenue to combat the drift of affairs in the South. He wrote to A. H. Slocomb, requesting the names of open-minded white citizens so that he could send them materials.[65] He wrote to literary friends, calling attention to what was going on: "You have probably read of the action taken by the Virginia legislature affecting injuriously the Virginia Collegiate and Normal Institute."[66] He worked on articles. But he clung to the belief that however prevalent prejudice might be, however tempting white Americans might find the further exploitation of Negro Americans, he still could do a life work to affect "the unjust spirit of caste." Only after the savage race riot at Wilmington did Chesnutt utterly despair of North Carolina. From that despair arose a conflict about methods of attack that beset him the rest of his life.

Chesnutt lived habitually at a pace that would have discouraged a man less dedicated. He had associated himself in 1887 with Henderson, Kline, & Tolles, a law firm where he awaited clients. His salary was slight or nonexistent, for he made himself available as a court reporter. From the beginning, Chesnutt experienced success in making money from stenography. He supported his family by it while studying law from 1885 to 1887, even though family needs were increasing. In 1886 the house on Ashland Avenue began to seem small. The *Cleveland City Directory* entry reads: "1886-1887, Chesnutt, Charles W. Stenographer, R. 85 Florence."

"This was a larger house on Florence Street," wrote Helen Chesnutt.

63.   Charles N. Hunter to Chesnutt, Durham, Sept. 13, 1889. CC, Fisk.

64.   Chesnutt to George W. Cable, May 24, 1889. George W. Cable Collection, Tulane University, New Orleans.

65.   A. H. Slocomb to Chesnutt, March 9, 1889. CC, Fisk.

66.   Chesnutt to George W. Cable, May 26, 1889. George W. Cable Collection, Tulane University, New Orleans.

"The neighbors were friendly people."[67] By then the Chesnutt's oldest daughter Ethel was seven and had started school. After Charles had taken the bar examinations, the listing changed: "1887-1888, Chesnutt, Charles W. Lawyer, room 8, 219 Superior. R." The listing for the following year, 1888-1889, is the same; but the year after that it changed again: "1889-1890, Chesnutt, Charles W. Attorney & Stenographer, 3 Blackstone Bld. tel. 861, Residence, 64 Brenton."

By 1889, The Chesnutts had moved again to a fourth house in their five Cleveland years. Charles had joined and left the law firm with which his name was listed, and he had moved into his own office. Paying legal clients appeared infrequently, but the demand for verbatim reporting had increased.

Charles Chesnutt found it impossible to support his family as he desired by practicing law. On March 4, 1889, he wrote to his literary acquaintance George W. Cable that he "had been chiefly employed in the past two years as a stenographic reporter in the courts of this county, intending to use this business as a means of support while awaiting the growth of a law practice, there being reasons why this process might be a little slower in my case than in some others."[68] But his stenographic business provided enough to allow him to move to the larger house on Florence Street, and then to build an even larger home at 64 Brenton Street. His daughter described the house:

There was a vacant lot halfway between Cedar and Central, and here Charles decided to build his house. He had found one on Hilburn Street that he liked very much and he had his house built on that plan. Unfortunately the cost seemed too great; so he economized by cutting off six feet from the width of the house.... There were nine rooms, two stairways, three fireplaces, a furnace with hot air heat, and gas for lighting. The bathroom was the last word in luxury—the woodwork of rich mahogany, the tub of shining zinc encased in mahogany. The floor was painted a dark red, and the window, which let down on a chain when one wanted to open it, had a border of red, yellow, blue and green glass squared around it.[69]

In May 1888 the Chesnutts moved in. All this had been arranged while Chesnutt was hoping to practice law, but while he was supplying

---

67. H. Chesnutt, Pioneer, p. 42.

68. Chesnutt to George W. Cable, March 4, 1889. George W. Cable Collection, Tulane University, New Orleans.

69. H. Chesnutt, Pioneer, p. 48.

his needs through stenography. "By a very natural process," he wrote Cable in 1889, "the things I have given most time to [the shorthand] hindered instead of helped the thing it was intended to assist [the law]. As a consequence, I have built up a business mainly as a stenographer which brought me in last year an income of two thousand dollars."[70]

People were beginning to realize that shorthand could be put to many uses—for taking depositions, for recording testimony, for reporting speeches, conventions, meetings, and political campaigns, as well as for reporting trials.

Sometimes there was more business than Chesnutt could handle. Before the Chesnutts moved from 85 Florence Street in 1888, Chesnutt's youngest sister Lilly came to make her home with them. Charles taught her to type and to write shorthand.[71] Still he needed more help. The *Cleveland City Directory* for 1891-1892 shows that Chesnutt moved his office from the Blackstone Building to an office with three rooms in the Society for Savings Building, and that J. C. Pomerene, 228 Lake Street, who had been listed alone in the 1890-1891 *Directory,* had become Chesnutt's associate. But Pomerene's name disappeared from the listing for 1892-1893: "Charles W. Chesnutt, Attorney and Stenographer, 736 Society for Savings Building, tel. 2228."[72] Chesnutt had to depend on himself. Not for several years would he find, in his association with Helen C. Moore, an enduring partnership.[73]

What Charles Chesnutt did must have seemed a dizzy round to ordinary hard-working people. He built a business in which he was the chief operator; he studied law and qualified himself brilliantly to practice. He located and relocated his family several times. He interested himself in political affairs in Cleveland, and in the situation of the Negro people of the United States. The rest of the time he wrote stories and poems and more stories and articles.

The Writing Begins in Earnest: The Stories Appear in Print

Charles began to send the fruits of his efforts to publishers. He preserved as carefully as he kept his occasional acceptances some of the

70. Chesnutt to George W. Cable, March 4, 1889. George W. Cable Collection, Tulane University, New Orleans.

71. Chesnutt to George W. Cable, Dec. 30, 1889. George W. Cable Collection, Tulane University, New Orleans; H. Chesnutt, *Pioneer,* p. 42.

72. *Cleveland City Directory,* 1910-11 and subsequent years.

73. *Cleveland Call and Post,* Aug. 5, 1933. Moorland-Spingarn Collection, Howard University, Washington. An article details a suit instituted by Miss Moore after Chesnutt's death.

discouraging correspondence new authors accumulate. While the editor of the *Detroit Free Press* felt "greatly obliged" for the privilege of reading a story, he returned it with the comment: "We consider it an advantage to have the situation suggested with brevity and to have the climax with directness. The heroine should not be prejudiced by indicating that she is in love with a man of a different race."[74] The editor of *Tid-Bits* could use Chesnutt's poems—his two poems, for a third poem had been lost. That editor made no mention of remuneration.[75] The editor of the *Chicago Ledger* was more encouraging; he would use Chesnutt's story, "The Dr.'s Wife" [sic]. He enclosed three dollars.[76]

About then an Irish-born entrepreneur was developing a publishing business. Less rapidly he was developing a capacity to pay contributors. His story provides another American idyll. The year before Chesnutt left Fayetteville, Samuel Sidney McClure graduated from Knox College in Galesburg, Illinois. He started for Boston, where he arrived "late at night, in a terrible storm," with $1.50 in his pocket. He "didn't know a soul."

McClure had no capital, but he had an idea. He expressed it in a prophetic innovation, a "Circular Letter," which he sent to "Young Ambitious Writers."[77] In this way Chesnutt heard of him. McClure was organizing "a newspaper syndicate" for the daily publication of short stories to average 1,500 words. McClure found the publishing field a challenge; the competition of radio, television, and motion pictures was not yet a problem. He perceived that he could build a market for the steady consumption of stories. Though he had realized the appetites of an expanding, spending public, McClure failed to convince the appropriate people that his idea was sound. So he undertook the enterprise without capital or experience. He intended "to establish on a broad basis my present scheme for the publication of good literature in mediums where the great masses of the people can read it." He thought that his remunerations of $3 per story would equal the average—for Chesnutt, they did—and that the "opportunities for extended reputation" would be far greater than any one paper or periodical could offer." So

74. Chesnutt from "The Editorial Rooms" of the *Detroit Free Press*, Nov. 1, 1888. CC, Fisk.

75. Editor of *Tid-Bits* to Chesnutt, Dec. 3, 1886. CC, Fisk.

76. Editor of the *Chicago Leader*, by "M" to Chesnutt, Dec. 11, 1886. CC, Fisk.

77. S. S. McClure, "Circular Letter to Writers," New York, No. 140 Nassau Street, Aug. 17, 1886. CC, Fisk.

it was that he began the creation of "a vast new readership for serious literature (and for bilge as well)."[78]

One day Charles learned of the competition, and he sent a story. McClure bought the story, "Uncle Peter's House." After that Chesnutt was among those "young and ambitious writers" who supplied the market for which McClure was developing a powerful organ. McClure paid Charles for these stories, but he did not overpay, and he did not always pay soon. Once McClure wrote that a story was too long—but that he would pay $10. "The fact is," he added, "that neither literature nor art is paid for sufficiently by the syndicate."[79] Another time McClure enclosed a check for $15: "The reason you have not received it sooner [is] because I find it hard to get hold of myself."[80] Yet McClure invented the Sunday Supplement, brought first-rank authors to the attention of readers, revolutionized American journalism through his syndicated materials, and even sponsored many muckraking progenitors of progressive legislation. Through these activities he accumulated a fortune. Briefly his path crossed that of Chesnutt; he syndicated seven Chesnutt stories, some so long that they required publication in successive issues.

At first Chesnutt was glad of scattered chances to be published, despite nominal compensation. Soon he made connections with other publications: the *Cleveland Voice, Family Fiction: The Great International Weekly Story Paper, Puck, Tid-Bits,* the *New Haven Register, Two Tales.* McClure's acceptance of his stories had offered opportunities to extend a new writer's "readership." But now Charles felt the dilemma of those who would enter the writing profession: if a writer is unknown, he cannot command pay, and if he cannot command pay, he cannot become known. But his first story was printed in 1885; five others appeared in 1886, and thirteen more appeared here and there in 1887.[81]

---

78. Peter Lyon, *Success Story: The Life and Times of S. S. McClure* (New York, 1963), "Prefatory Note." S. S. McClure, *My Autobiography* (New York, 1914). McClure introduced Robert Louis Stevenson, Rudyard Kipling, Conan Doyle, and Joseph Conrad; was first to print O. Henry, Damon Runyon, Booth Tarkington and others; was first to bring to national acclaim Willa Cather, Stephen Crane, Jack London, and Frank Norris, and to encourage muckrakers Samuel Hopkins Adams, Ray Stannard Baker, Lincoln Steffens, Ida Tarbell, and George Kebbe Turner; but no mention is given Chesnutt by Lyon or McClure. McClure published seven Chesnutt stories: "A Tight Boot," "A Bad Night," "Two Wives," "Secret Alley," "A Midnight Adventure," "A Doubtful Success," and "Cartwright's Mistake."

79. S. S. McClure to Chestnutt [sic], June 10, 1886. CC, Fisk.

80. S. S. McClure to Chestnutt [sic], March 1, 1886. CC, Fisk.

81. Freeney and Henry, *A List of Manuscripts, Published Works and Related Items in the Charles Waddell Chesnutt Collection.* CC, Fisk.

Six stories were published in 1888. Chesnutt did feel encouraged on July 20 when A. J. Wheeler of Houghton Mifflin Company sent a check for $40 for a story for the *Atlantic Monthly*.[82] The editor, Thomas Bailey Aldrich, had recognized the quality of "The Goophered Grapevine." Before another year, the same magazine had published a second story, "Po' Sandy." At last the door was open; the young writer could get consideration from an important publisher. Yet Aldrich was uninformed about Chesnutt's race when he took the stories.[83] In June 1889 the *Overland Monthly* published a story. That editor wrote two months later from San Francisco enclosing "the small check for ten dollars ($10.) agreed upon for 'The Conjurer's Revenge.' " He said they wished that the check were larger and that they could have sent it sooner.[84]

Though preoccupied with writing these stories, Charles was aware of the life in Cleveland. That year he noted that a statue of Moses Cleveland was belatedly raised in the Public Square. The first brick pavement was finally laid. In order to resolve the controversy over the admission of women to Western Reserve University, the Flora Stone Mather College for Women began to offer courses in the Ford homestead.[85] Charles approved of education for women. Now that his daughters were going to school, his interest increased. In November of 1888 the *Independent* published an important Chesnutt story, "The Sheriff's Children"; this one was destined to arouse controversy.

Though some have said that they kept to themselves, Charles and Susan made many personal associations—with German and English neighbors,[86] with teachers in the children's schools, and in church activities. Susan joined St. Mary's Episcopal Church on Woodland Avenue; when they moved to Brenton Street, she transferred to Emmanuel Church on Euclid Avenue. Charles became a member of that congregation—later than his wife, and perhaps rather reluctantly.[87]

Immigrant families were swarming into Cleveland. Few laws or cus-

---

82. A. J. Wheeler to Chesnutt, July 20, 1880. CC, Fisk.

83. Chesnutt to John Chamberlain, June 16, 1930. CC, WRHS, Container 1, Folder 5.

84. Overland Monthly Publishing Co. to Chestnutt [sic], Aug. 27, 1889. CC, Fisk. Walter Hines Page to Chesnutt, Oct. 28, 1898. Walter Hines Page Collection, Houghton Library, Harvard University.

85. Rose, *Cleveland*, pp. 487, 488.

86. H. Chesnutt, *Pioneer*, p. 41.

87. Emmanuel Episcopal Church records show Chesnutt confirmed the First Sunday in Advent (Dec. 2), 1900 with a class of 29. Bishop William Andrew Leonard presided. Rev. Wilson R. Stearly was in charge.

toms regulated the hours of labor, and scarcely any factory protective devices existed. As immigrants arrived, as workers crowded into tenements, as Cleveland exploded outward, one could find many young women who preferred to live away from the blighted sections and who were eager to support themselves in domestic service. Susan Chesnutt tried several servant girls.[88] Finally, she found a young woman named Julia Bash, who lived in and worked for the Chesnutt family for several years.

After a while the Chesnutts joined the Cleveland Social Circle, "a group of young colored people who wanted to promote social intercourse and cultural activities among the better-educated people of color."[89] Through this club, and through his shorthand reporting in the courtroom and about the city, Chesnutt came to know many prominent and lesser Cleveland figures of both races—lawyers, politicians, doctors, ministers of the gospel, businessmen, newspaper men and women, members of Emmanuel Church, and members of other churches about the city.[90]

Chesnutt Forms Some Literary Friendships

Through the stories appearing in local publications and in national magazines, Chesnutt formed a literary acquaintance.[91] He corresponded with publishers. He wrote to Editor Nick Childs of the *Topeka Plaindealer,* a weekly newspaper that circulated among 7,000 Negroes "over Twenty columns of original matter each week." Childs wrote Chesnutt that "If we shall succeed in interesting our people in the literature of our race I believe that we shall go a long ways towards making our people to walk uprightly before God and man."[92]

Through another acquaintance, then directly, Chesnutt came to know Richard Watson Gilder, editor of the *Century.* Gilder's sharp criticisms supplied intellectual stimulation, and they helped Chesnutt to deepen

---

88. Immigrants were often doomed to sweatshop conditions in their homes. William Ganson Rose, *Cleveland, the Making of a City,* commented: "The clothing industry began in the home and diligent housewives probably welcomed the day that garment-making moved into industrial plants" (p. 429). H. Chesnutt, *Pioneer,* p. 49.

89. This club was the model for the Blue Veins of "The Wife of His Youth." H. Chesnutt, *Pioneer,* p. 61; Chesnutt to John Chamberlain, June 16, 1930. CC, WRHS, Container 1, Folder 5.

90. Interviews given Frances Richardson Keller by Russell H. Davis, Sept. 30, 1971; Mrs. Louise Evans, Oct. 1, 1971; and Mrs. John R. Cornwell, Oct. 1, 1971, all in Cleveland.

91. Chesnutt to Mrs. Alice Haldeman, Feb. 1, 1898. CC, Fisk, p. 3.

92. Editor Childs to Chesnutt, March 8, 1890, and Jan. 26, 1890. CC, Fisk.

portrayals. Gilder provoked Chesnutt to greater efforts. Chesnutt knew that Gilder had published writers with whom he could feel sympathetic— George W. Cable, for example. But Gilder had also published the first story by Thomas Nelson Page, a writer whose picture of slavery was anathema to Chesnutt.[93] A little later Chesnutt corresponded with R. N. Johnson, associate editor of the *Century*. Johnson read and rejected a Chesnutt novel, *The Rainbow Chasers*, though he thought it had "striking good qualities."[94]

Chesnutt also came to know H. E. Scudder, then at the *Century* and later with Houghton Mifflin. Through this house he corresponded with Albert Bushnell Hart, the Harvard historian. He also conducted a long and lively correspondence with Walter Hines Page, who became an associate editor of Houghton Mifflin.[95]

Chesnutt's correspondence with publishers and editors was important for his future. But friendships he formed with writers were exciting.[96] He came to know George Washington Cable at the zenith of Cable's career; he corresponded with Judge Albion Tourgee, through whose example he had become interested in a writing career.

Since Chesnutt was writing stories about the South and was gaining a reputation, he and Tourgee found mutual interests. "I have kept track of your work and have noted the growth," Tourgee wrote to Chesnutt in 1888. "You may do much—I trust you will do much to solve the great question of the hour—the greatest question of the world's history—the future of the Negro race in America." Judge Tourgee described his uncomprehending disillusionment with American liberty, American civilization, and Protestant Christianity. He had hoped to behold these ideals fulfilled in his lifetime. But he had to concede that his attack on

---

93. Herbert F. Smith, *Richard Watson Gilder* (New York: Twayne Publishers, 1970), p. 73; Chesnutt to Richard Watson Gilder, April 24, 1899, May 19, 1899, and Jan. 1, 1901. Manuscripts and Archives Division, The Century Collection, New York Public Library, Astor, Lenox, and Tilden Foundations.

94. Chesnutt to R. N. Johnson, Esq., May 16, 1900. Manuscript and Archives Division, The Century Collection, New York Public Library, Astor, Lenox, and Tilden Foundations.

95. The two major collections of the Chesnutt-Page correspondence are at Fisk and at Harvard.

96. George Washington Cable Collection, Special Collections Division, Tulane University Library, New Orleans; Chesnutt to Richard Watson Gilder in the Century Collection, Manuscript and Archives Division, New York Public Library; Astor, Lenox, and Tilden Foundations: April 24, 1891, Jan. 1, 1901, April 11, 1895, and May 19, 1899. Chesnutt to R. N. Johnson, May 16, 1900. The Century Collection, Manuscript Division, New York Public Library; and Chesnutt to H. E. Scudder, March 28, 1900. Houghton Library, Harvard University.

the citadels of power had failed. He would like to see Negroes "erect a noble monument to the memory of John Brown." He would like to be remembered "as one who tried to have the nation redeem the injustice of the past and give them [Negroes] their due share of the glory of the future." "Pardon me," he continued, "for running off the subject. You see how I earned the name of 'Fool' by forgetting myself for the sake of an idea greater than I can ever become."

In discussing literature and the Negro future, Tourgee made a thoughtful prediction:

I incline to think that the climacteric of American literature will be ne-groloid [sic] in character. I do not mean in form—the dialect is a mere fleeting incident,—but in style of thought, intensity of color, fervency of passion and grandeur of aspiration. Literature rather than politics, science or government is the branch in which the American Negro—not the African for there is really but little of the African left—will win his earliest, perhaps his brightest laurels.

Fate has been kinder to him than he yet knows and has already avenged his wrongs upon the white race in ways as yet but half comprehended.

I do not think the dreams of their best men will at all be realized. Power will not flow to their hands for many generations, but art and literature will be the field of their achievement and triumphs.[97]

Many times Judge Tourgee had acted upon what he believed. In 1893 he made plans to establish a newspaper which would support the cause of the Negro, and which would be a forum for Negro writers. In attempting to raise money he approached Chesnutt. But Chesnutt thought the risk too great:

You have infinitely better opportunities for feeling the public pulse than I have [Chesnutt wrote]. Yet in my intercourse with the best white people of one of the most advanced communities of The United States, with whom my business brings me in daily contact, I have never, but once, to my recollection, heard the subject of wrongs of the Negro brought up; and when I bring it up myself, which I have frequently done, it is dismissed as quickly as decency will permit. They admit that the thing is all wrong, but they do not regard it as their concern, and do not see how they can remedy it.[98]

97. Albion W. Tourgee to Chesnutt, Dec. 8, 1888. CC, Fisk.

98. Chesnutt to Albion W. Tourgee, Nov. 27, 1893. CC, Fisk.

121

Chesnutt thought that some white men might subscribe to such a journal, but he feared it would have "a tendency to repel the average white man, rather than attract." Though Chesnutt did give Tourgee some names of Negroes who might become interested,[99] Tourgee had to drop this venture, as he had had to retreat from other commitments.

Chesnutt's powers were growing, and a sense of literary self was taking form. Contact with writers helped him to sharpen insights and to express ideas. Cable became a counselor, a friend who helped him to think, whether or not he took the advice. In this way he was able to crystallize insights. About a year and a half after the first letter from Tourgee, Chesnutt wrote Cable discussing Gilder's comments about a Chesnutt manuscript. Cable had sent the manuscript to Gilder, and then had relayed Gilder's comments to Chesnutt. Chesnutt compared the attitudes of writers toward their Negro characters. "Judge Tourgee's cultivated white negroes are always bewailing their fate, and cursing the drop of black blood that 'taints'—I hate the word, it implies corruption—their otherwise pure blood," Chesnutt wrote. He thought that "an English writer would not hesitate to say that race prejudice was mean and narrow and provincial and unchristian—something to which a free-born Briton was entirely superior; he would make his colored characters think no less of themselves because of their color but infinitely less of those who despise them on account of it." But American writers had taken a different posture:

Maurice Thompson's characters are generally an old, vulgar master, who, when not drunk or asleep, is amusing himself by beating an old negro. Thos. N. Page and H. S. Edwards and Joel C. Harris give us the sentimental and devoted negro who prefers kicks to half-pence.

"I notice," Chesnutt told Cable in this handwritten letter, "that all of the good negroes (excepting your own creations) whose virtues have been given to the world through the columns of The Century have been blacks, full-blooded, and their chief virtues have been their dog-like fidelity and devotion to their old masters:" "Such characters exist; not six months ago a negro in Raleigh, N.C. wrote to the Governor of the State offering to serve out the sentence of seven years in the penitentiary just imposed upon his old master for some crime. But I don't care to write about these people; I do not think these virtues by any means the crown of manhood."

---

99. Chesnutt suggested S. R. Scattron of Brooklyn and F. J. Loudin of Ravenna, Ohio. Chesnutt to Tourgee, Nov. 27, 1893. CC, Fisk.

Chesnutt had read a number of English and French writers who dealt with Negro characters:

They figure as lawyers, as judges, as doctors, botanists, musicians, as people of wealth and station. They love and they marry without reference to their race, or with only such reference to it as to other personal disabilities, like poverty or ugliness for instance. These writers seem to find nothing extraordinary in a talented well-bred colored man, nothing amorphous in a pretty, gentle-spirited colored girl.

Chesnutt told Cable that Gilder found that he lacked humor, or that

my characters have "a brutality, a lack of mellowness, a lack of spontaneous imaginative life, lack of outlook." I fear, alas! that those are exactly the things that do characterize them and just about the things that might be expected in them—the very qualities which government and society had for 300 years or so labored faithfully, zealously, and successfully to produce, the only qualities which would have rendered life at all endurable to them in the 19th century. But I suppose I shall have to drop the attempt at realism, and try to make my characters like other folks, for uninteresting people are not good subjects for fiction.[100]

In his early thirties, Chesnutt felt the difficulties of focusing his efforts; he had almost despaired of finding critiques and publishers. "While your letter is still warm, and I have just finished reading," replied Cable, in whose complex life the problems of publication, at least, had been solved,

I hasten to say that . . . in your own resolution—you must take back your proposition "to drop the attempt at realism and try to make your characters like other folks." You must not let yourself for a moment consent "to please the editors" as publishers but only as faithful critics and never let anything go to the public—which is all too easily pleased—until you have pleased and satisfied yourself. . . . Keep clearly in the reader's sight your own fully implied (rather than asserted) recognition of the "brutality, lack of mellowness, lack of spontaneous imaginative life, lack of outlook," of the people of the story.
In other words you must make the story of Rena Walden very much more what it is already rather than less. You must charge through the smoke and slaughter not retreat.

---

100. Excerpts and paraphrasing from Chesnutt to George W. Cable, June 13, 1890; signed letter in the George Washington Cable Collection, Special Collections Division, Tulane University Library, New Orleans.

Goodbye till next time.[101]

Early in their association Cable encouraged Chesnutt to write essays on political and racial topics. Cable had published *The Silent South* in 1885. He had counseled in the South as now he counseled in the North, an open approach to racial relations; he had set forth his conviction that a free society requires equal protection and equal opportunity for all black and white Americans.[102] For this, Cable found it "healthier to go north." But he continued his activities from Northampton, Massachusetts—he wrote more novels, he arranged lecture tours, he corresponded with political and literary figures, he was active in reform movements. The Open-Letter Club was a project. Cable, who was the guiding spirit, described the purpose: "to keep under public discussion every aspect of the great moral, political and industrial revolution going on in the South."

Cable hoped that the Open-Letter Club would be a channel for the exchange of ideas and would combat the worsening caste conditions of Southern life. Cable planned in large dimensions—he mailed three thousand copies of an address by Bishop Atticus G. Haygood to a list of people assembled from Open-Letter Club members. Earlier he had mailed seven hundred copies of his own article, "The Negro Question," enclosing an announcement that later pamphlets would be sent as requested. When a speech or article or symposium made sense from the liberal point of view, Cable intended to circulate it among Southern men disposed to consider the contents; this would be a campaign to educate influential people.[103]

Chesnutt valued this association. Often he considered ways to devote more time to writing and less time to shorthand. Perhaps he could become Cable's Secretary—for Cable needed assistance. Chesnutt thought of some arrangement that would permit him an opportunity for literary efforts. He asked Cable's opinion as to "the wisdom or rashness of my adopting literature as a means of support":

I can turn my hand to several kinds of literary work—can write a story, a funny skid [sic]; can turn a verse, or write a serious essay, and I have

---

101. George W. Cable to Chesnutt, June 17, 1890. Cable's copy, exactly like the signed original, is in George Washington Cable Collection, Special Collections Division, Tulane University Library, New Orleans.

102. George W. Cable, "The Southern Struggle for Pure Government," an address, Boston, 1890, pp. 15-19.

103. Arlin Turner, *George W. Cable, A Biography* (Baton Rouge: Louisiana State University Press, 1966), pp. 244, 264, 265. Haygood was President of Emory College and a Methodist Bishop.

heretofore been able to dispose of most that I have written, at prices which fairly compensated for the time spent in writing them, as compared with what I could have earned in the same time at something else. I have even written a novel, though I have never had time to revise it for publication, nor temerity enough to submit it to a publisher. I have a student's knowledge of German and French, can speak the former, and could translate either into grammatical English, and I trust into better English than many of the translations which are dumped upon the market.

Chesnutt was "impelled to this step by a deep and growing interest in the discussion and settlement of the Southern question, and all other questions which affect the happiness of the millions of colored people in this country." He ought to begin anything he could do: "I am only 31, but time flies rapidly."

It seems to me that there is a growing demand for literature dealing with the Negro, and for information concerning subjects with which he is in any manner connected; his progress in the United States, in Brazil, in the West Indies, in South America, and in other lands, the opening up of Africa. . . .

Chesnutt thought the time propitious. This seemed to be a field in which "a writer connected with these people by ties of blood and still stronger ties of sympathy, could be facile princeps, other things being equal; or in which such a writer of very ordinary powers could at least earn a livelihood." Chesnutt concluded that if he could earn twelve or fifteen hundred dollars a year at "literature or some collateral pursuit which would allow me some time to devote to letters" he would be interested.[104]

After this Chesnutt visited Cable at Northampton. "I want you now to think over the matter carefully and make up your mind for what salary you could come to Northampton as my secretary," Cable wrote on April 13, 1889. "I do not know that we can meet each other on the pecuniary basis, but I will try if you will."[105]

But Chesnutt decided against the change. He could not come for any amount Cable could offer: "You will see," he wrote on May 3, 1889, "that even $1200 or $1500 a year would, in comparison, be a sacrifice which I, personally, would not hesitate to make, in view of the com-

---

104.   Chesnutt to George W. Cable, March 4, 1889. George Washington Cable Collection, Special Collections Division, Tulane University Library, New Orleans.

105.   George W. Cable to Chesnutt, April 13, 1889. CC, Fisk.

pensating advantages, but which my duty to my family, and other considerations constrain me not to make." Chesnutt reaffirmed his eagerness to assist the Open-Letter Club: "you can command me for assistance in anything where distance will not be too great an obstacle."[106] So Cable employed Adeline Moffat, a student.[107] But they had to abandon the Open-Letter Club. The "great moral revolution" for which Cable hoped reversed itself. Daily the climate of opinion in the South grew more hostile. The idea of persuasion receded from possibility.

And Charles Chesnutt had made a decision; he had experienced an easy success in making money from court reporting. He and his family had grown accustomed to the advantages a good income affords. By this time he was psychologically unfit for the slow money-making of a beginning literary career. He turned back from the long, lonesome literary swim as the means for his livelihood. He could not entertain the idea of living precariously. He was unwilling to commit himself and his family to the difficulties the change would have imposed. There may have been another reason: Chesnutt wrote of "other considerations." Though he needed Cable's criticism and though he benefited from Cable's generous guidance, he may have thought that a dependent association with so prominent a figure would have presented problems.

Chesnutt Experiments with Non-Fiction

After this, as before, Cable encouraged Chesnutt. On January 10, 1889, Chesnutt had completed an essay on the Negro question; he and Cable exchanged letters about it.[108] "This is my first attempt at a serious composition," Chesnutt wrote. "I would not have ventured to trouble you with it, but for your friendly offer." In this still unpublished manuscript Chesnutt assessed what had happened by 1889, expressing anger about racial attitudes in the South:

The gentlemen who so loudly assert . . . that the Negro vote is cast without hindrance and honestly counted, and that the Negro is contented and happy are the same men, who, thirty years ago, maintained the essential righteousness of slavery, and assured the world that the Negro was contented and happy in bondage.

---

106. Chesnutt to George W. Cable, March 3, 1889. George Washington Cable Collection, Special Collections Division, Tulane University Library, New Orleans.

107. Turner, *George W. Cable*, p. 266.

108. Chesnutt to George W. Cable, Jan. 10, 1889; Chesnutt to Cable, Jan. 30, 1889; Cable to Chesnutt, Feb. 12, 1889; Chesnutt to Cable, Feb. 12, 1889; Chesnutt to Cable, Feb. 22, 1889, all in George Washington Cable Collection, Special Collections Division, Tulane University Library, New Orleans.

Negroes were discontented. The saw that in the old slave states political rights were nullified, and civil rights were disregarded and denied in theory. The Negro, Chesnutt argued,

sees a powerful faction using all the advantages derived from superb political organization, from wealth, from the habit of command, from high and assured social position, from skill in literary composition and the arts of debate, engaged in a desperate struggle to perpetuate in a free government and in the nineteenth century, a system of caste of which he is the victim, and to keep him for an indefinite period in a position of hopeless inferiority. He hears it solemnly asserted that the exercise of his right to vote means destruction to our political institutions; that the recognition of his right to decent and equal treatment in public institutions, in hotels, on railroads and steamboats, and in places of public amusement means the demoralization and ultimate destruction of the social fabric.

To the Negro the Negro question is the question of life itself:

The manner in which the question of [the Negro's] rights is decided in the United States will determine for him whether the peace and safety of the republic shall be menaced by the presence within its borders of a large and increasing portion of its population who have no share in its glory and no respect for its institutions.

How the Negro's rights are decided will determine how he feels about the Christian religion, Chesnutt continued in this 1889 piece. A black man, Dr. Edward Blyden, had written a book demonstrating the superiority of Islam to Christianity: "It is indeed hard for thinking men and women to look without disgust upon a religionism which makes a brave show of obedience to the Divine command to love God, and at the same time entirely ignores the companion precept, 'Thou shalt love thy neighbor as thyself.' " Chesnutt set forth what the Negro wants:

The Negro wants an equal share in all public benefits, and an equal right to share in the exercise of every public function. He wants the right, or rather the opportunity to cast his vote unmolested, for the candidate of his own choice, to have that vote honestly counted and accepted equally with the votes ot other citizens, as expressive of the will of the people. He wants to enjoy the right to accommodation in hotels and on public conveyances, and in places of public amusement; he wants an equal share in the benefits of public schools and colleges and asylums; and he wishes to be permitted to enjoy those rights equally and in common with other citizens. He demands the repeal of all laws

127

on the statute-books of Northern or Southern states which in any way limit or qualify his rights, or that recognize any distinctions of race and color; and of all contract or labor laws, and all harsh and oppressive penal laws which, while ostensibly applicable to all citizens alike, are in reality aimed at his liberties.

He wrote that "The intelligent Negro would spit upon any final settlemnt of his status which offered him less than this." He noted what the Negro does not ask:

The Negro does not ask for social equality with white people; that is to say, he does not ask for admission into private white society. The fear of intimate personal contact with the Negro on terms of equality seems the greatest bugbear to the Southern people.... They are afraid that Southern society will be "Africanized."... The much-dreaded "miscegenation," so freely condoned by a former generation of white people when it was the result of unbridled license, and so loudly condemned by the present generation when there is a possibility that it may some day receive the sanction of law will never be possible without the consent of the white people.... The Negro is quite willing to leave to time and to the operation of natural laws the question of his reception into private white society; he recognizes in every man an inalienable right to select his own associates. He can ask, however, that there be no legal barriers to his social advancement, and these matters be left entirely to nature and to social convention.

In character with all of his writing, Chesnutt made some comments about Southern history: he wrote that "the Negro has always been willing and anxious for intelligent white cooperation and leadership."

Even the much abused, and not always justly abused carpetbaggers are a shining example of this very fact. The Southern white people stood sullenly aloof, and threw every obstacle in the way of good government by their former slaves. The Negro, newly enfranchised, and finding no aid or guidance from those who under a free government should have been his natural leaders, availed himself of such assistance as the moment offered. The Negro has a tender place in his heart for the carpetbagger; he came to the once despised slave, and to the still scorned and hated freeman, like a ray of light through the outer darkness; he treated the Negro like a man, and guided his footsteps, not always wisely, alas! in the untried path of citizenship.

With that 1889 passage, Chesnutt revised the first round of Reconstruction Histories. "Henceforth," he concluded, upon having considered the carpetbaggers, "when the Negro vote is cast, it will be cast for such white men rooted in Southern soil as recognize the rights of the Negro, and are not afraid to express their convictions, and for such colored men as are qualified, by nature and by training, for leadership. If the Negro made great mistakes, if he should still make occasional blunders, he has only to go to his white fellow citizens for precedents innumerable."

For one hundred years the United States had freely conceded equal rights to "the very offscourings of European society." Why should it not do so? "The good, the wise, the great are the exceptions among all peoples. The slave-holding aristocracy which ruled the South and domineered over the country before the war was but a small portion of the white people of the South; behind it lay the vast, inert, illiterate, and poverty-stricken mass of poor whites of that society."

A race has a right to be judged by its best men. It is high time that this man of straw, the ignorant, degraded Negro who came out of slavery, always painted at his worst, should be knocked down, and something better set up in his place as the typical American Negro.[109]

For all his liberality Cable hesitated to approve some of Chesnutt's ideas. In the correspondence about "The Negro Question," Cable thought the section beginning "[the United States] had freely conceded rights to the very off-scourings of European society" through the comments about the need for a new "typical American Negro" should be cut. Cable's notes, written in longhand in the margin of the manuscript returned to Chesnutt in January 1889, and acknowledged in other communications, are: "All this were better left out. The brevity gained is worth more than the elucidation"; with reference to the section dealing with "the small portion of white people" who ruled the South, Cable wrote, "This would only sting & exasperate."[110]

In other parts of this eleven-page avant-garde manifesto, Chesnutt opposed any colonization and any Back-to-Africa movement: The greed of white men was an insurmountable obstacle:

It is almost impossible for the government to keep intact for Indian reservations a few thousand square miles of land in the Western states. The white race is forcing its way into Africa, the home of the black race,

109. Chesnutt, unpublished MS. Three copies in CC, Fisk. One title is "An Inside View of the Negro Question." A revised title is "The Negro's View of the Negro Question," p. 1; pp. 2-8.

110. Cable returned this manuscript to Chesnutt in January 1889, and acknowledged it in other communications. See n. 108.

*and is overrunning every spot of the globe not already fully occupied,
which is available for human habitation. It would break its record if it
permitted any desirable part of the world to be long monopolized by another race. [The] theory of colonization would hardly be worthy of refu-
tation, but for its periodical recurrence, even in the mouths of the Negro's best friends; its simplicity is alluring, but it is utterly and hopelessly
impracticable.*

In closing, Chesnutt advocated the return of the Republican Party in
national politics. And he thought that

*The Negro himself will do something toward the settlement of this ques-
tion. The Silent South will find speech. The Negro is learning his
strength, and the next step in the line of progress is to learn how to uti-
lize it. But the Negro also knows that in the United States his race
stands in the proportion of one to eight or ten of the white race. He is
well aware that he could never hope to lift himself one step higher in
the world if the fifty millions of white people in the United States were
so to decree.... He will adapt no policy that would alienate him from
this support; he will inaugurate no "race wars"; he will not draw the
dagger nor brandish the torch; such manifestations, if any occur, will be
merely local and temporary and provoked by white people. But the Negro will insist upon his rights, and will if needs be, die in the attempt to
exercise them and in defense of them, and he will endeavor to do this
in such a manner that the world will applaud instead of condemning.
... [The Negro] sees the country waking up to the importance and gravity of the situation. He sees the question of his rights dwarfing every
other subject of public discussion. He sees the dawn of a new school of
literature dealing with the Negro as a man, with hopes and passions
and aspirations as other men.*

He ended with the hope that the South will grow "unwilling to be, in the
matter of human rights, the most illiberal corner of the civilized
world."[111]

With this piece Chesnutt had begun writing serious essays. All would
be concerned with black people in the United States. Many were caustic;
some were exploratory; many were carefully researched. He wrote re-

---

111. This 1889 manuscript is quoted at length because it is important in evaluating Chesnutt. See J. Nowell Heermance, *Charles W. Chesnutt, The First Great Black American
Novelist* (Conn.: The Shoestring Press, 1974). Heermance dismisses the import of this and
other early essays crucial to Chesnutt's thought and work. See Earl Schenk Miers' Introduction to *The Wife of His Youth* (Ann Arbor: University of Michigan Press, Paperback
1968), p. xiv. Miers' impressions run contrary to Chesnutt's stands here and elsewhere.

plies to Southern publications for the Open-Letter Club;[112] he wrote on topics of his choosing. Through these essays Chesnutt developed a unique position on racial questions.

Chesnutt accepted Cable's suggestion to change the title of this first essay to "The Negro's View of the Negro Question." Cable sent the essay to *Forum,* which refused it, and then to the *Century,* which refused it.[113] The editor, Richard Watson Gilder, gave his reason: "Mr. Chesnutt's paper—'The Negro's Answer to the Negro Question,' is a timely political paper. So timely and so political—in fact so partisan—that we cannot handle it. It should appear at once somewhere."[114] Before giving up they tried the *North American Review,* which also refused it. "I fear that the public, as representd by the editors of the leading magazines, is not absolutely yearning for an opportunity to read the utterances of obscure colored writers upon the subject of the Negro's rights," Chesnutt remarked.[115]

But he was undeterred. In the first letter he had sent to Cable, he noted it was easy to see that the writer was a Negro. Though advised not to advertise the fact, Chesnutt wrote, "I am not afraid to make a frank avowal of my position, and to give the benefit of any possible success or reputation that I may by hard work win, to those who need it most."[116] A few days after the *North American Review* refused the essay, Chesnutt saw his carefully researched second essay printed in the *Independent* of May 30, 1889. The title was "What Is a White Man?". That essay compared the laws of the Southern states on who is a Negro. "Where the intermingling of the races has made such progress as it has in this country," Chesnutt wrote, "the line which separates the races must in many instances have been practically obliterated." The article showed how different legal interpretations arose. The Mississippi code of 1885 drew the color line at one-fourth Negro blood; by 1890 all persons of one-eighth Negro blood were legally white. In Louisiana, a descendant of a white and a quadroon was a white. Before the war in Ohio a person was legally white if he was more than half white. South Carolina

112. Chesnutt to Baskerville, Sept. 25, 1889, CC, Fisk, is such a reply.

113. Chesnutt to George W. Cable, Feb. 22, 1889. George Washington Cable Collection, Special Collections Division, Tulane University Library, New Orleans.

114. Quoted in Smith, *Richard Watson Gilder,* p. 71.

115. Chesnutt to George W. Cable, May 24, 1889. George Washington Cable Collection, Special Collections Division, Tulane University Library, New Orleans.

116. Chesnutt to George W. Cable, Jan. 10, 1889. George Washington Cable Collection, Special Collections Division, Tulane University Library, New Orleans.

concluded that "where color or feature is doubtful," the jury must decide by reputation, by reception into society, and by the exercise of the privileges of a white man, as well as by admixture of blood. In Georgia the term "person of color" meant "all such as have an admixture of Negro blood."

This essay was informed. It was sarcastic in tone: "In spite of the virulence and universality of race prejudice in the United States, the human intellect long ago revolted at the manifest absurdity of classifying men fifteen-sixteenths white as black men."

Chesnutt considered the marriage laws "to preserve the purity of the white race" and commented, "Nature, by some unaccountable oversight ... neglected a matter so important to the future prosperity and progress of mankind."

Chesnutt ended this first published essay by wondering if purity of the white race could not as well be preserved by virtue, and those natural laws so often quoted by Southern writers.[117]

The next day Cable wrote that he was planning a Western tour. Could Chesnutt secure engagements? He offered a commission.[118] On April 10, Chesnutt had not yet procured any engagements, but he was trying.[119]

The tour did not take place till fall, and Cable visited the South as well as the West. In Nashville he addressed students of Fisk University. Then he took supper in the home of a Negro attorney, J. C. Napier. He had gone to Napier's home to discuss the Open-Letter Club with several Negro men. He knew that they would not be permitted to sit down in the public room of any Nashville hotel. For this the *Nashville American* attacked him: "Mr. Cable has often urged social equality of the races, and we are glad to see him following his own advice on the subject. In the South, however, a man must choose the race with which he associates." The editorial occasioned subsequent communications, some of them Cable's, and a heated exchange. Cable's biographer Arlin Turner believes the affray doomed the Open-Letter Club; but Cable thought it was just as well the matter had been brought into the open:

I tell you [he wrote], this soothing and pacifying and conciliating these people intoxicated with prejudice and political bigotry is helping neither

117. Chesnutt, "What Is a White Man?" *The Independent*, May 30, 1889.

118. George W. Cable to Chesnutt, April 1, 1889. George Washington Cable Collection, Special Collections Division, Tulane University Library, New Orleans.

119. Chesnutt to George W. Cable, April 10, 1889. CC, Fisk.

them nor any worthy interest. I am glad my record is made and that I stand before them as unclothed with any reservation as a swimmer.[120]

Cable's action represented no change; Turner reported that a month earlier he had taken tea with Charles W. Chesnutt and his family while he was in their home reading a Chesnutt manuscript for the Open-Letter Club symposium.[121] Chesnutt's daughter gives a version of this occasion. One November afternoon during this tour her father had brought Cable to their new home on Brenton Street to show Cable his books and manuscripts, especially *Rena Walden*. It was "a very great occasion for the family." Charles and Susan decided to ask Cable to stay for supper. Though Neddie was sleepy, the children stayed up, for Chesnutt "wanted all the children to have this wonderful experience. They sat spellbound as they listened to the little bright-eyed man who seemed to be having such a delightful time with Papa."[122]

But Cable and Chesnutt did not know that the *Nashville American* would publish such criticisms of Cable's acts, nor did they realize how far Southern conditions were hardening.[123] They planned for the Open-Letter Club. Cable sent Chesnutt a letter from ex-Congressman Alfred Moore Waddell of North Carolina, a man who would lead a white supremacy campaign in 1898. Chesnutt wrote a reply for Open-Letter Club use. It began:

[Ex-Congressman Waddell's] statement of the County Government system, though brief, is correct; and from it may be readily gathered what Mr. Waddell does not directly say—that it centralizes the government of the state in the hands of the legislative majority, and entirely takes away the power of any local majority of the opposite political party.

In this letter, which he thought would be circulated through Open-Letter channels, Chesnutt developed the revisionist view of Reconstruction history that he outlined in his first essay, "An Inside View of the Negro Question."[124]

120. Quoted in Turner, *George W. Cable*, p. 268; Cable to Baskerville, p. 271. Arlin Turner, ed., *The Negro Question, A Selection of Writings on Civil Rights in the South by George W. Cable* (New York: Doubleday Anchor Books, 1958), pp. 179-180. Cable's essay "The Negro Question" is pp. 120-152.

121. Turner, *George W. Cable*, p. 269.

122. H. Chesnutt, *Pioneer*, p. 50.

123. Chesnutt to George W. Cable, Dec. 30, 1889. George Washington Cable Collection, Special Collection Division, Tulane University Library, New Orleans.

124. Chesnutt to Miss A. M. Moffat, Secretary, Nov. 14, 1889. George Washington Cable Collection, (Special Collections Division, Tulane University Library, New Orleans.

Chesnutt bent over backward to demonstrate fairmindedness in discussions for Open-Letter Club circulation; the plan was to persuade Southerners that their interests would best be protected in an open society. Chesnutt did not expect to convert ex-Congressman Waddell; he hoped to persuade other readers that Waddell's position was damaging to the South.[125] Charles Waddell Chesnutt did, as he said, "happen to know" something about ex-Congressman Waddell. It is likely that part of what he knew furnished material he used in his first novel, *The House Behind the Cedars*. Chesnutt worked on this novel for years.

Concurrently he took care of business, and in letters to Cable he expressed an increasingly dynamic philosophy of race. As conditions worsened, Chesnutt grew more forceful. Exasperated with the irresolution of government, he wrote on March 29, 1890, "I take it that every citizen is entitled to such protection as the government can extend to him in the enjoyment of his rights, and that he is entitled to that protection *now* and whenever his rights are invaded." He wrote of the lengthening record of Southern wrongs—"lawless and under the form of law." He told Cable it was time for Americans to give the Negro a show, "not five years hence or ten years hence, but *now* while he is alive and can appreciate it." He added that posthumous fame is glorious, but posthumous liberty is worthless.[126]

It was important to Chesnutt that he develop and express these ideas. Cable served Chesnutt by encouraging non-fiction as well as the novel that had long lain in Chesnutt's thoughts. This was the story of Rena Walden; it was published years later as *The House Behind the Cedars*.

Cable also served Chesnutt as a literary critic and as a knowledgeable adviser. Cable's literary ideas were sound; he urged Chesnutt to strip away unnecessary passages and to omit unnecessary words. And Cable's connections were helpful. Once Chesnutt noticed a story by Harry Stillwell Edwards, a writer with whose approach to racial questions Chesnutt disagreed.[127] Edwards' story, published in the *Century* and entitled "How Sal Came Through," bore too striking a resemblance to Chesnutt's story "How Dasdy Came Through," published in *Family Fiction* on February 12, 1887.[128]

---

125. In a 19-page "Appreciation" of Joseph C. Price (undated, unpublished MS in CC, WRHS), Chesnutt develops views on carpetbaggers in interpreting Reconstruction history.

126. Chesnutt to George W. Cable, March 29, 1890. George Washington Cable Collection, Special Collections Division, Tulane University Library, New Orleans.

127. Chesnutt to Cable, May 6, 1890. George Washington Cable Collection, Special Collections Division, Tulane University Library, New Orleans.

128. George W. Cable to Chesnutt, May 9, 1890. CC, Fisk. Harry Stillwell Edwards to Gilder, May 5, 1890. CC, Fisk. Chesnutt to Editor, *Family Fiction*, May 13, 1890. CC, Fisk.

Chesnutt believed that Edwards plagiarized his work. He sought Cable's advice; though he thought he had been wronged he did not wish to antagonize the editor of the *Century*. Cable contacted Gilder, who approached Edwards. He got an explanation that the resemblance was a coincidence. Cable advised Chesnutt to accept the explanation: "All you really need to have established is the fact that your story appeared before Edwards's and that therefore if there was plagiarism or unconscious reminiscence, it was his and not yours. . . . I would discourage the editor from further action in the matter."[129] Chesnutt dropped the matter.

Sometimes, however, Chesnutt disregarded Cable's advice. He did found his fiction on historical events, which Cable disapproved.[130] Yet Cable remained interested and helpful. He asked Gilder to read another Chesnutt manuscript. Gilder's comments were astringent.[131] With them, Cable sent a letter to Chesnutt. "I feel," Cable wrote, "that you and this story stand in a very important relation to the interests of a whole great nation. . . . If you—with your vantage ground of a point of view new to the world and impossible to any other known writer—can acquire Gilder's clear discernment of all ungenuineness, you will become an apostle of a new emancipation to millions. . . . I beg you to fall right to work upon 'Rena Walden' "[132] By thinking about Gilder's comments and Cable's remarks, Chesnutt deepened his portrayals.

But Rena must wait her turn. Chesnutt intended to write about her. He intended to affect "the unjust spirit of caste" through reaching a common humanity. But he appreciated now the complexities of that art. He had also discovered a strength in the writing of essays. This was another medium for developing views on racial questions. He felt disposed to try his powers.

Meanwhile Chesnutt's income from his shorthand practice steadily increased. He was earning over $3,000 per year, a good income at that time. When he tried to give up shorthand to devote himself to writing, he had saved between ten and fifteen thousand dollars. It was too little and it was too late. No amount of money that Chesnutt accumulated to

---

129. George W. Cable to Chesnutt, May 30, 1889. CC, Fisk.

130. George W. Cable to Chesnutt, June 17, 1890. CC, Fisk. Duplicate in Cable Collection, Tulane University, New Orleans.

131. George W. Cable to Chesnutt, May 31, 1890. CC, Fisk.

132. George W. Cable to Chesnutt, May 3, 1889. George Washington Cable Collection, Special Collections Division, Tulane University Library, New Orleans.

provide him leisure to write could have influenced the United States toward a different course in racial matters. Nevertheless, Chesnutt explored the possibilities through his next few essays.

AN AMERICAN CRUSADE

5

GROWING THROUGH TRIAL AND ACCOMPLISHMENT: TO THE END OF THE CENTURY, 1890-1900

*B*uilding Three Careers:
Business, Literature, Public Life

Blue-eyed, fine-featured, Charles Chesnutt stood about five feet nine.[1] At thirty-two he wore sideburns and a mustache, but by forty-two the sideburns were gone.[2] He was light-skinned, slender, lithe; about the city he dressed conservatively, almost fastidiously, wearing a vest and a coat. Sometimes he wore a polka-dotted bow tie, though as he grew older he often wore a cravat and a stickpin. Usually he carried a book or a pencil. To some who remembered him Chesnutt seemed gentle, quiet-mannered, even introverted; yet acquaintances mentioned his keenness of observation, his gift for story-telling, his turn of wit. Some noticed a somewhat stuffy concern that his foreign-language accomplishments be recognized. Many recalled his stamina: every day he conducted the shorthand business; almost every night he worked on writing.

By the 1890s Chesnutt had proved that his business would accomplish some goals. He could provide an easier, broader life. As his family expanded, he developed cosmopolitan tastes. In December 1890 his fourth child Dorothy was born. In her somewhat darker coloring, this child resembled her mother and her brother rather than her father and her sisters.[3]

---

1. Interview given Frances Richardson Keller by Russell H. Davis, September 30, 1971, Cleveland. Mr. Davis was many years a friend of the Chesnutt family.

2. Information from interviews and from photographs. Cleveland Public Library and Chesnutt Collection, Fisk.

3. Interview given Frances Richardson Keller by Louise Evans, stepdaughter of Chesnutt's brother Lewis. Oct. 2, 1971, Cleveland.

Despite the ups and downs of business, even in spite of the 1893 Panic, the Chesnutts lived comfortably. Susan Chesnutt was a restless person. She could afford help; everyone recalled her orderly house. Her children remembered "semi-annual orgies" of housecleaning, and conspiring with their father to persuade her to stop sewing their clothes. In August 1890, and for several summers, Susan took her children to Saybrook House, an old village inn in a town some fifty miles to the east. Charles spent the week doing business in Cleveland. At night he wrote. On Saturday afternoon he would go to Saybrook to be with his family until Monday morning.[4] He would bring presents. The Chesnutts appeared to be the incarnation of the American success ethic, as they increasingly enjoyed vacation and travel. Some acquaintances thought "they kept to themselves," and some Negroes covertly accused them of avoiding the race issue.[5] Others resented their membership in Emmanuel Church, which interested Susan, because it was a "social" church; some believed it remote from problems of black people.[6] But in fact the Chesnutts took an active part in the life about them.[7] They joined social clubs. They entertained in their home.[8] The children attended appropriate schools and took piano lessons. The whole family enrolled in dancing classes, which served for story settings.[9] To outward appearances the personable, quiet man who ran the shorthand office was a rock of business America. But he never avoided the race issue. Chesnutt believed in integration, not in separation; he lived accordingly.[10]

Though Chesnutt did well for his family, his commitments to himself

---

4. H. Chesnutt, *Pioneer*, pp. 111, 227; 66, 67, 79; 149.

5. Interview given Frances Richardson Keller by Russell H. Davis Sept. 30, 1971, Cleveland. Davis believed "The family was wrongly accused of avoiding the race issue."

6. Ibid. Mr. Davis related that at the death of Helen Chesnutt a request for a minister from Emmanuel Church was made. Five minutes before services a church employee telephoned that no minister was available. Other last-minute arrangements were made.

7. The Chesnutts joined the Social Circle, later the Euchre Club; later, the Tresart Club, the Chester Cliffs Club, a Country Club, and the Brenton Circle. Chesnutt joined Rowfanters in 1910.

8. Interview given Frances Richardson Keller by Helen G. Cornwell, Oct. 2, 1971, Cleveland. Ms. Cornwell was often present when the Chesnutts entertained on Brenton Street and Lamont Street.

9. Chesnutt, *The Wife of His Youth and Other Stories of the Color Line;* the story is "Her Virginia Mammy."

10. Chesnutt expressed this lifelong attitude often. He said it precisely August 13, 1925, in a letter to Thos. L. Dabney, CC, WRHS: "Of course I regard segregation as detrimental and cooperation as helpful to the solution of the race problems in America."

remained unfulfilled. His agenda required attacking color discrimination where it stood when he encountered it—in the minds and hearts of ordinary people. In youth he had conceived a project to realign the underpinnings of a caste society; he never changed this project. Chesnutt had even conceived a broader assignment; he would put his shoulder against the syndrome of exploitation.

In the 1890s publishers began to notice his existence. Probably the Negro community and most of Cleveland knew only a little about his literary activities. But Chesnutt was emerging as a spokesman for black people. He was producing searching articles and stories of powerful import.

The year before Dorothy was born, the *Atlantic* published a story distinguished by originality. It foreshadowed a technique Franz Kafka later used to reveal the psychological straits of twentieth-century man. Both stories turn on the processes by which a tragic delusion can possess a man's mind. Kafka's story, "The Metamorphosis," is a tale about a man who becomes an insect. In 1889, when Kafka was a lad of six, Chesnutt published "Dave's Neckliss." Dave was an intelligent, feeling slave. It seemed that "His had not been the lot of the petted house-servant, but that of the toiling field hand." Yet Dave had learned to read. He had even gained his master's permission to share his Bible-learning with the other slaves, and he was even going to be allowed to marry the slave girl he loved. A rival managed to make it appear that Dave had stolen a ham from the smokehouse, however. After his whipping, Dave's punishment began. The overseer forced him to wear the ham on a chain soldered about his neck. Despite his denials, the other slaves, as well as the white people, believed that Dave had stolen the ham. They laughed at him, they shunned him. His love would have him no more. Since everyone thought Dave guilty, he came by degrees to believe that he had become a ham. The rival at last confessed, but Dave was destroyed. He hung himself in the smokehouse.[11]

Chesnutt hoped such a story would be widely read and would arouse sympathy toward the character Dave, and shame and indignation toward the oppressors. Yet Chesnutt accounted the hardening climate. He groped to discover resolutions of the racial dilemma. He wrote more articles intended to be logical confrontations with attitudes that permit exploitation. In April 1891 the *Independent* published "A Multitude of Counselors." Chesnutt discussed the advice the black people attracted; most of it was impractical. He wrote of political alignments:

---

11. Chesnutt, "Dave's Neckliss," *Atlantic Monthly*, 64 (October, 1889): 501.

That any considerable number of colored people in the face of the torrent of vilification and abuse, to say nothing of the physical outrage, to which they are subjected, should support the [Democratic] party which at the South justifies and at the North excuses such a course toward them it is difficult to see.

This Democratic Party of the 1890s was "joined to its idols, the bigotry and lawlessness of the Bourbon Democracy of the South." He ruled out a race war. Never but once had such a war succeeded; it was unlikely that conditions of San Domingo (Haiti) would occur again. Someone advised that Negroes say nothing. Chesnutt opposed the idea:

This is asking too much of poor human nature. Perhaps white people . . . have reached that point of self-control where they could endure in silence such indignities and wrongs as are heaped upon the Negro—tho no such fact is apparent from a study of their history.

Chesnutt opposed emigration. No foreign state and no newly conceived American state would permit it. What could Negroes do? None of the other courses advised for them would help. But they could gradually spread over their own country. He began to develop what came to be a distinctive position: "The advantages of such dispersion are obvious. It would hasten the ultimate assimilation of the two races."

Chesnutt made an acid assessment about the Northern reaction to large numbers of Negroes in their midst:

The descendants of the Puritans, who direct the public sentiment of the North and West, would, if confronted with such a condition, find some other method than assassination and disfranchisement to counteract the alleged dangers of Negro ascendancy.

Reflecting a tortured search for a solution, he concluded this 1901 article with these words:

If the colored people of the South could voice in one cry all the agony of their twenty-five years of so-called freedom, the whole world would listen, and give back such an indignant protest as would startle this boasted land of the free into seeing itself, for a moment at least, as others see it—as a country where prejudice has usurped the domain of law, where justice is no longer impartial, and where the citizen deprived of his rights has no redress.[12]

---

12. Chesnutt, "A Multitude of Counselors," *Independent*, April, 1891.

142

The article was a vigorous criticism of social practice. Chesnutt had pushed his search into unexplored channels. Until this time no writer had suggested assimilation.

Throughout the next decade he developed his business and he turned out stories and articles. In the year of the *Independent* article (1891), he tried to interest Houghton Mifflin in a volume. He sent the manuscripts of eight stories, three of which they had published in the *Atlantic*, mentioning that he was an American "of acknowledged African descent":

These people have never been treated from a closely sympathetic standpoint. They have not had their day in court. Their friends have written of them, and their enemies; but this is, so far as I know, the first instance where a writer with any of their own blood has attempted a literary portrayal of them.[13]

But Houghton Mifflin thought Chesnutt should publish more stories before putting forth a volume. Chesnutt even thought of assuming the expense.[14] He longed to throw himself into a writing career. "The only question with me," he told Houghton Mifflin, "is that the money returns from literature are so small and so uncertain, that I have not had the time to spare from an absorbing and profitable business to devote to it."[15]

But he wrote in the time that he had. Amazingly, he also involved himself in political and racial activities. H. C. Smith, Negro editor of the *Cleveland Gazette*,[16] wrote Chesnutt that the Board of Negro Ministers had named him to their Resolutions Committee.[17] Chesnutt sometimes questioned Smith's judgment,[18] but on this and other occasions he accepted the invitation. The Resolutions he assisted in drafting were adopted at a "Meeting of Colored Citizens" on May 31, 1892. The group sent copies to members of the Senate and the House of Representatives. The Resolutions concluded:

13. Chesnutt to Houghton Mifflin Company, Sept. 8, 1891. CC, Fisk.

14. Chesnutt to Houghton Mifflin, Nov. 18, 1891. CC, Fisk. See Walter H. Page, *A Publisher's Confessions* (London: William Heinemann, 1924), Ch. 6, p. 107.

15. Chesnutt to Houghton Mifflin, Nov. 18, 1891. CC, Fisk.

16. Davis, *Memorable Negroes in Cleveland's Past*, p. 33; Kenneth L. Kusmer, "Black Cleveland: The Origins and Development of a Ghetto, 1890-1939" (unpublished Master's thesis, Kent State University, 1970).

17. H. C. Smith to Friend Chesnutt [sic], May 18, 1892. CC, Fisk.

18. Chesnutt to John P. Green, Dec. 7, 1897. John P. Green Collection, WRHS, Container 2.

RESOLVED that we earnestly invite and appeal to all citizens and God-fearing men and women who favor justice and abhor injustice and op-pressions to aid us, by their prayers and in every other lawful and con-sistent way, to stop the horrible butcheries and oppressions of colored citizens in the South and we demand as American citizens the enact-ment of proper laws and that our chief executive and the Judges of our Federal Courts do so construe the constitution and laws of this land as to protect all citizens at home as well as abroad.[19]

Chesnutt Travels to Europe

Chesnutt began to travel during the 1890s. In the summer of 1891 he took a vacation alone at Chautauqua, New York.[20] Despite the business decline of 1893, Chesnutt took his wife to the World's Fair in Chicago.[21] And in 1896 he made his first trip to Europe. At thirty-eight, Chesnutt relished every moment. On the seventh of August, 1896, he was in Paris, and he started a journal. He wanted to remember, though he noted that "There are so many things of interest to be seen that it seems like wasting time to write."[22] He used abbreviations, and punc-tuated carelessly if at all. The reader notices an easy confidence in con-trast to the preoccupations of the journals of his youth.

Because he brought the wealth of the Indies, Chesnutt discovered many treasures of Paris. The brief entries give a glimpse into his thoughts. He made the tourist rounds, visiting the cathedral of Notre Dame and Napoleon's Tomb. He took a drive through the countryside to visit Versailles:

Beautiful drive, Marvellously beautiful and gorgeous palace. "L'etat est moi" said Louis XIV & a look around the palace wd indicate that he had the state by the throat; it cost 3,000,000,000 [sic] dollars, and he was even ashamed of it himself.

Chesnutt saw Paris at night: "Visited the Moulin Rouge, The Elephant, The Café de Néant & several other cafes & went home."[23]

---

19. "Resolutions Drafted and Adopted at a Meeting of Colored Citizens." May 31, 1892. Copy in CC, Fisk.

20. "Charles to Susan, July 20, 1891, Point Chautauqua, N.Y.." Quoted in H. Chesnutt, *Pioneer*, p. 65.

21. H. Chesnutt, *Pioneer*, p. 65.

22. Chesnutt, Journal, First Trip to Europe, p. 4. This journal is in the Chesnutt papers, Western Reserve Historical Society, Cleveland. Hereinafter cited as *JFTE*, Western Reserve Container 2, Folder 2.

23. *JFTE*, Western Reserve, pp. 7, 8.

He made a point of inspecting the statue of the French Negro novelist Alexandre Dumas, as well as the home of another celebrity of this family, "Dumas, fils." In Paris, as elsewhere, Chesnutt's daily decisions arose from purposes defined in his youth.[24]

On another morning he "went to the Père Lachaise Cemetery & stood by the tomb of Abélard & Héloise & the great men of France; plucked a leaf from the grave of Molière & Racine, another from that of Balzac & another from that of Chopin." These were the graves of the tragic lovers and the literary figures Chesnutt had known and loved. "After Westminster Abbey," he wrote, "it thrilled me more than any other one thing in Europe."

He went to see "Les Ambassadeurs," and noticed a Negro girl in the cast. Though the French showed no particular interest, Chesnutt remarked that Parisians treated Negroes exactly as they treated others. This presented a contrast to the situation at home. Increasingly by 1896, and especially in the South, black people were denied accommodations.

He spent time watching people. "There are some very curious things in Paris," he wrote. "Last night a party of 3 danced nearly all the way from the Champs Elysee [sic] to the Louvre." The shop windows were "a show," but nothing was cheap.

Chesnutt savored the life of Paris. He returned to the Louvre. He shopped. He bought books, some about the Dumas family. He noticed that the ladies of Paris raise their dresses on a rainy day "the height depending slightly on the gracefulness of the ankle." He saw priests everywhere and "soldiers everywhere else."

He sat outside on the street and sipped lemonade, watching "the usual large & diligent assortment of the demimonde, including several colored women—creoles." "Three or four finely dressed colored fellows came along & sat down jabbering French & jesticulating [sic]." Had Chesnutt felt only a casual concern for black people at home, he would scarcely have noted their presence at the cafe.

On a "delightful" Sunday he attended a "very impressive and beautiful" mass at St. Roch. The girls of the Church School wore blue checked frocks with white straps and white caps. He noticed beggars. After church he took an omnibus for Montmartre, where he visited the graves of Alexandre Dumas, fils, and Heinrich Heine, the German poet.

He roamed about Paris. With his writer's eye he searched distinguishing, descriptive detail. He "studied the populace on the Champs

---

24. Ibid., p. 9. See Chesnutt to Mrs. S. Alice Halderman, Feb. 1, 1896, CC, Fisk, and an undated, unpublished manuscript on the Dumas family, CC, Fisk, where it is evident that the scientific aspects of race mixture were absorbing to Chesnutt.

de Mars. Soldiers in different uniforms—Legs, legs, legs,—children, stockings, nurses, (ribbons & caps.)" He made many reminder-jottings:

African villager. Very interesting. 6 or 8 rings in ears. Fraternizing. One Sitting down 2 sous. Pissoirs, Watercloset. 2 sous. Woman. Feeding birds in Champs Elysee. Roasting chickens before the window.

Chesnutt everywhere sensed a feeling of pride and veneration for the past. "Old fellows like Charlemagne & Clovis & St. Louis & St. Genevieve & St. Sebastian become living realities in this the scene of their exploits."

He experienced a "very rough" Channel crossing, then scribbled impressions from London:

Bells of St. Martins in the Fields, sounds of revelry. Dull distant roar. train, Eusten for Leamington. Went by Kenilworth unawares. Warwick! peacocks, ivy &c. Went to bed early. Noisy street, right on the parade.

Chesnutt traveled about England and spent time in Stratford-on-Avon. For a shilling a small boy guided him to Anne Hathaway's cottage, the old houses of Stratford, the tomb, the many memorials. Chesnutt visited the master's birthplace, the museum, and the Red Horse Inn where Washington Irving once stayed. He lingered where William Shakespeare lived and worked and observed his fellowmen.

After that, journal-keeping lapsed; Chesnutt wrote only a little, observing that houses were going up, but the people chose "to build in the old way."[25]

He took the train to Liverpool. Then, in a pleasurable—almost jaunty—frame of mind, he ended his first European trip and his diminishing jottings: "Went on board Lucania at 3:30 p.m. & sailed over the bright blue sea For Ameriky!"[26]

Chesnutt had early developed cosmopolitan habits of mind. By persevering, he had acquainted himself with creators in Latin, German, French, and his own language. The voyage permitted contact with the cultures from which these works of literature arose. His daughter saw the trip as a "lonely" time, but it appears that it was a deeply interesting, gratifying, and broadening experience.[27]

---

25. *JFTE,* Western Reserve, pp. 10, 12-13, 16-17, 19-20, 23-26, 28-32, 34.

26. Ibid. p. 34. The date is August, 1896.

27. H. Chesnutt, *Pioneer,* p. 248.

Chesnutt and Walter Hines Page Escalate the
Short Stories into Volumes

Chesnutt returned to a busy scene. Before he left, Cleveland celebrated a centenary. On the morning of July 19, 1896, the chimes of Tri-
nity Cathedral rang forth. Churches held services. The Mayor dedicated
an army post, Camp Moses Cleveland. In the Armory, Chairman of the
Chamber of Commerce Committee James H. Hoyt read a message
from Grover Cleveland, President of the United States. Then the Chamber of Commerce president announced gifts of $300,000 cash and land
from John D. Rockefeller to complete "Rockefeller Park" in a seven-
mile stretch of facilities. Major William McKinley, a former governor of
Ohio and a treasured friend of Cleveland industrialists, praised the great
achievements of Cleveland.[28]

It had been a time of industrialization, of new businesses, of new fortunes, of growing monopolies, and of trusts. Everywhere Chesnutt heard
the cry for a still greater future.

Yet there was dissatisfaction. One writer thought of an ancient heritage. In a *Centennial History of Cleveland*, C. A. Urann questioned the
benefits of industry. He wrote of the Indian mound remaining in Cleveland, between Seelye and Sawtell Avenues: It was "a priceless relic of
the past," and it was "the only one left untouched." "Would that proper
measures for its preservation might be a part of our grand Centennial
Celebration!"

*In what shall this much talked-of greatness consist? Shall the rising gen-
eration see our water-front of 7 or 8 miles built up with docks and
warehouses ...? ... Shall it be vouchsafed to them to breathe a pure,
smokeless atmosphere and to see the city streets kept clean by squads
of men such as are now supported in idleness in asylums or reforma-
tory institutions at public expense? Shall they see fewer great churches
and many greater congregations of true worshippers? See greater charity between the sects, or better yet—no sects and creeds? See greater
honesty in political, business and social life? Greater equality of sex and
greater respect for what is pure and good?[29]*

Chesnutt had returned to the most productive years of his writing career. The more he undertook, the more he seemed able to handle. He
met a dizzying round of obligations. He expanded his business. He in-

---

28. Rose, *Cleveland*, p. 572.

29. C. A. Urann, *Centennial History of Cleveland* (Cleveland: J. B. Savage, 1906), pp.
118-20.

volved himself in community activities, especially activities of Cleveland Negroes. He corresponded with Negroes and others, beginning many exchanges. T. Thomas Fortune wrote Chesnutt on stationery of the *New York Age,* an "Afro-American Journal of News and Opinion" of which Fortune was editor. He and Chesnutt found common ground:

I try to do my duty as God gives me light to see it in the place where I stand, and of course I am gratified when the friends can approve my course. We are at a very critical stage and I feel that we must speak out without fear or favor.[30]

Chesnutt took care of his family, supplying their needs and aiding with school work as the older girls, who attended Central High School, approached college age.

Despite these demands Chesnutt never ceased writing stories. He ventured into longer forms. He seemed driven to carry out his plans. To Cable's inquiry in 1895, he answered that he had written "last year a novel of about 60,000 to 70,000 words," and that he had just taken up the manuscript of an old story "with a view to re-writing it." "My years of silence have not been unfruitful," he said. "I believe I am much better qualified to write now than I was five years since and I have not used up a fund of interesting material which I might have expended on 'prentice work.' "[31]

Shortly before this a dynamic young Southerner—Walter Hines Page— had become editor of the *Atlantic Monthly.* As editor of the *Raleigh State Chronicle,* Page had distinguished himself by wit, energy, proficiency in the arts of language—and intolerance. He had berated the spirit that took comfort for present poverty in bygone achievements. Once Page had referred to a former Confederate officer as Thothmes II, an Egyptian ruler of the Eighteenth Dynasty. This was an effective jibe: the officer canceled his subscription. Page then elaborated in a series of "Mummy Letters."

It is an awfully discouraging business [Page wrote] to undertake to prove to a mummy that it is a mummy. You go up to it and say "Old fellow, the Egyptian dynasties crumbled several thousand years ago. You are a fish out of water. You have by accident or the Providence of God got a long way out of your time. This is America." The old thing grins that grin which death set on its solemn features when the world was

---

30. T. Thomas Fortune to Chesnutt, Dec. 14, 1898. CC, Fisk.

31. Chesnutt to George W. Cable, April 11, 1895. CC, Fisk.

young; and your task is so pitiful that even the humour of it is gone. Give it up.[32]

In his twenties, Page felt no hesitation in grappling with sacred cows that grazed in his native state. He disapproved the Daughters of the Confederacy: he thought the only meaningful measure of a civilization was whether it improved the condition of the common man. Later he titled an address with an inspired phrase, "The Forgotten Man." This speech was a striking plea for an improved North Carolina school system. Page would include women:

Let any man whose mind is not hardened by some worn-out theory of politics or of ecclesiasticism go to the country in almost any part of the State and make a study of life there, especially of the life of the women. He will see them thin and wrinkled in youth from ill prepared food, clad without warmth or grace, living in untidy houses, working from daylight till bed-time at the dull round of weary duties, the slaves of men of equal slovenliness, the mothers of joyless children—all uneducated if not illiterate.[33]

At a time when the idea was unpopular, Page would offer every boy and every girl an elementary education. He even took a stand for the education of Negroes, and was promptly accused of "promoting the social equality" of the races.[34]

People quoted Page's editorials in New England as well as in North Carolina. In the one place, they stirred interest, but in the other they aroused ire. The *Chronicle* was an editorial success, but Page learned a lesson. An article may be inspired, but it will have little influence if you cannot sell the paper that prints it. Page saw the *Chronicle* collapse. Despite the brilliance of his writing, or because of it, he could find no place in the South. Late in the summer of 1885 he left for the North, where he worked two years on the *New York Evening Post*. Never again did Page confront his dragons with disdain for the buying public. When he became editor of *Forum* he disciplined his efforts. The purpose was to "provoke discussion about subjects of contemporary interest." Page

---

32. Quoted in Hendrick, *Life and Letters of Walter H. Page*, 1, 46; pp. 43, 71.

33. Walter H. Page, *The Rebuilding of Old Commonwealths* (New York: Doubleday, Page & Co., 1902), p. 24. This speech was delivered in June, 1897.

34. Hendrick, *Life and Letters of Walter H. Page*, p. 43. Burton J. Hendrick, *The Training of an American: The Early Life and Letters of Walter H. Page* (Boston: Houghton Mifflin, 1928), pp. 261-72. Cf. Page, *The Rebuilding of Old Commonwealths*, pp. 124-26. Page evidently saw no contradiction between the need to elevate the Negro at home and the desire to dominate others abroad.

featured the magazine debate; the result was a publication of vitality and of broader acceptance. Within two years the *Forum* had a subscriber list of 30,000. During the eight years Page was editor, the magazine prospered. With the approval of the owners, he developed methods for ferreting out talent and for publishing those writers he selected—but only those writers.[35]

In 1895 H. E. Scudder resigned as senior editor for Houghton Mifflin. In the reshuffling, the company invited Page to succeed Thomas Bailey Aldrich, editor of the *Atlantic Monthly.* It was an assignment worthy of the talent and experience Page could bring; even the *Atlantic* could suffer from falling subscriptions. Page realized he must attract subscribers from many sections; he intended to substitute for the atmosphere of satisfaction a concern with urgent questions of American life.[36]

The *Atlantic* had published three Chesnutt stories before Page took over.[37] Two were stories recasting myths about slavery, and the third was a powerful indictment of that institution. Chesnutt had submitted other stories, and he wrote to Page that he was working on a short novel (it is one of the few Chesnutt pieces that deals with no race problem). He mentioned that *A Business Career* dealt "mainly with a very noble order of human nature, more or less modified by circumstances."[38] The novel remains unpublished. The next winter he worked on another novel, naming it for a character, Mandy Oxendine; at Page's invitation he submitted it. Houghton Mifflin rejected it on March 30, 1898.[39]

Yet it was a cheerful change when Walter Page walked into the Boston Park Street office and into the literary life of Charles Chesnutt. In important cases, Page's ideas worked to Chesnutt's advantage. The month before rejecting *Mandy Oxendine,* Page had accepted two of Chesnutt's best short stories—"The March of Progress" and the story that would make him famous, "The Wife of His Youth." Even then,

---

35. Hendrick, *Life and Letters of Walter H. Page,* p. 48, 49.

36. Hendrick, *The Training of an American,* pp. 233-44.

37. Chesnutt to John Chamberlin, critic of *The Bookman,* June 16, 1930. CC, WRHS. Chesnutt discusses his race and Houghton Mifflin's early attitudes.

38. *A Business Career.* CC, Fisk. The story concerns a young girl bent on revenge. She becomes secretary to the man who wronged her father, a talented executive; she discovers he was not guilty, but had been her father's benefactor. She marries him. There is no mention of race.

39. Houghton Mifflin & Co. to Chesnutt, Mar. 30, 1898. CC, Fisk.

Page wondered if the stories should be published together.[40] Encouraged, Chesnutt sent two more stories. Page liked both "The Bouquet" and "The Dumb Witness." But it had taken a long time to find space for the other Chesnutt stories, and they must not give Chesnutt's field "undue" attention; so Page returned the last two.[41]

Page thought that a magazine should deal with timely topics and that an editor should seek writers. Page seldom read unsolicited contributions. He would spread news items, memoranda, and manuscripts all over the top of a large, flat table, and about a month and a half before his deadline he would plan the magazine. He selected topics from current events—a lynching of unusual horror, the trial of a clergyman, a scientific discovery, a political nomination, a battleship sinking in Havana harbor. Remembering the *Raleigh State Chronicle*, Page aimed to attract readers of differing persuasions.[42] He varied his subjects. He would choose someone who could write authoritatively and set out to interest that person. He would take his prospect to lunch, discuss the question, and arrive at a shape for an article. More than once Page bought an article but never published it because he disliked the content or the literary quality, or both. He became an expert at shunting a man aside. "There isn't a man in New York who can write," he exclaimed in a moment of disappointment. "Not one!"[43] Yet if he found a good thing, he acted. When a good story seemed one too many of its kind, however, it was his practice to return it.

By then Chesnutt knew the difficulties of dealing with publishers. He saw advantages in being on the spot: "When one lives far from literary centers and is not in touch with literary people there are lots of interesting things one doesn't learn." He determined to keep in touch with Page. "I am not easily discouraged," he wrote.[44]

Nor was Walter Page discouraged. He never underestimated the

---

40. Editors of *The Atlantic Monthly* by WHP to Chesnutt, Feb. 10, 1897. CC, Fisk. Identical copy in Walter Hines Page Collection, Houghton Library, Harvard.

41. Walter Hines Page to Chesnutt, Oct. 2, 1897. Walter Hines Page Collection, Houghton Library, Harvard.

42. Dr. H. W. Lilly of Fayetteville, cited in Hendrick, *The Training of an American*, p. 175, relates how years later Page "repaid every dollar that had been invested [in the *Raleigh State Chronicle*] on his account. And this he did though [it was] an act not incumbent upon him nor desired or expected by his friends."

43. Hendrick, *The Training of an American*, pp. 193-282.

44. Chesnutt to Walter H. Page, April 4, 1898. CC, Fisk.

promise of Chesnutt's offerings.[45] "If you had enough 'conjure' stories to make a book, even a small book, I cannot help feeling that that should succeed," he wrote in late March, 1898. In this letter he refused to publish either a volume of short stories or the novel *A Business Career*.[46] Page was becoming preoccupied with the Spanish War and the prestige of the United States in the world, as Chesnutt was growing ever more concerned about the degradation of the Negro at home. Both Chesnutt and Page would have preferred to publish a Chesnutt novel. Page had repeatedly told Chesnutt so: "I am delighted to hear that you have got a long novel so far ahead," he had written in December 1897. "This seems to me a much more important step in your literary career than the book publication of any short stories whatever."[47] Still, when it appeared they might agree about a "Conjure" collection, Chesnutt wrote six more "Conjure" stories and had them in the Boston office two months later.[48] He also promised another novel.

Meanwhile Chesnutt had made a discovery which explained the editor's interest in the "Conjure" stories.[49] Page was a North Carolinian, " 'bawn en raise' within 50 or 60 miles of the town where I spent my own boyhood and early manhood, and where my own forebears have lived and died and laid their bones." When Chesnutt sent his additional "Conjure" stories, he told Page of this discovery.[50] Both men were Southerners who refused to live in the South, and who had reacted in their life-style to boyhood in North Carolina. Neither could countenance the anxieties of a closed society. Both understood the "Conjure" stories.[51]

---

45. Page showed greater insight than Gilder, Scudder, or McClure. See Larzer Ziff, *The American 1890's: Life and Times of a Lost Generation* (New York: Viking Press, 1966), pp. 120-45.

46. Walter H. Page to Chesnutt, March 30, 1898. CC, Fisk. Identical copy of Walter H. Page Collection, Houghton Library, Harvard.

47. Walter H. Page to Chesnutt, Dec. 15, 1897. Walter H. Page Collection, Houghton Library, Harvard.

48. Walter H. Page to Chesnutt, April 8, 1898, Walter H. Page Collection, Houghton Library, Harvard. The stories were "The Gray Wolf's Ha'nt," "Sis Becky's Pickaninny," "A Victim of Heredity," "Mars Jeems's Nightmare," "Tobe's Tribulations," and "Hot-Foot Hannibal." See Chesnutt to Walter H. Page, May 20, 1898, CC, Fisk, for Chesnutt's description of the origin of his "Conjure" stories; and manuscript for a reading, Nov. 15, 1900. CC, Fisk.

49. Walter H. Page to Chesnutt, April 8, 1898. Walter H. Page Collection, Houghton Library, Harvard.

50. Chesnutt to Walter H. Page, April 4, 1898. CC, Fisk.

51. S. P. Fullinwider, *The Mind and Mood of Black America, 20th Century Thought* (Homewood, Ill.: Dorsey Press, 1969) gives a superficial, often incorrect account of Chesnutt's life and thought. Fullinwider calls the "Conjure" stories "neutral." (p. 80.)

In each story, the ex-slave Uncle Julius relates a tale to the white Northerner John and his wife Annie. By this device, Chesnutt tells a tale within a tale. He shows differing responses to the slave situations of which Julius speaks. Typical of white reactions is John's tolerant paternalism, his preoccupation with business and family concerns, his inability to relate the cruelties of the slave system to a common humanity. John cannot see the wisdom that grew from the black man's experience in slavery; thus he perpetuates injustices. But Annie understands the black man's relationship with natural forces; she can look past superstition to relate her own humanity with that of the story characters. John points out that Julius is opportunistic, but Julius emerges as a sharp business observer as well as a compassionate participant with those who suffered. The stories move Annie as Chesnutt hoped that his characters would move white readers.

For Page the stories captured the white man's blundering responses to racial aspects of American life. For Chesnutt they revealed a wisdom of the heart that grew from the black man's centuries of toil and rejection. They were also Chesnutt's attempt to mingle rivers of experience. He hoped the stories would affect white society, for they showed that the white man's greed and his thirst for power still prevented the emergence of humanizing values. Beyond this, the "Conjure" stories provided a wealth of social history.

So Page and Chesnutt shared interests.[52] Because Page encouraged him, Chesnutt wrote additional stories. In July of 1898 while readers at Houghton Mifflin were going over the stories, the *Atlantic* published "The Wife of His Youth."

This story focuses on a choice forced upon Mr. Ryder, a light-skinned free Negro who emigrated to the North. There he found success and acceptance. He joined a club which was, like the Cleveland Social Circle to which the Chesnutts belonged, "a very exclusive organization." Chesnutt called the story club the "Blue Veins." By subtle comparisons Chesnutt revealed the standards to be like those of white social clubs. He satirized members for adopting color values from which they suffered.[53] Mr. Ryder, who had become president, was meticulous in upholding these standards. Living alone, Mr. Ryder had not considered marriage until a lovely visitor won his heart. She was the widow Mrs. Molly Dixon. Mr. Ryder planned to give a ball; at the end he would announce their

---

52. See Walter Hines Page to Chesnutt, April 8, 1898. Walter H. Page Collection, Houghton Library, Harvard.

53. William Dean Howells, "Mr. Charles W. Chesnutt's Stories," *Atlantic Monthly*, 85 (May, 1900): 701.

engagement. On the day of the event, however. the dark-skinned, ignorant, and aging but loyal and loving woman with whom he had been allied in his youth reappeared. From deep wellsprings of his being, Mr. Ryder chose to resume his life with her.

This story won notice and praise. So about two months before Houghton Mifflin decided to publish the "Conjure" volume, Chesnutt began to receive letters about "The Wife of His Youth"; he collected favorable reviews.[54]

Page also received letters. One letter came from James Lane Allen, whose collections of stories had made the Blue Grass region of Allen's Kentucky well known. "Who—in the name of the Lord!—" wrote Allen, "is Charles W. Chestnutt [sic]?" He related that he had

turned to the wife of my youth—I beg your pardon—to "The Wife of His Youth." I went through it without drawing breath—except to laugh out two or three times. It is the freshest, firmest, most admirably held in & wrought out little story that has gladdened—and moistened—my eyes in many months.[55]

Page sent the letter to Chesnutt. Possibly such letters aided Page in deciding to publish the Chesnutt volume. Chesnutt informed Page about the mail he received.[56] At the end of August, Chesnutt went to Boston,[57] taking along, no doubt, his notices and letters about "The Wife of His Youth." They discussed the "Conjure" stories.[58] Three days later a formal letter confirmed the agreement to publish the book, though it stated reservations:

Let us say first that it gives us unusual pleasure to add a book by you to our list; and then we ought frankly to say that this particular book we cannot help regarding with some doubt as to any great financial success. The workmanship is good—of some of the stories, indeed, we think it is exceedingly good; but whether the present interest in this side

54. Chesnutt scrapbooks. CC, Fisk.

55. James Lane Allen to Page, n.d., but for date see Walter H. Page to Chesnutt, June 28, 1898. Walter H. Page Collection, Houghton Library, Harvard.

56. Chesnutt to Walter H. Page, Aug. 14, 1898. CC, Fisk.

57. Walter H. Page to Chesnutt, Aug. 17, 1898. Walter H. Page Collection, Houghton Library, Harvard.

58. Walter H. Page to Chesnutt, Sept. 6, 1898. Walter H. Page Collection, Houghton Library, Harvard.

of the negro character is sufficient to carry the book to the success we hope for can be determined only by experiment.[59]

Page had temporized with the "Conjure" stories, for he remembered that the *Raleigh State Chronicle* collapsed because he defied the climate of opinion.[60] The reception accorded "The Wife of His Youth" made him feel there was a chance of publishing a "Conjure" volume without jeopardizing his financial position. But he was not too sure, and he said so.

Page did everything to develop a writer once he had made a decision.[61] He printed in the *Atlantic* certain "Conjure" stories which had not been published. He rearranged his publication plan: stories to be included in the volume needed prior exposure. He exchanged a story—which he considered a sketch—for a "Conjure" story.[62] Chesnutt worked well with Page; he sent that story-sketch, "The March of Progress," to Richard Watson Gilder of the *Century*. This time Gilder published his work.[63] Page advised Chesnutt ably on deletions and additions and other details of preparing the book.[64] He suggested a title, *The Conjure Woman*.[65] Continually Page encouraged Chesnutt to finish the novel he was rewriting.

Chesnutt worked at top speed. One day in November he heard an ugly story of events in Wilmington. He had feared that the 1898 North Carolina election was being conducted in a racist vein. Now the premeditated violence of this attack dismayed him, and he expressed deep pain and disgust.[66]

59. Walter H. Page to Chesnutt, Sept. 9, 1898. Walter H. Page Collection, Houghton Library, Harvard.

60. Dr. H. W. Lilly to Page, quoted in Hendrick, *The Training of an American*, p. 175.

61. Walter H. Page to Chesnutt, Nov. 22, 1898, Walter H. Page Collection, Houghton Library, Harvard; Chesnutt to Walter Hines Page, June 29, 1904. CC, Fisk.

62. Walter H. Page to Chesnutt, Nov. 22, 1898. Walter H. Page Collection, Houghton Library, Harvard.

63. Chesnutt to Mr. R. W. Gilder, April 24, 1899, May 19, 1899, Jan. 1, 1901. The Century Collection, Manuscripts and Archives Division, New York Public Library, Astor, Lenox, and Tilden Foundations. The "story-sketch" was "The March of Progress." It turns on the competition between a Northern white woman teacher and a mulatto former pupil for the Negro School. CC, WRHS.

64. Walter H. Page to Chesnutt, Sept. 9, Oct. 18, Oct. 24, and Oct. 28, 1898. Walter H. Page Collection, Houghton Library, Harvard.
ge to Chesnutt, Dec. 14, 1898. Walter H. Page Collection, Houghton Library, Harvard.

66. Chesnutt to Page, Nov. 10, 1898. CC, Fisk.

Page responded at once that occurrences in North Carolina "have given me also very deep concern."[67] But he again urged Chesnutt to send his novel: "I am especially glad to hear what you write about the novel, and we are looking to its coming with very great interest."[68]

The Conjure Woman was scheduled for February publication. Page prepared a reception. He wrote that he would "take great pleasure in doing all that is possible to further our common interests."[69] He turned over to his publishing department the many reviews of "The Wife of His Youth": "We'll do our share to keep the ball rolling!"[70]

Chesnutt was reworking his novel, as he had promised. Three days before the year's end he sent it. He, too, worked on advance publicity; he kept in touch with Page; they grew familiar with one another's views on literary and political subjects. "I have been reading the March Atlantic," Chesnutt wrote on March 22. He told Page there wasn't a dull line in the Atlantic, and noted "the contrast between slavery struggling for existence in an essentially free democracy and liberty struggling vainly for life in a despotism" in two pieces of that issue—Mrs. Julia Ward Howe's Reminiscences and Prince Kropotkin's Autobiography.[71]

He also commented on "Chief," a dialect story by James B. Hodkin.[72] Chief was a slave so devoted to his former master's family that after emancipation he used money he had garnered to purchase the old mansion. Chief then presented the deed to his impoverished former mistress. Chesnutt pointed out that this was "one of the sort of Southern stories that makes me feel it my duty to try to write a different sort."[73] Page may have printed it at that time to please readers who would be unsympathetic with Chesnutt's frequently appearing work. This policy did not escape Chesnutt's notice.[74]

---

67. Walter H. Page to Chesnutt, Nov. 14, 1898. CC, Fisk. Exact copy in Page Collection at Houghton Library, Harvard.

68. Walter H. Page to Chesnutt, Dec. 28, 1898. Walter H. Page Collection, Houghton Library, Harvard.

69. Walter H. Page to Chesnutt, Feb. 2, 1899. Walter H. Page Collection, Houghton Library, Harvard.

70. Walter H. Page to Chesnutt, Feb. 4, 1899. Walter H. Page Collection, Houghton Library, Harvard.

71. Chesnutt to Walter H. Page, March 22, 1899. CC, Fisk.

72. James B. Hodgkin, "Chief," Atlantic Monthly, March, 1899, pp. 374-82.

73. Chesnutt to Walter H. Page, March 22, 1898. CC, Fisk.

74. Atlantic Monthly to Chesnutt, Sept. 24, 1900. CC, Fisk. This attitude became an editorial policy.

Nor did he hesitate to discuss politics. Page had traveled to the South, Chesnutt guessed, to "help pour oil on the troubled waters in North Carolina." He told Page of whites exploiting and degrading black people for political purposes. "I could write on the subject for a week," he said, "and I therefore refrain." "I am really wasting time, for I know that whatever personal or editorial influence you may have will be thrown in on the side of justice and equity." But Chesnutt added a thought about tactics:

...the Supreme Court of the United States is in my opinion a dangerous place for a colored man to seek justice. He may go there with maimed rights; he is apt to come away with none at all, and with an adverse decision shutting out even the hope of future protection there; for the doctrine of stare decisis is as strongly intrenched [sic] there as the hopeless superiority of the Anglo-Saxon is in the Southern States.[75]

The Conjure Woman was well received. But shortly before it appeared, readers of the novel Rena rejected the new version. Still, publication of The Conjure Woman assuaged Chesnutt's disappointment and strengthened his determination to follow up this success. The volume attracted notice so that the author felt a warmth of approval. Members of the Rowfant Literary Club and other Clevelanders subscribed to a special edition of The Conjure Woman, a beautiful book, which was displayed about the city.[76] Cleveland papers featured articles. Alice E. Hanscom, a reviewer for Town Topics and Index, wrote of her "sincere wishes for your supreme success in a work that challenges the past, educates the present and appeals to the future, a work whose art addresses itself irresistibly alike to mind and heart,—a work 'whereto you have been called' by a Voice that makes no mistakes."[77] Chesnutt began to give readings. He would send clippings about them to Houghton Mifflin.

There were notices in many parts of the country. Chesnutt supplied information for articles; he answered inquiries, furnishing material to publications—the New York Age, the Boston Transcript,[78] the Guardian,

---

75. Chesnutt to Walter H. Page, March 22, 1899. CC, Fisk. See also unpublished manuscript on "Courts and the Negro," n.d.. CC, Fisk.

76. Judge Madison W. Beacom, a charter member, suggested this. See Chesnutt, "Post-Bellum—Pre-Harlem," p. 4.

77. Alice E. Hanscom to Chesnutt, Dec. 17, 1899, Feb. 4, 1899, and Feb. 8, 1899. CC, Fisk.

78. Walter H. Page to Chesnutt, March 24, 1899, Walter H. Page Collection, Houghton Library, Harvard.

the *Bookman,* the *Book Buyer.*[79] He provided Oscar Fay Adams of Boston with information for a *Dictionary of American Authors.*[80] When Emmett J. Scott, Secretary to Booker Washington, sent him a copy of a letter to the *Atlanta Constitution* protesting the omission of his race in a review, Chesnutt replied:

I agree entirely with you that the colored race is entitled to and needs all proper credit for whatever any one of its members may accomplish. . . . It is substantial equity that credit should go where, under different circumstances, blame would probably be placed. I am entirely willing that the race should have full credit for anything I may accomplish.[81]

Chesnutt sent a copy of *The Conjure Woman* to James Lane Allen, whose comments about "The Wife of His Youth" had proved helpful. He even received a request for his portrait from the woman's fashion magazine *Vogue.*[82]

Chesnutt realized that recognition accorded *The Conjure Woman* would produce a receptive climate at Houghton Mifflin; if he could not interest them in *Rena,* they might publish a second volume of stories. He determined to go to Boston, so he again supplied his publishers with an avalanche of clippings. It was "an embarrassment of riches," according to their acknowledgment.[83]

Then he wrote Page suggesting they discuss a second volume of stories "along the line of 'The Wife of His Youth.' " Page answered that he would probably be there, but if because of "unsettled" plans he should be away, the others at Houghton Mifflin would be "heartily glad" to talk over the possibility.[84] Page realized that until he owned a substantial share of a company in which he did the editing, his judgment could be ignored, his decisions reversed. And Chesnutt realized that he must put forth sustained efforts to be published at all.

---

79. *The Book Buyer,* 18 (June, 1899). This reporter learned from Chesnutt that "It is very gratifying to him [Chesnutt] that the publication of 'The Wife of His Youth' in the *Atlantic Monthly* for July 1898 marked almost the exact time at which he had for years intended to begin definitely a literary career."

80. Oscar Fay Adams to Chesnutt, May 12, 1899. CC, Fisk.

81. Emmett J. Scott to Mr. Lucian L. Knight, June 21, 1899; Chesnutt to Mr. Emmett J. Scott, June 29, 1899. CC, Fisk.

82. *Vogue* to Chesnutt, July 5, 1899. CC, Fisk.

83. Houghton Mifflin & Company to Chesnutt, April 12, 1899, and May 6, 1899. CC, Fisk.

84. Walter H. Page to Chesnutt, July 18, 1899. CC, Fisk.

But Page was in the Boston office when Chesnutt arrived in early August. Page gave no indication of planning a change. He received Chesnutt cordially and introduced him to H. D. Robins, Francis J. Garrison, W. B. Parker, and Bliss Perry,[85] as well as to others in the publishing field. Page requested Chesnutt to substitute for him on a summer program at Greenacre, Maine. Page then assisted Houghton Mifflin to decide on publishing a second collection of Chesnutt stories. He suggested a title, *The Wife of His Youth and Other Stories of the Color Line.*[86] This was one of his last acts at Houghton Mifflin.

Beyond doubt Page's interest had proved decisive in Chesnutt's fiction-publishing career. Before Chesnutt got to Cleveland, Page had resigned to begin anew in New York; he would be part owner of a firm, Doubleday, Page & Company. Of this impending change Page had said nothing. But George A. Mifflin at once assured Chesnutt of Houghton Mifflin's intention to publish as planned *The Wife of His Youth and Other Stories of the Color Line.*[87] Chesnutt congratulated Page in the next mail. He reported a favorable reception at Greenacre, and he wished Page well: "I am sure," he wrote, "that the world will be the gainer by enlargement of your field of opportunity."[88] Page replied as quickly: "Good! I congratulate myself on my substitute. All good luck to you. You shall hear from me soon about *Rena.*"[89]

From the Douglass Biography to the Transcript Articles

Chesnutt's trip proved profitable in several ways, for a gentleman offered him another opportunity. Chesnutt learned that M. A. DeWolfe Howe edited a series of thumbnail biographies of eminent Americans; these books were an effort to expand into "Youth" and "Textbook" fields. "The Beacon Biographies" were red-bound volumes with gold lettering on the back. Three by 4½ inches in size, and containing fewer than 150 scholarly pages, the little books could be held width-wise in one hand.

---

85. Walter H. Page to Chesnutt, July 18, 1899. Walter H. Page Collection, Houghton Library, Harvard.

86. Chesnutt to Houghton Mifflin & Company, Aug. 23, 1899. CC, Fisk.

87. Chesnutt wrote of George A. Mifflin as "a liberal and generous gentleman trained in the best New England tradition." Chesnutt, "Post-Bellum—Pre-Harlem," p. 4.

88. Chesnutt to Walter H. Page, Aug. 15, 1899. CC, Fisk.

89. Walter H. Page to Chesnutt, Aug. 17, 1899. Walter H. Page Collection, Houghton Library, Harvard.

In a chance conversation Chesnutt and Howe agreed that a "Life" of the abolitionist-orator Frederick Douglass would be a distinctive addition, and that Chesnutt would write it. Chesnutt admired Douglass. On two occasions he had heard Douglass speak. Before the end of August he set about writing, for he promised to finish in ten weeks. He told Howe that he was "working away at the Douglass Biography, and making as I think, very fair headway." "It is a new line for me," he wrote, "but I am not at all apalled [sic] by it, and shall I think do very well with it."[90]

Chesnutt did so well within the "Beacon" limitations that Walter Page offered him an opportunity to write a full biography of Douglass.[91] They never came to terms,[92] although Page realized the project would take at least a year. But the little red "Beacon" book—called by an eminent reviewer a "simple, solid, straight piece of work"—was distinguished by interpretations of the role of Douglass in American life.[93] Chesnutt wrote movingly of Douglass's mother. She was

a negro slave, tall, erect, and well-proportioned, of a deep black and glossy complexion, with regular features, and manners of a natural dignity and sedateness. Though a field hand and compelled to toil many hours a day, she had in some mysterious way learned to read, being the only person of color in Tuckahoe, slave or free, who possessed that accomplishment.

Douglass's father was a white man. It was the nature of things that historians should attempt to discover the sources of Douglass's talent, and that the question should be raised whether he owed it to the black or the white half of his mixed ancestry:

But Douglass himself... ascribed such powers as he possessed to the negro half of his blood; and, as to it certainly he owed the experience which gave his anti-slavery work its peculiar distinction and value, he doubtless believed it only fair that the credit for what he accomplished should go to those who needed it most and could justly be proud of it.

---

90.   Chesnutt to M. A. DeWolfe Howe, Aug. 29, 1899. CC, Fisk.

91.   Walter H. Page to Chesnutt, Feb. 17, 1900. Walter H. Page Collection, Houghton Library, Harvard.

92.   Walter H. Page to Chesnutt, Feb. 7, and March 9, 1900. Walter H. Page Collection, Houghton Library, Harvard.

93.   The reviewer was William Dean Howells, "Mr. Charles W. Chesnutt's Stories," *Atlantic Monthly*, 85 (May, 1900): 700. The biography is Chesnutt, *Frederick Douglass, The Beacon Biographies*, ed. by M. A. DeWolfe Howe (Boston: Small, Maynard & Co., 1899), pp. 3, 4.

Chesnutt wrote that "it was the curious fate of Douglass to pass through almost every phase of slavery, as though to prepare him the more thoroughly for his future career." Chesnutt traced his subject's movements: In Boston Douglass was legally equal to every person, but he could work only as a laborer: "Caste prejudice prevented him from finding work at his trade of calker." Chesnutt wrote of ways free Negroes helped others escape bondage. "But it was reserved for Douglass, by virtue of his marvellous gift of oratory, to become pre-eminently the personal representative of his people for a generation." Chesnutt penetrated some of that generation's problems:

While it was true enough that the Church and the State were, generally speaking, the obsequious tools of slavery, it was not easy for an abolitionist to say so in vehement language without incurring the charge of treason or blasphemy—an old trick of bigotry and tyranny to curb freedom of thought and freedom of speech.

Chesnutt even commented about reformers:

The little personal idiosyncrasies which some of the reformers affected, such as long hair in the men and short hair in the women—there is surely some psychological reason why reformers run to such things— served as convenient excuses for gibes and unseemly interruptions at their public meetings.

Chesnutt's thinking on the question of assimilation emerges in his discussion of the second marriage of Frederick Douglass to Miss Helen Pitts, a white woman:

There was some criticism of this step by white people who did not approve of the admixture of the races, and by colored persons who thought their leader had slighted his own people when he overlooked the many worthy and accomplished women among them. But Douglass, to the extent that he noticed these strictures at all, declared that he had devoted his life to breaking down the color line, and that he did not know any more effectual way to accomplish it; that he was white by half his blood, and, as he had given most of his life to his mother's race, he claimed the right to dispose of the remnant as he saw fit.[94]

The little Beacon book was published on November 27, 1899.[95] Chesnutt expected the publication of The Wife of His Youth and Other Sto-

---

94. Chesnutt, Frederick Douglass, pp. 4, 15, 29, 30, 37, 38, 128.
95. Herbert Small to Chesnutt, Nov. 27, 1899. CC, Fisk.

ries of the Color Line during the next month. Houghton Mifflin asked his thoughts on the efforts they were planning.[96] He told them the New England cities "wouldn't be a bad field," but he expected to incur adverse criticism in Southern cities—"any discussion of the race problem from any but the ultra Southern point of view naturally would," he wrote.[97]

Not long before this, Chesnutt wrote to tell Page in New York that he had retired from stenography. This decision turned on money receipts. He hoped there would be adequate returns from his writings, but he felt many needs. He wanted to educate his children. The two older girls were at Smith College,[98] and there were two younger children. The family were living well, enjoying a spacious house, servants, travel, and stays at vacation places. Frequently they entertained friends. "I am quite convinced that I cannot stay in town this summer, so have decided to rent the house out near Willoughby."[99] So Susan wrote her daughters at Smith on April 30, 1900. This was six months after Charles had retired. But in May 1900 Charles wrote Edward Williams: "I was busy last week, at vulgar toil, earning the money, in an old matter downtown, to pay the rent for our summer cottage."[100]

Whether Chesnutt ever felt free of stenography is a question. But officially he had "retired" on October 1, 1899, to devote his time to "literary pursuits of one kind or another." On October 10 he had sent off the manuscript of his life of Douglass, on which he had done "a conscientious piece of work, that I am not ashamed of"; he was by then reading the proof sheets of *The Wife of His Youth.*[101] "I would be very glad to know your candid opinion about my novel 'Rena,'" he wrote to Page. "I should like to think you had read it, even if it should take more time for you to get around to it.[102] If Chesnutt could make ends meet by writing, he would not return to stenography. In early December

96. Houghton Mifflin & Company to Chesnutt, Dec. 8, 1899. CC, Fisk.

97. Chesnutt to Houghton Mifflin & Company, Dec. 12, 1899. CC, Fisk.

98. Transcripts in the archives of Smith College, Northampton, Massachusetts, show Ethel and Helen Chesnutt as entering students, Fall 1897.

99. Quoted in H. Chesnutt, *Pioneer,* p. 148, but not presented to Fisk.

100. Ibid., p. 149. Edward C. Williams married Chesnutt's oldest daughter, Ethel. See Davis, *Memorable Negroes in Cleveland's Past,* pp. 40-41.

101. Chesnutt to Walter H. Page, Oct. 11, 1899. Walter H. Page Collection, Houghton Library, Harvard.

102. Chesnutt to Walter H. Page, Oct. 11, 1899. Walter H. Page Collection, Houghton Library, Harvard.

Houghton Mifflin published his second volume, as they had planned while Page was there.

When his publishers requested names of prominent Negroes to whom the book might be sent for an opinion, Chesnutt suggested Professor W. E. B. DuBois of Atlanta University. "I do not know him personally," wrote Chesnutt on December 12, 1899, "tho we have had some slight correspondence." The connection of DuBois with Houghton Mifflin through *Atlantic* articles, as well as his interest "ought to elicit a good opinion." "About Booker Washington I don't know," Chesnutt wrote. "Anything he might say would doubtless be valuable, if he would venture to express himself favorably of a book supposed from the Southern standpoint to preach heretical doctrine. . . . As I have reviewed his book on the F. of the A. N. [*The Future of the American Negro*] and have been asked to write a signed article on it for *The Critic,* one good turn ought to deserve another."[103]

The New York Mail & Express, for which Chesnutt had written a column years before, printed one of the first reviews:

We have a variation of most of the methods employed by American story writers in handling the characterizations of our colored population—from a humorous or a pathetic point of view, and one that is so striking and so novel that it may fairly be called a new departure in art. . . . It simply seems to interest us in him [the Negro] as an individual human being.[104]

The reviewer also spoke of Chesnutt's art as "so fine, so elusive, so shadowy, and yet so sincere and real, that one is compelled to feel it, without quite understanding it."

A few days later an appreciative review appeared in the *Boston Transcript:*

The simple art with which Chesnutt tells his tales is not unbefitting the primitive motives which make their pathetic interest. . . . The narrator is never bitter, his experience and his observation force him to use his undoubted gift of expression in illustrating the facts which are brought before us more vividly in this way than in any other. . . . The name story is the most finished of these racial narratives, but the simplest of them all. "The Bouquet" is the most perfect—a touching homely idyl.[105]

---

103. Chesnutt to Houghton Mifflin & Company, Dec. 12, 1899. CC, Fisk.

104. *New York Mail and Express,* Dec. 9, 1899.

105. *Boston Transcript,* Dec. 16, 1899.

Many reviews followed. Alice E. Hanscom wrote in the Cleveland *Town Topics* that Chesnutt was "fortunate to stand alone in command of a rich field." Another writer said the book was "a contribution to the literature of the race question—not the least serious problem before the American people for solution."[106] Hamilton Wright Mabie wrote for the *Outlook:*

It is safe to say that no finer psychological study of the Negro in his new life has been presented than that which is found in the story which gives its title to this volume—a story which in keenness of perception, in restraint and balance, in true feeling and artistic construction must take its place among the best short stories in American literature.[107]

This was praise from a man whose professional purpose was to foster a distinctive literary culture in the United States.[108]

For the May *Atlantic* William Dean Howells wrote an article entitled "Mr. Charles W. Chesnutt's Stories." Of *The Wife of His Youth*, Howells wrote:

Any one accustomed to study methods in fiction, to distinguish between good and bad art, to feel the joy which the delicate skill possible only from a love of truth can give, must have known a high pleasure in the quiet self-restraint of the performance.

. . . [Chesnutt] touches all the stops, and with equal delicacy in stories of real tragedy and comedy and pathos, so that it would be hard to say which is the finest in such admirably rendered effects as "The Web of Circumstance," "The Bouquet," and "Uncle Wellington's Wives." In some others the comedy degenerates into satire, with a look in the reader's direction which the author's friend must deplore.

Of other Chesnutt stories, Howells wrote:

It is not from their racial interest that we could first wish to speak of them, though that must have a very great and very just claim upon the critic. It is much more simply as works of art that they make their appeal, and we must allow the force of this quite independently of the other interest.

Howells noticed that occasionally Chesnutt seemed detached, that occasionally simplicity lapsed and style became pompous, or again, report-

---

106. Chesnutt, Scrapbook. CC, Fisk.

107. Hamilton Wright Mabie, *Outlook*, Feb. 25, 1899.

108. Lyman Abott, *Outlook*, Jan. 10, 1917; the article was written upon Mabie's death.

orial; but he thought these faults were minor: For "these occasions were 'exceptional.' " The stories were "new and fresh and strong as life always is and fable never is." If Chesnutt had the courage to deny himself "the glories of the cheap success which awaits the charlatan in fiction," "one of the places at the top is open to him." Howells believed there was—"happily"—"no color line in literature."[109]

There were few in the United States whose opinion carried greater weight. Howells wrote these comments during that quarter of a century when he was the acknowledged leader of American letters. At a turning point in 1891, Howells had put forth a manifesto suggesting a criterion: "Everything real in human nature is valuable and nothing unreal is valuable." Howells had by then mastered and progressed beyond the short-story form; he had become a first-rank novelist and a generous, principled critic.[110] His approval was a milestone for Chesnutt.

Despite this, some denigrated Howells's belief that in 1900 places at the top were reserved for the deserving of whatever color. Chesnutt was correct in anticipating severe criticism in the South; Southern reviewers objected in varying degrees. Nancy Banks could appreciate the first story; it was "The first publication of a subtle psychological study of the negro's spiritual nature," and it revealed "those secret depths of the dusky soul which no white writer might hope to approach through his own intuition." But she found the other stories "hardly worthy of mention by comparison":

A graver fault than [the volume's] lack of literary quality is its careless approach to the all but unapproachable ground of sentimental relations between the black race and the white race. Touching this and still more dangerous and darker race problems, Mr. Chesnutt shows a lamentable lack of tact of a kindred sort, an incomprehensible want of the good taste and dignified reserve which characterizes his first beautiful story and the greater part of all his work.[111]

"The Sheriff's Children" most shocked Miss Banks. That story showed a "reckless disregard of matters respected by more experienced writers." The matters which "more experienced writers" would avoid concerned the conflict which arose when a respected white sheriff and his white

---

109. Quotations from Howells's "Mr. Charles W. Chesnutt's Stories," *Atlantic Monthly*, May, 1900.

110. See Mildred Howells, ed., *The Life in Letters of William Dean Howells* (New York: Russell & Russell, 1968), Vols. 1 and 2.

111. Nancy Huston Banks, *The Bookman*, February, 1900.

daughter confronted his unacknowledged mulatto son. The son had been accused of murder. Tragedy resulted when the sheriff repelled a lynch mob, only to find that his white daughter, unaware of the relationship, had fatally wounded his innocent mulatto son, her brother.

When Chesnutt retired from stenography to devote himself to "literary pursuits of one kind and another," he may have little realized some of the demands he would meet.[112] He planned displays. He wrote letters. He furnished lists for publishers.[113] He gave lectures and readings. Before this he had written stories, articles, and a biography; and he had worked on novels. In Howell's words, he had "sounded a fresh note, boldly, not blantantly, and he [had] won the ear of the more intelligent public."[114]

But Chesnutt had failed to win the interest of ordinary readers or the approval of Southern reviewers. Though he expected an adverse response, Chesnutt could not be indifferent when it came. Too much of his life commitment was involved. The Southern reviews produced a greater urgency to achieve some modification of the attitudes behind them. So Chesnutt felt inclined to accept the suggestion contained in a letter of May 1900 from a Boston acquaintance. Joseph Edgar Chamberlin had been a staff member of the *Youth's Companion* till he left to become chief editor of literary "features" for the *Boston Transcript*. Chamberlin remembered a conversation with Chesnutt about the future American race; what would it be like after amalgamation of African and Indian elements had advanced? Both expected that in long evolutionary stretches—in hundreds of years—this would take place.

Chamberlin asked Chesnutt for two or three signed articles; he wanted facts, not a plea.[115] Chesnutt had thought that caste constructions could be affected only through alleviating those deep subconscious fears that precipitate exploitation. Fears could be tempered through familiarity, and literature could accomplish this. But he began to suspect that familiarity would be more surely achieved by blood relatedness than by education or literature. What fears of blacks or Indians could remain when they should no longer be markedly unlike other Americans?

---

112.   Chesnutt to Walter H. Page, Oct. 11, 1899. Walter H. Page Collection, Houghton Library, Harvard.

113.   Chesnutt to Houghton Mifflin & Company, Dec. 14, 1899. CC, Fisk. This letter contains a list of Afro-American newspapers. Chesnutt compiled it for Small, Maynard & Company. There are 33 papers on the list.

114.   W. Howells, "Mr. Charles W. Chesnutt's Stories," p. 701.

115.   J. E. Chamberlin to Chesnutt, May 8, 1900. CC, Fisk.

Chesnutt spent a busy summer at Willoughby, where his family stayed in a cottage by the shore of Lake Erie.[116] He helped entertain guests. He spent time with his children. He kept in touch with publishers. In August he wrote to Hamilton Holt of the *Independent* that he disapproved the "imperialism" and the "McKinley worship" implied in their sponsoring certain letters. But the *Independent* remained in the swing, replying that they defended their position in their publication, which he could read.[117]

He decided to do the articles for Chamberlin. By August 15 he sent them. Chamberlin was "very glad indeed to get them"; though he would have amplified certain conclusions, Chamberlain was sure they would be "widely read."[118]

Chamberlin published the three articles in late August and early September, and his prediction proved correct. In point of view, the articles were more revolutionary than the Chesnutt stories. They frankly approached the subject of racial admixture. In contrast to the "elusive," "shadowy" art of the stories, and the "wild, indigenous poetry," the articles were based upon scientific findings, and they displayed an astringent sarcasm:

The popular theory is that the future American race will consist of a harmonious fusion of the various European elements which now make up our heterogenous population.... This perfection of type—for no good American could for a moment doubt that it will be as perfect as everything else American—is to be brought about by a combination of all the best characteristics of the different European races, and the elimination, by some alchemy, of all their undesirable traits...for even a good American will admit that European races, now and then, have some undesirable traits when they first come over.

The first article touched on scientific research, on the incorrectness of any concept of racial purity, on the unity of the human race. The future American race (Chesnutt used the word to mean "a people who look substantially alike and are moulded by the same culture and dominated by the same ideals") will be formed by a mingling of the racial varieties of the United States. He looked for no sudden amalgamation, but the

---

116. H. Chesnutt, *Pioneer*, p. 149.

117. Hamilton Holt to Chesnutt, Aug. 4, 1900. CC, Fisk.

118. J. E. Chamberlin to Chesnutt, Aug. 4, 1900. CC, Fisk.

Negro race was destined to "play its part in the formation of this new [American] type."[119]

Chesnutt devoted the second article to the amalgamation that had taken place; the subtitle was "A Stream of Dark Blood in the Veins of the Southern Whites." Slavery had been a rich soil for the production of a mixed race; if the literature of the past two generations would not prove this, the laws of the present generation would. He cited Grace King's *Story of New Orleans*, the "creole" stories of George Washington Cable, and Colonel T. W. Higginson's *Cheerful Yesterdays*. Laws are made when there is a need, and judicial decisions are taken only as the result of litigation. Chesnutt reviewed the laws as to who is a Negro; he showed how various interpretations arose from the widespread intermixture of the races.[120]

The third article, subtitled "A Complete Race Amalgamation Likely To Occur," is an able, bitter summation of conditions as against inevitabilities. The Southern laws on intermarriage were a powerful deterrent "to any honest or dignified amalgamation," but they will not prevent it because the forces for absorption are vastly stronger. The white people of the South did not make their civilization; they inherited it. Much of their wealth was erected by the unpaid labor of colored people. There is one "distinctly American institution" that this generation has brought to a high state of development; the South may claim such credit as it wishes. "I refer," Chesnutt wrote, "to the custom of lynching." He noted that "the possession of a million dollars... would throw such a golden glow over a dark complexion as to override anything but a very obdurate prejudice." Religion is the only force that ever kept two races on the same soil apart and with the Jews, this is only "superficially" successful.

There can manifestly be no such thing as a peaceful and progressive civilization in a nation divided by two warring races, and homogeneity of type, at least in externals, is a necessary condition of harmonious social progress.[121]

It is easy to imagine the reaction of Southern readers. It is also easy to foresee the reaction of many Northerners. This was 1900. The South was bent upon holding to legal white supremacy. A frightened editorial

---

119. Chesnutt, "The Future American: What the Race Is Likely To Become in the Process of Time," *Boston Transcript*, Aug. 18, 1900.

120. Chesnutt, "The Future American: A Stream of Dark Blood in the Veins of the Southern Whites," *Boston Transcript*, Aug. 25, 1900.

121. Chesnutt, "The Future American: A Complete Race Amalgamation Likely To Occur," *Boston Transcript*, Sept. 1, 1900.

in the *Washington Times* of October 5, 1900, ventured that the articles are "worth the reading of anyone interested in that phase of the country's development." The articles "face the possibility of race amalgamation squarely, and speak more frankly on the subject than most other writers have dared to do." The editorial warned that to stop amalgamation, the public "must give colored workmen and artists a chance to make the most of themselves, they must not shut them out of everything, until those who could pass as white were compelled to do so."

For some time Chesnutt had been coming to the view that neither toil nor education would produce for his people the average chance that others enjoyed. In these articles he reasoned his way to the verge of a solution by assimilation. It was a third intellectual approach to the resolution of the American racial dilemma. Chesnutt could not have been more original had he slashed a Gordian knot or discovered a cure for cancer. Like Galileo, who saw the stars in a different context through the use of his telescope, Chesnutt was castigated for his daring in looking at human beings.

AN AMERICAN CRUSADE

6

NOVEL PUBLISHING:
THREE BOOKS IN
FIVE YEARS
1900-1905

Literary Love: Rena and *The House Behind the Cedars*

Chesnutt's reputation brought opportunities for speeches and articles. He developed an incisive style. Whatever the vehicle, he wrote to deal with racial disadvantage. All the time he had been pushing his story-telling into longer ventures. He had spent many waking hours in making a living, yet novel-writing remained a grand challenge. On October 1, 1899, Chesnutt closed his stenographic office.[1] He believed he could rise to the demands of the novel form.

One character rose with him. Many characters had taken shape from perceptions about personalities whose lives he had shared. By the end of the century, he had pushed the story art beyond contrivances of plot and dilemmas of the spirit to explore social-cultural dimensions. Through this, one character remained prominent; her story had lain close to the source of his creative energies. He titled his first published novel with her name, and he worked on her story more than fifteen years. "Rena" was Chesnutt's literary love. Like her storied life, Rena's literary life traced a tortuous course.

Rena appeared white. Beautiful, complex, sensitive, of a deep emotional nature, she lived the tragedy of the outcast struggling to discover an acceptable style of life. Rena was the daughter of a white father and a light-skinned Negro woman of pre-Civil War days. Chesnutt called Rena's mother "Mis' Molly Walden." Because she could never hope for marriage, Mis' Molly lived as a lonely exile in a house provided by her white paramour at the edge of town. Her daughter Rena watched an

---

1. Chesnutt to Walter Hines Page, Oct. 1, 1899. CC, Fisk.

173

older brother John learn law while working as office boy for a well-enough disposed white man; then John left their "Patesville" home—the house well hidden behind the cedar trees—and went to South Carolina to live as a white attorney. Despite his success, John felt some discomfiture. He returned to "Patesville," where he persuaded Mis' Molly to let him offer Rena a home; he wished to share with her the advantages of his success.

The character George Tryon was a young man of wealth and position and a client of John's. Moved by Rena's beauty and her natural dignity, Tryon soon found himself in love, and asked her hand in marriage. Inevitably the tragedy unfolded. Because Rena could not forget her mother, Tryon learned of Rena's Negro blood, and he rejected her. Still, he desired her, though only for what she knew to be the supreme insult, a liaison without a marriage. Sick from this proof that her fears were justified, Rena returned to her childhood home. She tried to make a life as a teacher in a colored school, only to be nearly victimized by a mulatto villain. In a desperate effort to escape both men, Rena set out through the dangerous cypress swamps of the North Carolina lands surrounding the Cape Fear River. There she met her death. Only Frank Fowler, a dark-brown young Negro, remained trustworthy. Though he had long hopelessly loved Rena, Frank's efforts to save her sanity and her life proved futile.

Chesnutt composed the character Rena of dreams and despairs, of knowledge of complexities, and of strictures that he and the society exacted. By revealing the hostility this gentle girl encountered he hoped to reach depths where fears abide and cruelties originate. He hoped to arouse feelings of concern that must precede change. When finally the novel was published, Chesnutt hoped that Rena would touch the sympathies of a wide public as the characters Jean Valjean and Cosette, David Copperfield and Oliver Twist, Liza and Little Eva had found their ways into the fabric of their cultures.[2] Rena's story epitomized the anguish attendant on blameless disadvantage.

The records of Fayetteville, in Cumberland County, reveal that Chesnutt's concern with the situation of the part-Negro woman arose from parallels in his family and in situations he knew. Helen Chesnutt wrote that "Chloe Sampson" and her daughter Ann Maria—who was Chesnutt's mother—left Fayetteville in 1856.[3] Yet census records of Cumberland County, Fayetteville District, show no entries under the name

---

2. Chesnutt to Walter Hines Page, June 29, 1904. CC, Fisk.

3. H. Chesnutt, *Pioneer*, p. 1.

Sampson for the census of 1850, and none for the census of 1840. The census of 1830, however, includes two interesting entries. Families are listed under the head of each household, and persons are listed with notations of age, sex, and color. The entries are:

1830 Jacob Harris, Head of Household   age between 24 and 35—6 free colored persons:
    2 male under 10
    3 male between 10 and 24 [possibly Moses Harris]
    4 female between 24 and 35
    5 female under 10
    6 female under 10

and

Henry E. Sampson, Head of Household—3 white persons and 3 slaves
    2 wife
    3 child
    4 female slave 24-35 [possibly Chloe]
    5 female slave under 10 [possibly Ann Maria]
    6 male slave under 10 [this person disappeared].[4]

Since Henry E. Sampson does not appear in the census of 1840 or that of 1850, he could have moved or died and a will might have been probated; yet there is no record of a will of Henry E. Sampson in Cumberland County. Nor is there a record of his having received or given property deeds. There could have been a record of manumission of the Sampson slaves, yet among the twenty or so manumission records preserved in Cumberland County there is no mention of Henry E. Sampson's having manumitted any slaves.[5] Nor did a check of records of the General Assembly of North Carolina from 1827 through 1857 yield evidence of a Sampson manumission;[6] likewise, minutes of the Cumberland County Superior Court for 1831-1839 failed to show any reference to a Sampson manumission.[7] There were no birth certificates or records of death in North Carolina until 1913; there is no record of any Samp-

4. *Fifth Census of the United States, Cumberland County, North Carolina, Fayetteville District*, 1830. North Carolina Archives, Raleigh.

5. Records of manumission. North Carolina Archives, Raleigh.

6. Records of the General Assembly of North Carolina. North Carolina Archives, Raleigh.

7. Minutes of the Cumberland County Superior Court, 1831-39. North Carolina Archives, Raleigh.

son marriage. Henry E. Sampson appears as a shadowy presence through the listing in the census of 1830 and through Helen Chesnutt's use of the name Sampson.[8] Apart from Sampson's slaves, his estate and the disposition of it remain a mystery.

An item in the 1840 census, however, appears related to the Sampson and Harris entries of the 1830 census. The item lists the family of Moses Harris as follows:

1840   Moses Harris—age 24-36, Head of Household.
        3 free colored persons:
        2 female 24-36 [possibly Chloe, who would have been 34]
        3 female under 10 [possibly Ann Maria]

A further item of the 1850 census appears thus:

1850   Moses Harris, 45, Black Male, carpenter, unable to read and write
            2 Chloe 40 Mulatto female, literate [Chloe would have been 44]
            3 Anne M. Sampson, 18, Mulatto female, unable to read and write.[9]

The next pertinent census is that of 1870, since the Chesnutts, Sampsons, and Harrises had migrated to Cleveland and were unlisted in Cumberland County in 1860. After these families had returned to Fayetteville, we find them listed in the 1870 census:

1870
Entry No. 20, June 28: [entries were by then numbered in the order of visitation by the census-taker]
        Jackson Chesnutt, Head of Household, 37, mulatto ret Grocer, Value of real estate, $500. Personal estate, $200. Literate. U.S. citizen.
            2 Ann Maria Chesnutt mulatto, literate, 35 [but Ann Maria would have been 38] born in North Carolina

---

8.   Chesnutt made one reference to the name "Sampson." See Chesnutt to Victor K. Chesnut, Aug. 4, 1924, CC, WRHS: "My ancestors, somewhat prior to 1775, lived in Sampson County, North Carolina, and my great-grandfather was at one time sheriff of that county." If Chesnutt was correct that prior to 1775 some of his ancestors lived in Sampson County. Henry E. Sampson—if descended from Sampsons of Sampson County— could have migrated to Fayetteville, there to have been counted in the census of 1830. Chesnutt does not say his ancestors living in Sampson County bore the name Sampson, however.

9.   Sixth Census of the United States, Fayetteville District, 1840, and Seventh Census of the United States, Fayetteville District, 1850.

3 Charles 12, in school [this is Charles Waddell Chesnutt]
4 minor in school [this is Lewis]
5 minor in school [this is Andrew]
6 minor not of school age
7 minor not of school age
[All the Chesnutt children, including Charles, are typed "M" for mulatto.]

Entry No. 21

Moses Harris, Head of Household, 60, Black carpenter able to read and write [but this age should be 65].

2 Chloe, 50, Mulatto housekeeper able to read and write [but this age should be 64].[10]

These records show some age discrepancies, and this casts some question about the identity of persons. And they show that Chloe lived as the wife of Moses Harris six years before she and her daughter left Fayetteville (in 1856) although Helen Chesnutt implies that Chloe met Moses Harris in Cleveland, and states that she married him there.[11] Whatever the facts it is at least possible that Charles Chesnutt's maternal grandmother Chloe was once the slave of Henry E. Sampson and that in some manner she gained her freedom.[12] It is unclear who was the father of Chloe's daughter Ann Maria; this child appears to be listed with Chloe on three occasions—once in the Sampson household in 1830, once in the Harris household in 1840, and again in the Harris household in 1850, but that year under the name of Ann Maria Sampson. Ann Maria, who became the mother of Charles Waddell Chesnutt, was then (in 1850) a girl of eighteen. It is easy to find parallels to Rena's story in the real-life situations of Chloe and Moses Harris and Chloe's daughter Ann Maria.

Evidence exists for inferring that an even more poignant parallel to Rena's story existed on the paternal side of Chesnutt's ancestry. A heading in the Cumberland County census of 1840 is "Name of Heads of Families." One of the entries is "Ann Chesnutt." At that time the census taker entered only the approximate age, number, sex, color, and status of persons:

---

10. *Ninth Census of the United States, Fayetteville District,* 1870. Harris is listed as literate, though a deed, April 25, 1871, says, "Moses Harris, his mark." Respondents often concealed literacy or illiteracy, age, or illegitimacy.

11. Helen Chesnutt, *Charles Waddell Chesnutt's Pioneer of the Color Line,* p. 6.

12. She is listed as a free person of color in the *Sixth Census of the United States, Cumberland County, North Carolina, Fayetteville District,* 1840.

1840   Ann Chesnutt, Head of Household, age 24-36
6 free colored persons
2 male under 10 [this was George Washington Chesnutt]
3 male under 10 [this was Andrew Jackson Chesnutt, father
of Charles Chesnutt]
4 male under 10 [this was Stephen]
5 female under 10 [probably Mary Ann or Abram]
6 female under 10 [Sophia]

The census showed no husband or means of livelihood for Ann Chesnutt.[13]

The same family appears in the 1850 census of Cumberland County, Fayetteville District, dated July 24, 1850. By that time more information was requested, and the entry records that "Anna M. Chestnut," age 37, female, mulatto, was born in North Carolina. The census shows no occupation and no real estate value and no husband. Beneath the heading "Persons over 20 years of age who cannot read or write," the box for her name is left vacant; apparently she was literate. Seven persons are listed:

1850

Entry No. 39. Anna M. Chestnut
2 George 19 mulatto barber $100 Real Estate Literate
3 Jackson 17 mulatto laborer $100 Real Estate Literate,
had not been in school that year
4 Stephen $150 Real Estate
5 Mary Ann 7 $150 Real Estate
6 Sophia $150 Real Estate
7 Dallas 3 $250 Real Estate

No husband is mentioned and no means of livelihood is noted.[14]

Through other references, it becomes clear that "Jackson Chesnutt" of this entry was Charles Chesnutt's father. The question of the identity of (Andrew) Jackson Chesnutt's father, who was the father of the children of "Anna M. Chestnut" (Or "Ann Chesnutt," as it is spelled in the 1840 census) is interesting because it contributed to Charles Chesnutt's writing and thinking.

Andrew Jackson Chesnutt's will mentions a "house & lot on C Street which was given me by my father."[15] The list of taxable persons in Cum-

---

13. *Sixth Census of the United States, Fayetteville District,* 1840.

14. *Seventh Census of the United States, Fayetteville District,* 1850.

15. Probate Records of Cumberland County, North Carolina Archives, Raleigh. Andrew Jackson Chesnutt's will is dated June 21, 1920.

berland County covers only the years 1824-29, 1837-49, and some of the years from 1857 to 1884.[16] The records from 1837 to 1849 reveal that from the year 1829 the name of W. Cade, for Waddle Cade, is frequently connected with the names of the "Chestnut" children. Though there is no record of Waddle Cade's having left a will, and though there are no Cumberland County Estate papers in his name, the index of deeds shows that Waddle Cade often bought or sold land. He started acquiring land in 1805; twenty-five recorded deeds show that he is the grantee. The earliest date is 1821; in that year he got a "Lot Russell St. Fay" from Thos. D. Burgh. In 1836 Cade deeded to Andrew Jackson Chesnutt a "lot Morgan-Russell Sts. Fayetteville."[17]

Surveying the list of taxable persons for the district of Fayetteville from the year 1849 and working backward reveals the following information:

For the year 1849	Property Listed	Valuation
Ann Chesnut	"Russell Street Improved"	200
Stephen Chesnutt	"Wilmington Road Improved"	150
Sophia Chesnutt	"Wilmington Road Improved"	
Mary Chesnutt	"Wilmington Road Improved"	

For the year 1848		
"Chesnutte Washington by Ann Chesnutte"	Russell Street improved	200
for Stephen Chesnutte	Wilmington Road improved	150
for Mary Chesnutte	Wilmington Road improved	150

[In this year Andrew Jackson Chesnutt was not mentioned, nor was Sophia. "Chesnutte Washington" was George Washington Chesnutt, Andrew Jackson Chesnutt's older brother; see the census of 1850.]

For the year 1847	Property Listed	Valuation
Chestnutt Ann for G. W. and A. J. Chestnutt [father of Charles]	improved Russell Street	200
Chestnutt Ann for Mary Chesnutt	improved Wilmington Road	150
Chestnutt Ann for Sophia Chesnutt	improved Wilmington Road	150

16. North Carolina Archives, Raleigh.

17. Cumberland County Index of Deeds, North Carolina Archives, Raleigh.

Chestnutt Ann for
Stephen Chesnutt   improved Wilmington Road   150

For the year 1846 Ann Chesnutt's name does not appear in the list of taxable persons for the district of Fayetteville. The following year, 1847, is the first year in which the list includes her name. Though her name may appear elsewhere, it is unlisted in 1844, for example, in any North Carolina district. The Chesnutt name occurs, however, as follows:[18]

For the year 1846	**Property Listed**	**Valuation**
Cade, Waddill for	60 acres on	
James W. Cade	Wilmington Road	1200
Cade, Waddill for	on Wilmington Road,	
William Cade	Campbelton	200
Cade, Waddill for		
Sarah Cade	Campbelton	150
Cade, Waddill for		
Washington and	in Campbelton on	
Jackson Chesnutt	Russell St.	150
Cade, Waddill for		
Sophia and Abram		
Chesnutt	on Wilmington Road	100
Cade, Waddill for		
Stephen Chesnutt	on Wilmington Road	100

Although there is no reference to Ann Chesnutt for the year 1846, her children appear, and they are connected with the family of Waddill Cade. For whatever reason, he deeded these properties to the children of Ann Chesnutt. These children also appear connected with the land that Helen Chesnutt's book mentions[19] and which, in the case of "Washington and Jackson Chesnutt," appears to be the land spoken of in Andrew Jackson Chesnutt's will. When Ann Chesnutt appears as a taxable person in the list of 1847, Waddill Cade ceased listing the Chesnutt children under his name. Thus in 1847 Cade (whose first name had variously appeared as Waddell, Waddle, Waddill, Waddel, or just W) listed only the 60-acre lot on the Wilmington Road for James W. Cade, and the land "in campbelton" valued at $300 for William Cade. And in 1848

18.   List of Taxable Persons, Fayetteville District, Cumberland County, North Carolina Archives, Raleigh. These tax books cover 1824-29, 1837-49. From 1857 to 1884 only miscellaneous tax lists have been preserved.

19.   H. Chesnutt, *Pioneer*, pp. 4, 8.

and 1849 Cade listed only one piece of property for "Wm." It was an "old Thames store" in "lower Fayetteville," valued at $300. This could have been the store turned over to Andrew Jackson Chesnutt on his return to Fayetteville after the Civil War.

It appears that 1846 was a crucial year; apparently Ann Chesnutt went on her own that year. It is possible to trace the listings for Waddle Cade further.[20]

For the year 1845	Property Listed	Valuation
Cade, Waddle for	60 acres on Wilmington	
James Cade	Road, improved	1200
Cade, Waddle for		
William Cade	Campbelton	300
Cade, Waddle for		
Sarah Cade	Campbelton	150
Cade, Waddle for		
W. & J. Chesnutt	Russell Street	150
Cade, Waddle for		
S. & A. Chesnutt	Wilmington Road	100

For the year 1844

The list of taxable persons is almost identical for "Cade, Waddell" with James, William, and Sarah Cade listed for the properties as they appear above. Sarah and William are listed so that ditto marks are used, creating an ambiguity when the Chesnutt listings appear below. Thus William Cade's property shows:[21]

Cade, Waddle		
for William Cade	Houses & Lots Campbelton	
for Sarah Cade	Houses & Lots	
for W. & Jackson		
Chesnutt	Houses & Lots Russell St.	150
for Sophia and Abram	Houses & Lots Wilmington	
Chesnutt	Road & known as the Lot	
	Stephens Lot & 1 other lot	100

It is difficult to tell whether there was more than one house and lot on Russell Street or whether the recorder used ditto marks carelessly. But the valuations remain the same.

---

20. List of Taxable Persons, Fayetteville District, Cumberland County, North Carolina Archives, Raleigh.

21. Ibid. A better description of the property owned on Wilmington Road, though still inconclusive.

For the year 1843

The list of taxable persons under "Cade, Waddel" shows the same properties for the Cade children and for "Washington and Jackson Chesnutt": "house and lot on Russell St." at the same valuation of $150. This is the first year in which "Sophia" and "Abram" are not mentioned, although the 1840 census shows that they had been born. It appears that Cade waited for a time before ceding land to these children.

For the years 1842 back through 1837

Washington and Jackson are mentioned in each of these years under a listing of Waddle Cade as owning this "House and Lot in Campbelton"; the valuation is always $150.[22] In the year 1836 Cade deeded to Andrew Jackson Chesnutt a "Lot Morgan-Russell Sts. Fayetteville."

For the year 1829 the following entry occurs: "Cade, Ino for W. Cade 'vacant [property] Russell Street, joins Davis,' Valuation $20." Since this is the only reference to Waddle Cade in 1829, this probably refers to the original deed to W. Cade of the land that he eventually improved and gave to Andrew Jackson Chesnutt, as stated in the Chesnutt will of 1920.[23]

According to these many instruments and the clause in Andrew Jackson Chesnutt's will identifying his father as the person who gave him his property, it seems clear that Waddell Cade was that father and that Ann M. Chesnutt was his mother. Though Cade was never legally connected with this family, he remained for many years interested to some extent in them, and he provided property for each of the children, as well as for his children bearing the Cade name. It is neither surprising nor coincidental that Charles Chesnutt, the first child of Andrew Jackson Chesnutt, was given the middle name "Waddell."

Most of the people involved in this dramatic situation lived in or near Fayetteville for most of their lives. Both of Charles Chesnutt's grandmothers found themselves in the situation Rena struggled to escape in *The House Behind the Cedars*. To all appearances both of Chesnutt's grandfathers were white men of property married to white women who bore them children and not married to the "other" women who bore their mulatto children. The sanctity of marriage was a pillar of the white

---

22. Workers of the WPA Writers' Program of the Work Projects Administration, North Carolina, *How They Began—The Story of North Carolina County, Town and Other Place Names* (New York: Harian Publications, 1941), p. 33. The entry explains "Campbelton" in the tax records.

23. Cumberland County Index of Deeds, North Carolina Archives, Raleigh.

caste structure; it is easy to imagine the pain and the embarrassment that must have been the life of the nameless white wives of Henry E. Sampson and Waddell Cade[24] and the humiliation, the insecurity, and the sense of futility that must have been the lot of Chloe (Sampson) Harris and Ann M. Chesnutt and their many children and grand-children.[25]

Such census figures attest that this situation was typical of Southern communities, as do observations of travelers like Frederick Law Olmsted; in 1855 he wrote of the many "nearly white colored persons" he saw.[26] Property laws excluding women indicate how far the governing elite sanctioned these practices; even more convincingly tradition defined for all women a role supremely submissive to all indignities.[27] The situation of Charles Chesnutt's forebears worked to the deprivation of men as well as to that of women. Charles Chesnutt—and his white male relatives as well as his mulatto male relatives of several generations—never escaped the consequences of these partially covert relationships.

The records also reveal parallels to situations in other Chesnutt works. Living in and near Fayetteville were sisters and brothers whose relationship was unacknowledged. Sometimes they resembled one another; it is likely that, like characters in The Marrow of Tradition, they became entangled in financial difficulties.[28] As the character Frank Fowler remained loving and reliable in the novel about Rena, it appears that the real Moses Harris remained faithful to the real Chloe through many trials. Several persons disappeared from the records. Like the fictional John and Rena Walden, these real victims moved away and lived as white persons. Chesnutt noted that close relatives took this path in efforts to escape consequences.[29]

---

24.   Ray Stannard Baker, Following the Colour Line (New York: Harper & Row, 1964), p. 166.

25.   See Cooper, A Voice from the South, pp. 90, 111. June Sochen, ed., The Black Man and the American Dream (Chicago: Quadrangle Books, 1971), p. 213; anonymous article, "The Race Problem—An Autobiography" by a Southern Colored Woman (Repr. from the Independent, March 17, 1904).

26.   Frederick Law Olmsted, A Journey in the Seaboard Slave States (New York, 1856), p. 18.

27.   Women could not own property separate from that of their husbands, nor enter into transactions concerning property they owned prior to marriage, nor sue nor be sued in their own names.

28.   A subplot turns upon lost papers determining the property inheritance of unacknow-ledged sisters.

29.   Chesnutt to Dr. Park, Dec. 19, 1908, CC, WRHS, p. 3: "Several of my own near rela-tives, as nearly related to me as uncles, and aunts, have taken this course [passing as

Chesnutt's ancestral background documents a sexual situation of black and white and mulatto women which was characteristic of Southern tradition. Nor is the experience of his forebears unrelated to Chesnutt's conclusion that only intermarriage and open assimilation will finally solve American racial dilemmas. Chesnutt wrote about Southern civilization from the point of view of the many who suffered from it rather than from that of the few who maintained it.[30]

Several legends have arisen about Chesnutt and Rena. One is that Rowena Bryant, daughter of the free Negro farmer David Bryant, lived in the house that Chesnutt described, and that she was the prototype for the character Rena.[31] Another is that Chesnutt's concern with Rena's situation is related to an earlier, dimmer era. In an autobiography titled *Fact Stranger than Fiction*, Chesnutt's cousin, John P. Green, disclosed another tale. In grammar more convoluted than his usual style, Green traced his mother's family, through whom he was related to the Chesnutts. Though they cannot conceal the human tolls, Green's commas, asides, and intricate subordinate classes almost conceal the last statement:

In the latter part of the eighteenth century, 1792, to be specific, there resided near the town of Clinton, in Sampson county, North Carolina, about thirty miles from the city (then town) of Fayetteville, in the same state, a family, containing two beautiful daughters, of which a man, Chesnut (or Chestnutt) by name, was the head. This pater familias was known and respected far and wide, by persons of his class; moreover, since his daughters were young and comely, they were, frequently favored by the calls of young gentlemen, in the vicinage, who, socially and financially, deemed themselves their superiors.

In the course of time, the young ladies became greatly enamored of two of these young men; but since they did not hasten to make to them proposals of marriage, they had recourse to the advice and services of

---

white persons]. Some I have kept track of, others have been swallowed up in the great majority. I hope they have won distinction. I am sure that their children will have a better opportunity in life, other things being equal, than had they taken a different course."

30. Alfred H. Benners, *Slavery and Its Results* (Macon: J. W. Burke Co., 1923). p. 36; Chesnutt, "Age of Problems," November, 1906, CC, Fisk, MS, address delivered before the Cleveland Council of Sociology: "All of which leads to the serious question, 'Is there really in the South any such exaggerated respect for white womanhood before which all other laws must give way, or is it founded purely upon race and caste hatred?' I yield to no one in my respect for womanhood (and I don't judge it by its color either), but I have never yet been able to see why the virtue of a woman is more valuable than the life of a man."

31. Suggested by Sylvia Lyons Render, "Tar Heelia in Chesnutt," *College Language Association Journal*, 9 (September, 1965).

a "likely" young colored man (the slave of their father), who advised them, in the premises, with the result that, ere long, each became the mother of a little colored girl. . . .

A glance will suggest that these two babies, being the offspring of one father by two sisters, were, at once, sisters and cousins!! This condition during the womanhood of these two colored girls was doubly complicated, when each girl presented to two white brothers, severally, a child, one of whom was my mother.

Bede 96 when died, Alice almost 90. Both left behind them a numerous progeny thus proving the fallacy of that "scientific" dogma—that mulattoes cannot reproduce their species; for both were mulattoes, having white mothers and a Negro father.[32]

Whatever ancient and contemporary racial complexities influenced Chesnutt, and there were many, he could never have escaped a knowledge of his immediate family, nor a deep concern for their welfare. He had too many opportunities to observe their dilemmas. From them he provided in *The House Behind the Cedars* an impressive historical-cultural study. Chesnutt's literary love for Rena began with a profound comprehension of his personal situation.[33] It progressed to an understanding that the situation was meaningful to the future of the American nation.

Nor did the novel about Rena spring forth in a burst of creative fulfillment. Chesnutt first composed a short story; then *Rena Walden* became a "novelette," then again a short story, and finally a novel. Five manuscripts of 39, 91, 55, 51, and 231 pages respectively still exist.[34] Chesnutt showed an early manuscript to George W. Cable. Then Richard Watson Gilder of the *Century* criticized *Rena* and returned it. Cable had

---

32. John P. Green, *Fact Stranger Than Fiction, Seventy-Five Years of a Busy Life with Reminiscences of Many Great and Good Men and Women* (Cleveland: Riehl Printing Co., 1920), pp. 6-7, 69, 147. Green shows that the relationship to Chesnutt was on his mother's side: "Was my spirit broken? Had the Stanley-Chesnutt blood ever quailed before that of another? Never!" (Green's parental grandfather was John Stanley, a lawyer, Speaker of the North Carolina House for seven sessions; pp. 2-4.) Chesnutt and Green exchanged many letters; see Chesnutt to Green, Feb. 13, 1899, John P. Green Papers, Container 5, Folder 4, Western Reserve Historical Society, Cleveland. This is written in French, evidently for the pleasure of the exercise.

33. Chesnutt to John Chamberlin, June 16, 1930. CC, WRHS. Late in life Chesnutt wrote Chamberlin, critic of *The Bookman:* "With reference to 'The House Behind the Cedars,' it is, in a way, my favorite child, for Rena was of "mine own people." Like myself, she was a white person with an attenuated streak of dark blood, from the disadvantages of which she tried in vain to escape, while I never did."

34. Freeney and Henry, *A List of Manuscripts,* p. 13.

felt that the story stood "in a very important relation to the interests of a whole great nation," that Chesnutt could "become an apostle of a new emancipation to millions."[35] Chesnutt sent the novel more than once to Houghton Mifflin, whose readers more than once decided against publication.[36] Again and again Chesnutt reworked it; it was the story that would accomplish his lifetime goals.

Chesnutt even tested responses by reading it aloud. He considered bearing publication expenses.[37] More than once he sent the story to Walter Hines Page: "I have not slept with that story for ten years without falling in love with it and believing in it," he wrote.[38] Page answered:

While I had a feeling that the story would probably succeed, I could not throw away another feeling that you had not by any means, even yet, done your best work on it, or had developed to the fullest extent the possibilities of the story. . . . I believe that a year hence if you read it over again you will agree with me that it is not even yet sufficiently elaborated and filled in with relieving incidents—not sufficiently mellowed— there is not sufficient atmosphere poured round it somehow—to make a full-fledged novel. . . . You had so long and so successfully accustomed yourself to the construction of short stories that you have not yet, so to speak, got away from the short story measurement and the short story habit.[39]

Chesnutt worked incessantly on writing and intermittently on structure. Professionally he grew from short-story-teller to novelist. "A novel," Page had said, "is . . . not simply a longer thing. It must also be a much more elaborate thing."

Chesnutt had known acclaim; but he experienced frustration over Rena. He felt tantalizingly close to convincing a first-rank editor that he had a superior novel; many times he received the answer that he almost did. Like a human love, this literary love became an anvil upon which quality would be defined and purpose tested. Chesnutt never abandoned Rena.

---

35. George W. Cable to Chesnutt, May 3, 1899. George W. Cable Collection, Tulane University, New Orleans.

36. See Walter Hines Page to Chesnutt, March 31, 1899. CC, Fisk.

37. Chesnutt to Houghton Mifflin & Company, probably early 1899. CC, Fisk.

38. Chesnutt to Walter Hines Page, March, 1899. CC, Fisk.

39. Walter Hines Page to Chesnutt, March 31, 1899, CC, Fisk; Walter Hines Page to Chesnutt, Jan. 24, 1904. Walter Hines Page Papers, Houghton Library, Harvard.

On January 24, 1900, Walter Page wrote to Chesnutt. Would Chesnutt care to have *Rena* brought out by Doubleday, Page? Three days later Chesnutt sat in Page's office. Outside interest turned the trick. Houghton Mifflin were considering another Chesnutt novel, *The Rainbow Chasers*. Though Bliss Perry and W. B. Parker liked the "homely sincerity," and the "freedom from affectation," they concluded that story was unsuitable as a serial.[40] Propitiously Chesnutt visited Boston, giving readings, dining with Joseph Edgar Chamberlin of the *Boston Transcript,* and with Professor Albert Bushnell Hart of Harvard.[41]

Surely Chesnutt informed Houghton Mifflin of the recently departed Page's offer. On March 24, Francis J. Garrison, son of William Lloyd Garrison, wrote Chesnutt: "We have decided to take *Rena* (under the title *The House Behind the Cedars*) in place of *The Rainbow Chasers*, and to publish it next fall."[42] On hearing all—especially on learning of Page's offer—and though they had many times refused it, Houghton Mifflin asked "the privilege of reconsidering *Rena*."[43] So Chesnutt's tragic story entered the American literary-historical treasury. Except for critical praise and a negligible sale, there it has languished. People seldom bought the book because it was inopportune to entertain equitable solutions to racial problems. Like Americans at the drafting of the Constitution, and like their descendants, Americans of Chesnutt's time turned away. The reasons lie deep in the human psyche.

The Historians and *The Marrow of Tradition:* Chesnutt's Dilemma

Charles Chesnutt had done what he could with Rena's story. In November of 1898, while he was rewriting *Rena*, he planned his next work. It would be rooted not so much in hushed happenings of generations gone as in an immediate nightmare—the race riot that occurred in Wilmington, North Carolina, after the election of 1898.[44]

Contacts of urban industrialization had precipitated a new violence. Horrified, ashamed, shaken, finding his worst fears exceeded, Chesnutt

---

40. W. B. Parker to Chesnutt, Feb. 27, 1900. Quoted in H. Chesnutt, *Pioneer,* pp. 141-42.

41. Albert Bushnell Hart to Chesnutt, March 13, 1899, CC, Fisk.

42. "FJG" to Chesnutt, March 24, 1900. Quoted in H. Chesnutt, *Pioneer,* p. 146.

43. Chesnutt to Daughters, March 24, 1900. Quoted in H. Chesnutt, *Pioneer,* p. 146.

44. Chesnutt to Mrs. W. E. Henderson, Nov. 11, 1905, CC, Fisk: "The book was suggested by the Wilmington riot.... [and] by a vivid description given me by Dr. Mask... of the events of the riot, and a ride which he took across the city during its progress."

conceived a truthful tale. He became the first writer to offer a sociological study of the Wilmington riot.[45] Since then politicians have questioned Chesnutt's account. But journalists and scholars have confirmed it.

Chesnutt wrote *The Marrow of Tradition* with the conviction of a man defending his home. The character Major Carteret was the only descendant of a family which had long possessed land, slaves, and prestige. He returned from Appomattox to share the common displacement. Through marriage and the establishment of a newspaper he gradually found his way back to a position of influence. Yet he felt insecure because the Negroes—"an inferior and servile race"—were in the majority in "Wellington," and because the Fusionists retained some political organization. A few Negroes held office and had risen in professions, and he foresaw that this would force upon "Wellington" a social equality. His wife Olivia had other reasons for a grievance, reasons that tortured her when her unacknowledged mulatto sister Janet Miller passed by, or when Janet's Negro husband, a physician, provided well for Janet and contributed to the welfare of his race.

Soon Major Carteret found common cause with General Belmont, a tricky demagogue, and with Captain McBane, whose "cracker" (disadvantaged) background had rendered him eager to do the dirty work of the power struggle. Using Carteret's newspaper, the three conspirators launched a campaign to fan white fears and to terrify black people. They fostered a plan to lynch the Negro servant Sandy, who had been accused of murder. Though Sandy had no trial, they planned to strike terror into the black residents. This would hold some in check and reduce the rest to impotence. But Sandy's white employer believed in Sandy's innocence and thwarted their plan.

Thinking that as the nation rushed toward world dominion, the suppression of an inferior race at home would go unquestioned, the Wellington Democrats labored to win the election of 1898 and to disfranchise black people. They stepped up their newspaper campaign. They organized committees. They pointed out the dangers of "Negro domination" and the necessity to enact strict suffrage laws. Negroes might understand that white Democrats would tolerate them if they acquiesced in their own disfranchisement.

But most Negroes realized that acquiescence meant the loss of opportunity. Outraged, they considered courses of action. Fearing disaster,

---

45. W. E. B. DuBois to Houghton Mifflin & Co., March 8, 1902. DuBois credits *The Marrow of Tradition* as "one of the best sociological studies of the Wilmington Riot which I have seen."

some left. Others—like the "unmanageable" Josh Green—armed themselves, though no white merchant would sell them firearms, and the best they could do was to oil up old guns. But white people procured arms in great quantities. As Josh Green and other Negroes frantically sought leaders, the "Wellington" Grays drilled incessantly at the armory.

Meanwhile the Negro editor of the *Afro-American Banner,* a character Chesnutt called Barber, began a newspaper attack of his own. He replied to a white woman of Georgia who clamored for vengeance on some Georgia Negroes accused of rape. Major Carteret reprinted Editor Barber's reply in his *Chronicle,* with comments condemning the Negro editor's answer as an insolent attack on white womanhood. Feelings grew more intense. Local Democrats publicly resented Negro "prosperity." Passions rose, as committees of white men prepared for action. In desperation a few Negroes gathered at the office of a Negro newspaper, while others assembled near Dr. Miller's hospital.

By November of 1898 the city had reached a dangerous tension. The white Democrats were unappeased by success in the election, and unwilling to wait out the term. Convinced that they had a sacred duty to remove white Republicans and Negroes from office, they prepared a mass assault, intending to wrest the city government immediately from Fusionist white and Negro incumbents and take charge. At the same time they would get rid of "undesirable" Negroes by driving from the city or killing those who resisted.

"The Wellington riot began at three o'clock in the afternoon of a day as fair as was ever selected for a deed of darkness," Chesnutt wrote.[46] When the storm broke, gangs of white men and boys stopped every Negro passing by on the street; in disarming the Negroes, they killed several. Then a prominent Democrat led a group to the office of the Negro newspaper and destroyed it. They ordered half a dozen prominent Negroes to leave within forty-eight hours or die. During a harrowing ride across the city to find his wife Janet, Dr. Miller learned that if he offered no resistance they would permit him to remain.

By night the "revolution" had become a murderous riot. Chesnutt wrote that "crowds of white men and half-grown boys, drunk with whiskey or with license, raged through the streets, beating, chasing or killing any black person so unfortunate as to fall into their hands."[47] Wild rumors circulated: the Negroes were up in arms. They were threatening to exterminate the white population. Yet in the cold November, many Ne-

---

46. Chesnutt, *The Marrow of Tradition,* p. 274.

47. Ibid., p. 298.

groes had taken refuge in woods and swamps. When a little band of desperate Negroes sought protection inside Dr. Miller's hospital, the mob became so rabid that the perpetrators were unable to prevent them from burning the building. Before he died in the holocaust, the militant Josh Green took vengeance by killing Captain McBane.

Chesnutt thus wrote the history of a power struggle. He used a respected Confederate general and his debauched grandson, an ex-slave driver, a displaced Southern aristocrat turned editor and his wife, a liberal young newsman, a white-supremacist politician, an aging woman of good family and little humanity. He used as varied a group of Negro characters: a militant young working man who would die before he would yield, a skillful physician and his near-white wife, a cowed serving-boy depending, to his ruin, on white protectors, a "mammy," glorying in her "place," an independent young nurse, a successful attorney, an editor, an honorable old servant.

First-rank historians have corroborated these happenings.[48] "Riots [in the United States] displayed patterns," said John Hope Franklin.[49] He described the patterns of the riot that is the background for Chesnutt's book and that was repeated in Atlanta and in other racial riots North and South in the late nineteenth and early twentieth centuries: No isolated incident could be pinpointed as a cause; a substantial segment of the population was involved, and events were related to the fanning of suspicions, fears, and hatreds by a previously responsible element of the white community. When emotions were inflamed, a real or fancied happening that might have passed unnoticed at another time became the precipitating incident. An orgy of violence followed; it tapered off, and sometimes ended in remorse.[50] Every case history of a riot exhibited resentment of a repressive act by some segment of the black community.

In 1951 Helen G. Edmonds provided a description of the particular riot that Chesnutt used in *The Marrow of Tradition.* Working from sources, Edmonds assembled evidence of the stages that Franklin out-

48. Helen G. Edmonds, *The Negro and Fusion Politics in North Carolina, 1894-1901* (Chapel Hill: University of North Carolina Press, 1951), pp. 136-177; J. Allen Kirk, "A Statement of Facts Concerning the Bloody Riot in Wilmington, North Carolina, Thursday, November 10, 1898," *Forum,* January, 1899, p. 580; Jack Thorne, *Hanover: The Persecution of the Lowly: A Story of the Wilmington Massacre* (New York: Arno Publishers, 1970), p. 13; Mabry, "The Negro in North Carolina Politics Since Reconstruction," pp. 31-56.

49. Remarks from notes made by Frances Richardson Keller, January 9, 1965, University of Chicago.

50. A. J. McKelway of Atlanta, in *Outlook,* Nov. 3, 1906, pp. 557-66, expresses satisfaction, not remorse.

lined and Chesnutt described. Whereas Chesnutt traveled to Wilmington in February of 1901 to collect "a great deal of material for the new novel"[51] and then used fictional names, Edmonds searched the records of half a century and identified persons who lived this terrible drama: Alfred Moore Waddell was a white supremacist orator to whom Chesnutt had years before addressed a letter intended for "Open-Letter Club" circulation. Edmonds quoted an address Waddell delivered at Durham at the end of the campaign of 1898. Waddell said:

We in Wilmington extend a Macedonian call to you to come over and help us. We will not live under these intolerable conditions. No society can stand it. We intend to change it, if we have to choke the current of Cape Fear River with negro carcasses.[52]

Edmonds designated Waddell as a "staunch democrat and defeated office-seeker" and as the "leader of the riot." Chesnutt called him General Belmont.[53] Josephus Daniels—whose role is taken by the editor Major Carteret—edited in fact the *Raleigh News and Observer;* three days after the riot, on November 13, 1898, Daniels's paper hailed this murderous vendetta as "the salvation of the city of Wilmington from degradation." Alex Manly, the Negro editor of the *Daily Record*—whose part is played by the character Barber—witnessed the destruction of his office and presses, and narrowly escaped lynching.[54]

Though Edmonds revealed a more complex interrelatedness than Chesnutt developed, she confirmed the attitudes and actions that Chesnutt highlighted. Her conclusions were that "the yellow journalism of the press made the city a veritable boiling pot"; that "the orators of the 'white supremacy' campaign fanned the flames of passion"; that "rumors played as large a part in intensifying racial antagonism in Wilmington as any other single factor"; and that for six to twelve months "the white citizens of Wilmington prepared quietly but effectively for the day when action would be necessary."[55] She found white Democrats chiefly interested "in eliminating [Negro] men of college training, some wealth, and local renown," men who not only "excelled in Wilmington," but who,

---

51. H. Chesnutt, *Pioneer,* p. 159.

52. Quoted in Edmonds, *The Negro and Fusion Politics,* p. 165.

53. The white supremacist politician Furnifold Simmons and others mentioned by Edmonds may have contributed to Chesnutt's portrait of General Belmont.

54. (J. Max) Barber was the Negro editor of an Atlanta newspaper, *The Negro Voice.*

55. Edmonds, *The Negro and Fusion Politics,* pp. 164-66; Mabry, "The Negro in North Carolina Politics Since Reconstruction," pp. 46-48.

191

when driven away, "continued to excel in other areas." Their migration left "an apathetic Negro citizenry, fearful of and resentful toward the whites."[56]

Racial conflagrations more violent than the Wilmington riot have occurred since Chesnutt wrote. They have interested editors, scores of "media" commentators, and teams of investigators. Not the least conspicuous were commissions chaired by Daniel Walker, Governor of Illinois, and by former Governor Otto Kerner. Yet no one approached the subject with greater good will than a journalist of the period when Chesnutt produced *The Marrow of Tradition.* This man's work underscores Chesnutt's contribution.[57]

Ray Stannard Baker's book, *Following the Color Line,* dealt with the 1906 riot in Atlanta.[58] Baker went to Atlanta a few weeks after the riot. He interviewed persons of both races, of both sexes, of all ages. He pieced information together, uncovering much, and leaving a valuable record. Though he never grasped the extent to which politicians shared responsibility, Baker revealed a duplication of the Wilmington events of Chesnutt's story as well as an example of the pattern Franklin delineated.

From early 1901 till July, Chesnutt worked on *The Marrow of Tradition.* The novel represents the emergence of the conflict that developed in Chesnutt's novel writing. That Chesnutt hoped that he could touch the hearts of readers, that he could allay fears, that he could call forth a fellow feeling is evident in his use of the sisters, white and Negro, in the tragic peril that came to their babies, and in other subplots. He wanted *The Marrow of Tradition* to "become lodged in the popular mind as the legitimate successor of *Uncle Tom's Cabin* and *A Fool's Errand.*" Yet his accurate approach to events represented a technique more akin to the analytical framework of his essays than to a story-teller's techniques; he wanted the book to depict "an epoch in our national history."[59] Chesnutt pushed relentlessly along both channels. Perhaps he abandoned some hope that he could "mine the garrison" of white supremacy, that he could lay bare the decaying props of establishment custom.

---

56. Edmonds, *The Negro and Fusion Politics,* p. 174.

57. Chesnutt to Judge U. L. Marvin, Sept. 17, 1908. CC, Fisk.

58. Dewey Grantham, Jr., ed., "Introduction," in Ray Stannard Baker, *Following the Color Line* (New York: Harper & Row, 1964).

59. Chesnutt to Houghton Mifflin & Company, Oct. 26, 1901. CC, Fisk. Chesnutt to Booker T. Washington, Oct. 8, 1901. Booker T. Washington Collection, Library of Congress.

Whatever his tensions, he used the novel to work out conflicts between commitments of his youth and the likely reception of them. *The Marrow of Tradition* resulted from a struggle over means to accomplish his purposes. It represents a confrontation between what Chesnutt believed possible by reaching reservoirs of empathy and his realization that forces of greed and reaction need be met by sterner measures. Writing *The Marrow of Tradition* taxed Chesnutt's psychic energies. He cherished his belief that man can be touched by the plight of his fellows, but he realized the necessity for countermeasures more stringent than those of the exploiters. It may be that Chesnutt overshot his mark: he laid open a recent event too discomfiting to contemplate. Or it may be that timing was crucial. The novel appeared just when the white man, having disfranchised the black man, or having by silence consented to it, could only reject a novel exposing the means used to do the thing and exposing as well the sufferings of victims.

Francis J. Garrison wrote that they were "much impressed by [the novel's] power and intensity"; and Houghton Mifflin enthusiastically prepared promotions.[60] Yet Chesnutt felt depleted, and he felt forebodings: "You must join me in hopes for the success of my book," he wrote to his oldest daughter, Ethel, "for upon its reception will depend in some measure whether I shall write for the present any more 'Afro-American' novels; for a man must live and consider his family."[61]

The Colonel's Dream and the Society of the South

Chesnutt did need to live, and he did consider his family. This required attention, for the income from his two novels was disappointing.[62] But he also wrote more "Afro-American" novels.[63] The last of his published novels quivers with the unresolved conflict that emerged in *The*

---

60. Houghton Mifflin & Company by Francis J. Garrison to Chesnutt, July 31, 1901. CC, Fisk.

61. Quoted in H. Chesnutt, *Pioneer*, p. 176. Chesnutt to Rev. Benjamin G. Brawley, March 24, 1922. CC, WRHS, Container 1, Folder 1.

62. H. Chesnutt, *Pioneer*, p. 176; Chesnutt to Houghton Mifflin & Company, Dec. 28, 1901, CC, Fisk: "I am pretty well convinced that the color line runs everywhere so far as the United States is concerned."

63. Only three Chesnutt novels were published: *The House Behind the Cedars*, 1900; *The Marrow of Tradition*, 1901; *The Colonel's Dream*, 1905. He wrote novels before this time: *A Business Career*, c. 1898, and *Mandy Oxendine*, c. 1897. He wrote other novels during this time: *Evelyn's Husband*, c. 1900, and *The Rainbow Chasers*, c. 1900. Chesnutt submitted *Evelyn's Husband* to McClure, Phillips & Co. in 1903, Witter Brynner to Chesnutt, Nov. 6, 1903, CC, Fisk. He wrote two, possibly more, after this time: *Paul Marchand,*

Marrow of Tradition.[64] *The House Behind the Cedars* and *The Marrow of Tradition* present historic situations into which Chesnutt wove the tragedies of characters with whom readers can sympathize. *The Colonel's Dream* leans more heavily toward the presentation of a thesis: When a community permits interests to hold power by fostering racial disadvantage, it sounds its knell; thenceforth it can only deteriorate. *The Colonel's Dream* details the cultural rot that became the post-war way of life in the Southern town of Clarendon. Chesnutt inscribed this volume:

To the great number of those who are seeking, in whatever manner or degree, from near at hand or far away, to bring the forces of enlightenment to bear upon the vexed problems which harass the South.[65]

Yet Chesnutt still endeavored to present appealing portrayals of people. The character Colonel Henry French was born in Clarendon;[66] he grew to manhood there, and served the Confederacy in a regiment of which he was the only survivor. Dispossessed, he sought his fortune in New York. He found partners, and built a business; in his forties he retired in possession of substantial holdings. He returned to Clarendon because he needed a place of convalescence for his motherless son. The Colonel intended a brief stay; instead he found himself lured by some fragrance from his childhood, and he found himself confronting a challenge: Clarendon had fallen prey to a general blight. The people were impoverished, and most were indebted to William Fetters, son of a "poor-white" slave-driver. When both were boys, French had despised

---

F.M.C., c. 1921, and *The Quarry*, c. 1928. *Paul Marchand, F.M.C.* is dated 1928 in Freeney and Henry's *A List of Manuscripts.* This appears erroneous. Chesnutt submitted this novel to Houghton Mifflin with a letter October 8, 1921. Chesnutt to Houghton Mifflin & Company, Oct. 8, 1921. Reserved papers of Houghton Mifflin Company, Houghton Library, Harvard.

Possibly Chesnutt wrote another novel after he submitted *The Quarry.* See James Weldon Johnson to Chesnutt, Jan. 31, and April 6, 1928; Chesnutt to Johnson, Dec. 28, 1928, all. CC, Fisk. Further correspondence, Johnson and Chesnutt, is in the James Weldon Johnson Collection, Beineke Library, Yale; access is prohibited by Mrs. Johnson. See James Weldon Johnson to Chesnutt, Dec. 28, 1928, Library of Congress; Chesnutt to Ferris Greenslet, Oct. 15, 1930, CC, WRHS; Ralph T. Hale to Chesnutt, Aug. 8, 1919, CC, WRHS.

64. Chesnutt never quit writing "race problem stories." Chesnutt to Walter H. Page, June 29, 1904, CC, Fisk; Chesnutt to Ferris Greenslet, Oct. 15, 1930. CC, WRHS.

65. Chesnutt, *The Colonel's Dream;* quotation from "Dedication."

66. Page believed that "Clarendon" and "Patesville" were both Fayetteville. Page to Chesnutt, June 24, 1904. CC, Fisk.

Fetters; now Fetters was founding a fortune upon the convict-lease arrangements that replaced the prewar plantation system.

The dream that took shape was that the Colonel would rehabilitate the old town, that he would rescue its white people and its black people from peonage. He began to plan a model operation, which would supply good wages and living improvements for both races. The Colonel sought reforms; through this device, Chesnutt revealed the role of churches in controlling people, and the backward schools of both races. He explored the courts and the financial structures. He exposed the degrading wage-slavery of a cotton mill where white women and children sat at spinning spools long hours for starvation pay.

The Colonel's activities led to a damning exposure of the convict-lease system. Finding his former slave, old Peter, accused of vagrancy, French learned the machinations of lawmakers and of courts. He discovered a conspiracy to shackle the indigent for the benefit of the state and the enrichment of men like Fetters. On a trip into the country to deal with Fetters, French passed a gang of convict laborers:

Upon the ankles of some was riveted an iron band to which was soldered a chain, at the end of which in turn an iron ball was fastened. Accompanying them was a white man, in whose belt was stuck a revolver, and who carried in one hand a stout leather strap, about two inches in width with a handle by which to grasp it. The gang paused momentarily to look at the traveller, but at a meaning glance from the overseer fell again to their work of hoeing cotton.

Failing to find Fetters at the plantation house, French passed the same gang on the return trip. This time

The Colonel saw four Negroes, in response to an imperative gesture from the overseer, seize one of their number, a short, thickset fellow, overpower some small resistance which he seemed to make, throw him down with his face to the ground, and sit upon his extremities while the overseer applied the broad leathern thong vigorously to his bare back.[67]

Despite such scenes, when white people discovered that French meant to include the Negroes in new opportunities, his plans were doomed. So successfully had caste conditions of life enslaved the residents that French had to realize his dream was vain. In a tragic conclusion he left forever.

---

67. Chesnutt, *The Colonel's Dream*, pp. 217, 18.

Into this social study Chesnutt wove a tapestry of characterizations and subplots. One tale of interlocked destinies of a mulatto slave woman, Viney, and her former master Malcolm Dudley is moving. Viney symbolizes the black race, Malcolm the white race. The decaying mansion where they are trapped is the South, and their pitiable inability to communicate is the harbinger of their destruction.[68] Yet it appears that though Chesnutt never altogether consciously decided, he was becoming more dedicated to setting forth realities than to eliciting the reader's response on behalf of the oppressed. *The Colonel's Dream* reflects a rising desperation. Though Chesnutt was unable to resolve the tension, he made further efforts. He prepared another novel manuscript titled *Paul Marchand, F.M.C.* (Free Man of Color). Four years before his death he submitted a 277-page manuscript titled *The Quarry*.[69]

Southern reviewers deplored Chesnutt's "bitter passionate arraignment of the white people of the South in their treatment of the Negro," or found that the book "told stories of the practice of peonage and prevalent cruelty and injustice to negroes not only false, but impossible."[70] Though early historians ignored or explained away those conditions, subsequent scholarship has confirmed Chesnutt's observations. Jesse F. Steiner and Roy M. Brown studied *The North Carolina Chain Gang;*[71] Vernon L. Wharton detailed the practices Chesnutt described in *The Negro in Mississippi;*[72] Fletcher M. Green provided an essay on the convict lease system;[73] and C. Vann Woodward remarked that "The degradation and brutality produced by this system would be incredible but for the amount of evidence from official sources."

One of the mightiest strongholds of privilege and social evil besieged by the welfare reformers was the convict lease system, still in existence in one form or another in all the Southern states in 1900.[74]

---

68. Ibid. pp. 170-78.

69. See n. 63.

70. Scrapbooks of newspaper reviews. CC, Fisk.

71. Jesse F. Steiner and Roy M. Brown, *The North Carolina Chain Gang* (Chapel Hill: University of North Carolina Press, 1949), p. 41.

72. Vernon L. Wharton, *The Negro in Mississippi, 1865-1890* (Chapel Hill, 1967).

73. Fletcher M. Green, ed., *Essays in Southern History Presented to Joseph Gregoire de Roulhac Hamilton* (Chapel Hill: University of North Carolina Press, 1949), p. 122.

74. Woodward, *Origins of the New South,* p. 212; See *The Twentieth Annual Report of the Commissioner of Labor, 1905, Convict Labor* (Washington, D.C.: Government Printing Office, 1905).

The Colonel's discoveries can be as thoroughly documented as Rena's situation and the Wilmington riot. Yet with three honestly founded novels, Chesnutt failed to move the hearts of Americans, as he failed to persuade them by evidence of damage to their society that they needed to alleviate racial injustice. Instead, Americans stifled his voice, chorusing support for disfranchisement, peonage, and the supremacy of those born white.

Chesnutt and the Literary Art

Chesnutt plainly said that he wanted to reveal to the public the racial cruelties that were common in American life by writing a novel that would win concern for the plight of Negro Americans and that would incline the hearts of many readers toward fair treatment. He wanted to pour out one story that would grip the nation. He believed that the question of racial justice was so central to American life that it would decide the survival of the Republic. In his youth he had selected two literary models, *Uncle Tom's Cabin* and *A Fool's Errand*. Both took the adversities of the Negro as central concerns, the one during slavery, the other during Reconstruction. Though Stowe's book gained a broader acceptance than Tourgee's, both reached a wide audience.

By 1900 Chesnutt had developed literary skills probably beyond those of Stowe or Tourgee, but his novels never sold well. He published three between 1900 and 1905, at the apex of racial hostilities. He wrote six additional still-unpublished novels before, during, and after that period.[75] But he failed to bring off what he wanted to do. In none of the nine novels did he marshal the literary skills to achieve the desired results. When it came to novels Chesnutt was unsuccessful in discerning which techniques to use and which to abandon in order to set an appeal to public sympathies in motion. Chesnutt was an accomplished author. Yet in novel writing he displayed less involvement with literary craftsmanship and more concern with social action than he had shown in his earlier imaginative writings.

With the possible exception of *The House Behind the Cedars,* Chesnutt's novels turned out to be different kinds of products than anything else to which he had turned his hand. This is why a confusion arose in early attempts to understand them; it cannot be done by applying formal literary criticism.

The confusion persists. One of the first to realize what Chesnutt had done was Sterling Brown, a Professor of English at Howard University.

---

75. See footnote 63.

197

Five years after Chesnutt's death, Brown wrote that "There is no gain-saying his knowledge of the southern scene, or of the Negro upper class in northern cities":

Unlike Dunbar [Chesnutt] is opposed to the plantation tradition, sharply critical of southern injustice, and aware of the sinister forces at work in Reconstruction. . . . He shows exploitation, riots and lynching mobs, as well as the more refined exercising of prejudice.[76]

To this extent, and in a departure from his usual critical approach, Brown refrained from writing of the novels as literary works.

So did the critic Hugh M. Gloster. Ten years after Chesnutt's death he summarized seven "themes" that Chesnutt treated in *The Marrow of Tradition:*

1. Intra-family strife, sometimes caused by miscegenation
2. The affection of the white gentleman for the black servant
3. The clash between Northern and Southern opinion relative to social contacts with the Negro
4. The advantages of jim crowism
5. The handicaps of the colored professional man in a prejudice-ridden environment
6. The destructive course of mob passion
7. The consequences of Negro efforts to acquire full civil rights.[77]

Thus Gloster saw Chesnutt's novels more nearly as social history than as works of fiction that could be understood through the study of the literary techniques employed.

In another ten years, Chauncey B. Ives discussed the "Development in the Fictional Themes of Negro Authors." He discovered six major "themes"; all can be found in Chesnutt's works:

1. Color desires of Negroes within their separate society
2. The adventure of passing for white
3. The betrayals and excitement of miscegenation
4. Violence as a primary weapon of the enemy
5. Law as a corrupted tool of injustice
6. American ideals of freedom and equality.

---

76. Sterling Brown, *The Negro in American Fiction* (Washington, D.C.: Associates in Negro Folk Education, 1937), p. 82.

77. Hugh M. Gloster, "Charles W. Chesnutt, Pioneer in the Fiction of Negro Life," *Phylon*, 2 (1941), 63-64.

But there was small concern for the literary techniques Chesnutt used to convey these themes, nor for the specific works in which they could be found.[78]

Five years later in 1962 the literary ctitic Sylvia Lyons Render wrote a dissertation titled "Charles Waddell Chesnutt, Eagle with Clipped Wings, A Study of Form and Feeling in the Fiction of Charles Waddell Chesnutt."[79] To be sure, Render noted that Chesnutt "touches upon every major aspect of Southern society as it related to North Carolina in the latter half of the nineteenth century." And she also observed that the "incorporation of famous landmarks, outstanding personages, memorable events, principal arteries of travel and geographic conditions indigenous to the region is a technique which Chesnutt used masterfully to give his settings the very essence of reality." But Render was writing primarily about the anecdotes, tales and short stories; in this study she began to apply to them the standards of literary criticism. Later she edited a collection, *The Short Fiction of Charles W. Chesnutt;* in an "Introduction" she confined herself almost exclusively to commenting upon Chesnutt's short imaginative works, and here she successfully used the criteria of literary criticism to discover the superb artist and original contributor that Chesnutt was.[80]

Of the earlier literary critics, only Hamilton Wright Mabie had also been able to apply literary criticism successfully to Chesnutt's work. Mabie wrote in February 1900 before the publication of any of Chesnutt's novels. He said in the *Outlook* that the first two Chesnutt volumes (*The Conjure Woman* and *The Wife of His Youth,* both collections of short stories) "constitute not only an important addition to our literature, but to our knowledge of the Negro race." It is in such work, wrote Mabie, that

The advancing movement of the American literary spirit is to be discerned. For this work has its roots in reality; its chief concern is the portrayal of life; it deals at first hand with original materials; it gives us new

78. Chauncey B. Ives, "The Development in the Fictional Themes of Negro Authors" (unpublished Ph.D. dissertation, University of North Carolina, 1957), pp. 3, 6.

79. Sylvia Lyons Render, "Charles Waddell Chesnutt, Eagle with Clipped Wings, A Study of Form and Feeling in the Fiction of Charles Waddell Chesnutt" (unpublished Ph.D. dissertation, George Peabody College, Nashville, Tennessee, 1962), p. 56.

80. Sylvia Lyons Render, *The Short Fiction of Charles W. Chesnutt* (Washington, D.C.: Howard University Press, 1974), pp. 11-56.

aspects of American life; it is the expression of what is going on in the spirit of man on this continent.[81]

But the literary critic Robert Bone perpetuated the confusions because he attempted to apply literary criticism to Chesnutt's novels. Bone did remark in passing that the short stories "raised the standards of Negro fiction to a new and higher plane." But he passed quickly over that discovery to say that Chesnutt "pioneered in his 'problem' novels," which were "incredibly overwritten." He found that the novels presented a fiction that is "merely a scaffolding through which Chesnutt can present his views on contemporary race relations." He commented that *The Marrow of Tradition* was "heavily overplotted," and that "an element of melodrama pervades the whole novel." Bone did note that the novels are of "considerable historical if not literary importance," and he did remark that "An appraisal of Chesnutt's novels is hardly a fair measure of his talent."[82] But he failed to give proper weight to the separate importance of Chesnutt's many works of short fiction.

More insightfully, John M. Reilly suggested that *The Marrow of Tradition* is Chesnutt's attempt to work out the historical-social dilemma of racial caste, as well as his own psychological problems in writing novels about it. Reilly refers to "a complex of subtly graded inclinations and conceptions which are continuously modifying and canceling each other."[83]

From the point of view of literary historians and literary technicians, Chesnutt never solved those difficulties in the writing of full-length novels. What the novels are to the social historian is another matter. But Chesnutt did successfully master the problems of literary craftsmanship in his anecdotes, tales, groups of related tales, and short stories. In all he wrote some eighty of them. They constitute a significant literary achievement. Had Chesnutt written no novels, no essays, no articles, no speeches, the short fiction alone insures him a place in American letters. It grew from an inheritance of European, American and African backgrounds operating upon the particular racial complexities of Chesnutt's situation in Fayetteville, North Carolina, and in Cleveland, Ohio. There was only the expectable Southern disagreement about the worth and

---

81. Mabie, "Two New Novelists," *Outlook,* Feb. 24, 1900. See also Hamilton Wright Mabie to Chesnutt, May 8, 1900. CC, Fisk.

82. Robert Bone, *The Negro Novel in America* (New Haven: Yale University Press, 1966), p. 38.

83. John M. Reilly, "The Dilemma in Chesnutt's *The Marrow of Tradition,*" Phylon, 32 (Spring, 1971), 37.

the drama of these short stories in Chesnutt's lifetime, and there is little or no disagreement now. The confusion in evaluating Chesnutt's literary efforts has arisen because critics either ignored the imaginative short works or attempted to judge the novels as if they were of a piece with the rest of Chesnutt's fiction. But from a literary point of view the novels, as much as the essays, were a departure; they verged toward social history, hanging sometimes somewhat awkwardly between disciplines.

In writing novels, Chesnutt shared a dilemma common among writers of his time. Many who attempted the longer forms were travelers on the roads between romanticism and realism. Many encountered as well the hazards that beset trans-disciplinary adventurers; they produced works of varying literary viability. Some were soon forgotten. Some still hover as harbingers over several disciplines. The muckraker Lincoln Steffans, for example, wrote an *Autobiography* that is almost a novel. Henry Adams wrote an immensely ironic book about his *Education* that is part biography, part essay, part fiction, a polyglot compendium.

These developments are understandable because this was the period when the United States was emerging from a divided adolescence to a continental togetherness. The eighties and nineties were uncomfortable for writers. They could no longer conceive a mercantile North and an agrarian South, each with a limitless West. This meant trial, withdrawal, groping, testing, experimenting, discarding. It meant transition.[84]

Some discovered formulas. They hoped to bring New England religion and Southern paternalism into adjustment with the wider American scene. Perhaps to ease anxieties, sometimes in the hope that the writers had discovered how to preserve illusions while guiding society to a safe course, people bought their books.

Some successes came out of the West. Vulgar, bumptious, earthy, power-hungry, hostile, violent—these were the qualities of characters peopling the pages of Bret Harte and Jack London and Frank Norris and Joaquin Miller and Mark Twain. These authors fascinated readers with a concept of a noble humanity underlying whatever rough exterior. The writers reconciled the old idealism with the Western adventure; some of their novels carried the appeal of a sea breeze on a summer day. But in the end, readers found the new brutality disturbing; the Western books lacked attributes a literature ought to possess.[85] The

---

84. Vernon L. Parrington, *The Beginnings of Critical Realism in America 1860-1920*, Vol. 3 of *Main Currents in American Thought* (New York and Burlingame: Harcourt, Brace & World, Inc., 1930), Ch. 4.

85. Robert E. Spiller *et al.*, eds., *Literary History of the United States* (London: Macmillan Co., 1963), pp. 789-952, deals with roads to realism. See pp. 792-94. Chesnutt's work is slightly considered, pp. 854-55; unfortunately the discussion contains inaccuracies.

great interpreter of America—and some of the others—moved to the East; Mark Twain established residence and wrote in Connecticut.[86]

But other writers consistently delivered a Southern theme. Thomas Nelson Page and Harry Stillwell Edwards and Joel Chandler Harris and Reverend Thomas Dixon all published when Chesnutt was writing. They expanded the "New South" sentiments of the journalists Richard Hathaway Edmonds and Henry Grady, the promoters Daniel Tompkins and Atticus Haygood, and even the politicians Benjamin Tillman of South Carolina and Tom Watson of Georgia. With varying emphasis, they accepted an indissoluble union; they lauded industrial advance; but they glamorized the old relations of the races, whether under slavery or the creeping white supremacy of the eighties and nineties. Their message was that the Negro would best remain what he had been—the serf of the nation. Each of these writers romanticized the plantation tradition, attempting to bring the social system inherited from it into congruence with industrial development. These writers ventured few new techniques nor would they explore a new philosophy of the literary art. Their books sold well.

But they had achieved a precarious adjustment. Science and business were jolting the United States toward preeminence. As their enterprises spun off technologies more portentous for people than any technology in memory, no tenuous literary balance would hold. It became urgent for writers to find a new rationale.

Part of the development would lie in choice of subject, as the Western writers—and Chesnutt—had understood; but more of it would arise from discovery of appropriate attitudes. The Southern writers failed to grasp that need. Or perhaps their intention of leading readers toward ideologies of the past was too far out of line with rising conflicts. Unsettled, many transition writers migrated East while Easterners traveled to Europe for vision and perspective. The "new" American Realism was being born. It would owe much to a European inheritance that came filtering through galaxies of works by John William De Forest, William Dean Howells, and Henry James.[87]

Charles Chesnutt belongs among those writers who were moving through these treacherous narrows from the genteel and the romantic toward the new realism. Chesnutt's special concern, his special contribution, was the literary blending of African and American strains as they

---

86. Parrington, *The Beginnings of Critical Realism*, pp. 91-101.

87. Spiller et al., eds., *Literary History of the United States;* on Howells, see especially pp. 878-98.

flowed through this nation, South and North. In this, as in confrontations with racial problems in other areas, Chesnutt was ahead of his time. From his vantage ground as a Negro-American who appeared white, he derived insight impossible to most fiction writers, as well as a lonely, distinguished foresight that nearly doomed his output among the people for whom he undertook it. His most effective expressions came out as ironic realism; he interpreted American race relations as the color-blind would see them, and, at the same time, as those suffering from racial injustice would understand them. His best short fiction reaches a unique verisimilitude. It stops before it gets to the didactic hammering home of themes that critics deplored in the novels. From the tentative efforts in the journals of his youth through the sometimes too contrived and too coincidental explorations of his early Cleveland stories Chesnutt rose to the superb and sophisticated artistry of the *Conjure Woman* collection and the stories of *The Wife of His Youth*.

But Chesnutt was trapped between the new literary realism as he applied it to racial subjects and the negative response of the society that must receive it. He wrote as the South rushed toward legal white supremacy and as the United States extended its dominion around the world.

Through his use of dialect, and sometimes through his rejection of it, through bestowing the whole range of human reactions upon his black characters in slavery and in freedom, through plot developments, through the sensitive rendering of settings, Chesnutt offers a new version of American Negro experience. Sharp criticisms of Southern injustice are implicit, as is Chesnutt's opposition to everything smacking of the plantation tradition in literature and in life. He exposes lynching, exploitation, political sabotage and murder, as well as the subtle, persistent personal cruelties that erupted over the color line, North and South.

In Chesnutt's work there is a progression of philosophies. Chesnutt never changed his point of view—that racial proscription is immoral—nor his goal of demolishing racial prejudice. But he did alter his approach. He first thought he could affect the spirit of racial prejudice through "imaginative" writings, which would reveal truths based on situations he knew.[88] Black people of his time scarcely knew and little appreciated his stories, perhaps because they themselves were as much victims of white literary traditions as of white cultural practices. That black people did know the contemporary black writer Paul Lawrence Dunbar, who wrote fiction countenancing the ideals of the past, bears out this possibility.

---

88. Chesnutt, Journal 2, May 8, 1880, pp. 196-98. CC, Fisk.

There were some white people and important white critics who understood the subtle artistry of Chesnutt's short fiction. But as Chesnutt felt ever more pressingly the extent to which race proscription was conquering American society, he abandoned the literary posture of ironic realism. He undertook longer fiction and a great deal of non-fiction, revealing increasingly the forthright social observer exposing and interpreting attitudes.[89] The depth of his insights and the accuracy of his observations made his work as welcome as a finding of guilt at an international bar. The social conditions of American life rendered the further development of Chesnutt's strength in fiction writing impossible and perhaps even undesirable; the literary posture of ironic realism, to however fine an edge it could come, proved not to be the answer to Chesnutt's search for means of confronting American racial wrongs. Yet on the way to the best he could give in this service, Chesnutt left an impressive legacy in his short fiction; by it he has earned recognition as a first-rate literary artist.

---

89. Chesnutt to Professor Richardson, Feb. 21, 1906. CC, Fisk. This letter shows the change in Chesnutt's thought.

AN AMERICAN CRUSADE

7

CHESNUTT CONFRONTS
NATIONAL ISSUES
1905-15

The Politics of Race:
Chesnutt Searches His Role

Late in Chesnutt's life a committee of eminent Americans recognized his "pioneer services as a literary artist" and his "distinguished career as a public spirited citizen."[1] The members realized that Chesnutt had developed both careers. He had spent the twenty-two years from 1883 to the publication of *The Colonel's Dream* in 1905 making a name as a writer; he spent the next twenty-odd years in public service increasingly national in scope. In some respects the careers overlapped; in some they merged. He began the second career of public service by writing articles when he was writing stories and novels in the 1890s; from 1905 to the end of his life, a period when he turned toward activities furthering racial equality in Cleveland and in the nation, he was still writing stories and novels. Perhaps this came about because Chesnutt never resolved the conflict that developed in his novel writing; probably he saw both careers as means to the same end.

While he was writing *The Marrow of Tradition*, Chesnutt increased the commitments on his calendar. He was forty-two. His older daughters expected to graduate from Smith College in June.[2] For financial reasons he picked up the threads of his shorthand business.

This was easy. Cleveland displayed signs of profitable enterprise. New companies were incorporating: the Ferro Machine and Foundry Company began to operate. Vinson and Korner started a book business. The Hunkin-Conkey Construction Company incorporated. Members of the

---

1. James Weldon Johnson to Chesnutt, telegram, June 8, 1928. CC, Fisk.

2. Archives of Smith College, Northampton, Massachusetts.

207

National Electric Lamp Association combined operations. Six automobile factories prepared to open. The Cleveland Automobile Club estimated in 1905 that 150 automobiles were in use, although an editor protested that "For all except people with generous incomes the cost of a horseless carriage is really prohibitive." He added that "As long as an auto costs as much as a team of horses with the carriage attached, it cannot be expected that the craze will grow with any marked degree of rapidity."

Old concerns were extending operations. United States Steel acquired Standard Oil's ore and transportation facilities. Fifteen iron and steel producers reported increased valuations, as did 77 women's clothing firms, 10 malt liquor firms, 10 meat-packing firms, and countless other enterprises. In one year the city issued more than 2,500 building permits.[3]

Cleveland produced politicians to fascinate cartoonists: There were Tom L. Johnson, of the bird-bright glance and the imperious manner, a genial entrepreneur turned people's man, who rode to the Mayor's office on the slogan "A three-cent street-car fare!";[4] Newton D. Baker, the city solicitor, a slight, smooth-countenanced lawyer, preoccupied and scholarly bent, who delivered speeches on unfortunate jail conditions;[5] Mark A. Hanna, a heavy-handed, money-raising Senator, the politician who convinced voters that business prosperity quarantees general welfare;[6] John D. Rockefeller, the absentee steel-eyed Baptist, who dealt out destinies. Chesnutt did reporting for concerns with which these men were associated; his firm did stenographic assignments.[7]

Chesnutt described one such experience. During a bitter traction affray, Tom Johnson's opponents employed Chesnutt to follow Johnson from one tent meeting to another, reporting what he said. Johnson tried to hire Chesnutt away from the other street car company. Chesnutt an-

---

3. Rose, *Cleveland*, pp. 622, 617.

4. Lorenz, *Tom L. Johnson*, pp. 83, 85, 125; Hendrick, *The Training of an American*, p. 209.

5. Rose, *Cleveland*, p. 621.

6. Lorenz, *Tom L. Johnson*, p. 86.

7. Interview given Ellen Holland Keller, Instructor in English Literature, Western Reserve University, by Peter Keisogloff, proprietor of the Keisogloff Bookstore, June 8, 1971. Newton D. Baker and Chesnutt had browsed there; Chesnutt to Walter White, Feb. 10, 1932, CC, WRHS; Interview given the writer by Russell Davis, September 30, 1971. Davis referred to a list of firms with which Chesnutt did business. The writer was unable to locate this list.

swered that he would split his services; but, he recalled, "That proposition didn't suit Tom. He wanted my exclusive services or nothing."[8]

A presidential election year came around. Twenty thousand persons took part in the McKinley-Roosevelt parade as it surged over Euclid Avenue on the third of November. Those who possessed the fortitude could listen to thirty-eight bands. An elephant lumbered along. Some carried canes decorated with red, white, and blue streamers. Others shouldered symbols of Hanna's wisdom—"full dinner pails." Still others sported more prophetic symbols, the broad-brimmed "rough-rider" sombreros of San Juan Hill.[9]

Chesnutt took an interest in the political life of the city and the nation. Less than a year later, President William McKinley lay dead; Chesnutt delivered a speech at memorial services in the Central Armory.[10]

But Chesnutt's deepest concern was the welfare of black people. Since Chesnutt had come to Cleveland in the 1880s, the South had experienced a reversion to violence. Occasionally there was a dissenting voice, like that of Samuel W. Boardman, President Emeritus of Maryville College in Tennessee. Boardman told Chesnutt that his college refused Negro students in 1904 though it had been endowed on the condition, "over and over pledged, in the strongest possible language by Synod, Directors and Faculty, that *all* citizens should have equal rights." Boardman deplored conditions when all this "had not a feather's weight with the Gov. & Legislature of Tenn."[11]

Nor had white men like Boardman more influence throughout the South. Politicians had engineered the legalization of white supremacy. Chesnutt's extra-literary activities increasingly demonstrated that he would never ignore nor condone any part of it.[12] Even during preparation of *The Marrow of Tradition,* he sought political involvement in this sector of the national life.

Chesnutt was aware that some black leaders disagreed with his remedies.[13] He used a review of Booker T. Washington's book *The Future*

8. *Cleveland Plain Dealer,* March 17, 1927. The paper sent a reporter to interview Chesnutt, who related this incident. Chesnutt did verbatim reports of series of lectures; See Thomas Wentworth Higginson, *American Orators and Oratory* (Imperial Press, 1901). "Reported by Charles W. Chesnutt."

9. Rose, *Cleveland,* p. 615.

10. The Cleveland Gazette, Sept. 16, 1901 and Nov. 16, 1901; Chesnutt to Ryadon Ritchie, Nov. 5, 1901. CC, Fisk.

11. Samuel W. Boardman to Chesnutt, April 14, 1904. CC, Fisk.

12. William H. H. Hart to Chesnutt, March 29, 1901. CC, Fisk.

13. Four Chesnutt articles appeared: *Boston Transcript,* February, 1900, "On the Future

of the American Negro to confront Washington's notions. "The author has practically nothing to say about caste prejudice, the admixture of the races or the remote future of the Negro," he wrote. Yet "the student of history and current events can scarcely escape the impression that it is the firm and unwavering determination of Southern whites to keep the Negro in a permanent position of vassalage and subordination." Perhaps Washington could convince the South it was under a "sacred trust" to be just to the Negro, but the facts were that "the lines of caste in the South are being drawn tighter and tighter." The whole nation is "directly responsible." Chesnutt stated that so long as we have laws determining rights by standards of race, that long the race question will vex our republic.[14]

One day Chesnutt read in the *Boston Transcript* an unsigned favorable review of another book, *The American Negro*. The author, William Hannibal Thomas, was pastor of a colored church in Everett, Massachusetts. It was rumored that he lost an arm during his Civil War service, that he had been a member of General Garfield's staff, that after the war he had been elected to the North Carolina Legislature, where he served on important committees.[15] It was said he had written his book "in trying to uplift the colored race."[16] But the book contained such abusive attacks upon Negroes that some believed a white man had written them.[17]

Chesnutt asked J. E. Chamberlin of the *Transcript* who could have given that book a favorable notice. To his surprise, Chamberlin had written the review. Chamberlin answered: "I was bound to assume that the house of Macmillan would not publish a book which was not genuine, or allow a preface to be put forth which contained a false statement of the author's life."[18] He thought the book went much further in condemning Negroes than Southern whites go; therefore it should bring Southern whites to the Negro's support: "if Thomas is a fraud he

of His People". *Saturday Evening Post*, April, 1901, "A Defamer of His Race"; *Critic*, March, 1901, "A Visit to Tuskegee," *Southern Workman*, April, 1902, "Free People of North Carolina."

14. Chesnutt, "A Plea for the American Negro," *Critic*, February, 1900, pp. 160-63.

15. *The Boston Globe*, July, 1901.

16. J. E. Chamberlin to Chesnutt, Feb. 1, 1901. CC, Fisk. Evidently the preface to the unavailable Thomas book said this.

17. *The Boston Globe*, July, 1901, upheld Thomas's pretensions, reporting a suit brought by Thomas against another critic, Rev. S. T. Tice.

18. J. E. Chamberlin to Chesnutt, Feb. 1, 1901. CC, Fisk.

should be fully exposed, and the house of Macmillan should be riddled for giving him the hearing." But he thought that if Thomas was what he claimed, he was entitled to the hearing.

Chesnutt thought that Thomas was a fraud, that the book would harm the Negro, and that Macmillan should withdraw the book. He compiled data on Thomas, obtaining court records. In a letter to Macmillan Chesnutt presented evidence that Thomas was "a man notoriously untruthful, without character or standing anywhere, and with a long record in the criminal courts and on the threshold of them."[19]

After this Chesnutt wrote an article exposing Thomas. The *Critic* published it in April 1901, though the editor, Jeannette L. Gilder, "trimmed it down a little, as the wicked Thomas might have us up for libel if we printed it just as it stands."[20]

Chesnutt's friends applauded. Professor Kelley Miller of the Howard University mathematics department expected to "read with much pleasure your flaying of the traitor Thomas,"[21] and Booker Washington thanked Chesnutt for sending a transcript of evidence "describing the character of the execrable William Hannibal Thomas."[22]

Macmillan answered defensively: No publisher should "inquire into the private or moral life of the author"; their readers were associated with famous institutions of higher learning.[23] But Booker Washington reported that "the Macmillans are not pushing it in any of their advertisements as I have taken pains to notice."[24] "I hope that we have spiked Mr. Thomas's guns," Chesnutt told J. E. Bruce when he thanked Bruce for a review in the *Colored American*. "Our own work is the best answer to his complaints, & the best antidote for his libellous statements."[25]

Eventually Chesnutt learned that Macmillan withdrew the book and sought to retrieve copies they had distributed.[26] This was one of several

19. Chesnutt to The Macmillan Company, April 20, 1901. CC, Fisk. Chesnutt to Robert C. Ogden, CC, Fisk.

20. Jeannette L. Gilder to Chesnutt, March 15, 1901. CC, Fisk. Chesnutt, "A Defamer of His Race," *Critic*, April, 1901, pp. 350-51.

21. Kelley Miller to Chesnutt, April 5, 1901. CC, Fisk.

22. Booker T. Washington To Chesnutt, May 3, 1901. CC, Fisk.

23. Macmillan Company to Chesnutt, May 10, 1901. CC, Fisk.

24. Booker T. Washington to Chesnutt, May 3, 1901. CC, Fisk.

25. Chesnutt to J. E. Bruce, May 6, 1901. John Bruce Manuscripts, Schomburg Collection, New York Public Library.

26. H. Chesnutt, *Pioneer*, p. 163. Booker T. Washington to Robert Ogden, May 24, 1904. CC, Fisk.

successful attempts to prevent libel; Chesnutt made it while working on *The Marrow of Tradition.*[27]

Chesnutt made efforts to place his own books in the hands of Congressional leaders who could be encouraged to work or vote for Negro causes. He had reason to think that Cleveland Representative Theodore E. Burton might be sympathetic.[28] The Congressman did suggest names of Representatives and others interested in terminating Negro disfranchisement.[29] But, he added, "The tendency is rather against doing anything," for "it is thought that any measure which the House might pass would go to the Senate and there be delayed indefinitely and finally defeated." Nevertheless, Chesnutt sent copies to several gentlemen. To Burton he wrote, "I do not imagine that legislation will materially affect the situation one way or the other, but it would at least have the effect of putting the South in the wrong." Chesnutt foresaw that the South would for some time disfranchise Negroes; but "the transaction should be branded theft," and the Southern states "should take their plunder subject to the same terms as those upon which other thieves enjoy their ill-gotten gains."[30]

William H. Moody, Roosevelt's Secretary of the Navy, responded to his copy of Chesnutt's book:

It has seemed to me that the problem of the races is the most serious domestic question which we have with us. It is evident that in some parts of the country there is a determination that the colored race shall be in a permanently subordinate condition. Leaving out all moral questions it has seemed to me that such a relation can no more permanently endure under our system than slavery. . . [31]

Representative Edgar D. Crumpacker wrote that "Whatever legislation there may be, the colored man must in a large measure work out his

---

27. Chesnutt's efforts paid off. Robert C. Ogden to Booker T. Washington, May 21, 1904; Ogden had seen a Thomas Nelson Page article "very unfavorable to the interests of our Negro population upon alleged facts drawn from that book." Ogden wished to furnish Carl Schurz with information on Thomas. In Washington To Ogden, May 24, 1904, CC, Fisk, Washington referred Ogden's letter to Chesnutt.

28. T. E. Burton to John P. Green, Sept. 3, 1898. John P. Green Papers, WRHS, Container 5, Folder 2.

29. T. E. Burton to Chesnutt, Feb. 19, 1902. CC, Fisk.

30. Chesnutt to T. E. Burton, March 26, 1902. CC, WRHS, Container 3, Series 1.

31. W. H. Moody to Chesnutt, March 29, 1902. CC, Fisk.

own destiny."[32] He wrote again, as did Charles E. Littlefield.[33] Both had also read Thomas Dixon's novel, a paean of hatred called *The Leopard's Spots;* both wrote politely but inconclusively.[34]

Chesnutt wanted President Roosevelt to read his book; he sent a copy and a thoughtful, brief letter to the President.[35] He also asked Booker Washington to suggest that the President read the book: "He has shown himself very friendly, so far to our people, and I should like to help brace him up in this particular."[36]

There was no acknowledgment from the President, but Chesnutt heard from influential persons. Cyrus Field Adams, Registrar of the United States Treasury, thought Chesnutt had written "a book which will live."[37] Charles W. Anderson, black supervisor of Racing Accounts of New York State, expressed admiration. Though he knew Negroes like the character Dr. Miller, Anderson confessed admiration for "that fellow who dies, rifle in hand, before the burning hospital. He is certainly one of the many types of which we are in need, as a race."[38] Louis F. Post, editor of the Chicago *Public,* thought the story superior to any other Southern story in truthfulness.[39] Charles S. Deneen, state's attorney of Cook County, Illinois, found the story "intensely interesting." He had told a friend about the book. The friend was "one white man who seems almost separate and apart from all of his kind." This friend had read Chesnutt's books:

He [the friend] said he often desired to meet you and made me promise that if you ever came to this city [Chicago] I would see that you were his guest at dinner some day, so he could have a good talk with you. He is one of the leading lawyers of the bar in this city, by name Clarence Darrow.[40]

---

32. Edgar D. Crumpacker to Chesnutt, March 31, 1902. CC, Fisk. Crumpacker was the author of a Resolution for the investigation of Southern election laws.

33. Edgar D. Crumpacker to Chesnutt, May 5, 1902. CC, Fisk. C. E. Littlefield to Chestnutt [sic], April 22, 1902. CC, Fisk.

34. On Dixon see Sterling Brown, *The Negro in American Fiction,* pp. 93-94.

35. Chesnutt to President Theodore Roosevelt, Nov. 25, 1901. CC, Fisk.

36. Chesnutt to Booker T. Washington, Nov. 25, 1901. CC, Fisk. Booker T. Washington to Chesnutt, Dec. 5, 1901. CC, Fisk.

37. Cyrus Field Adams to Chesnutt, Dec. 2, 1902. CC, Fisk.

38. Charles W. Anderson to Chesnutt, Dec. 11, 1901. CC, Fisk.

39. Louis F. Post to Chesnutt, Jan. 21, 1902. CC, Fisk. See also Francis J. Garrison to Chesnutt, Feb. 15, 1902.

40. Charles F. Deneen to Chesnutt, Nov. 5, 1901. CC, Fisk.

Chesnutt worked with white men and black men "to stem the adverse tide." He took seriously the comment of his friend T. Thomas Fortune, Editor of the *New York Age*, who thought there would be solutions "if the race or the leaders of it could be got to understand each other and stand together." But Fortune had found no way:

I have demonstrated through twenty years of effort that that is out of the question. I see nothing but long years of up hill fighting in every direction for the race. But I shall fight it out to the end of my chapter, because it is the nature of me.[41]

Chesnutt believed that a united leadership would elicit change. He also believed that black leaders could "be got to understand each other and stand together." This could be accomplished with mutual respect and without perfect agreement. His relationship with Booker Washington testifies that he hoped differences could be thrashed out.

Chesnutt and Booker T. Washington Address the Issues and Each Other

Since the Cotton States and International Exposition in Atlanta on September 18, 1895, Washington's prestige had grown. Asked to describe his feelings, Washington recalled that he had been a slave, and that his early years had been spent in poverty. This would be the first time any Negro spoke from the same platform with white Southerners on a national occasion; while most of his audience would be white Southern people, there would be white Northern people, and men and women of his own race. Washington assessed attitudes. He intended that all should feel placated or exonerated or encouraged, and hopeful that a solution to racial perplexities was possible. From that moment Washington's influence grew. White people soon regarded him as the leading advocate of vocational education for Negroes. Many viewed him as spokesman of his people.[42]

Though Chesnutt realized he and Washington desired the true emancipation of the Negro, he disagreed with Washington. Chesnutt distrusted the idea that a conciliatory posture toward the South was in the interest of the Negro. He saw the deterioration of the Negro's position there as a threat to the liberties of every citizen. When he had reviewed Washington's book in 1900, Chesnutt made it clear that Washington im-

---

41. T. Thomas Fortune to Chesnutt, Oct. 7, 1902. CC, Fisk.

42. For recent definitive treatment of the complexities of the Washington posture, see Louis R. Harlan, *Booker T. Washington, The Making of a Black Leader, 1856-1901* (New York: Oxford University Press, 1972), pp. 204-28.

plied acceptance of Southern tyranny. Chesnutt thought it suicidal to approve the loss of the ballot.

Yet when he visited Washington at Tuskegee in the spring of 1901, Chesnutt realized the valuable work of the school. He wrote an article for the *Cleveland Leader*.[43] "Tuskegee was a revelation, as it must be to anyone upon the first visit," Chesnutt said. He described his pleasure in being entertained in Washington's "handsome house," in attending the conference, in visiting impressive projects. "One who comes and sees is conquered," Chesnutt wrote. "The work is done on a scale which impresses the imagination."

The present writer does not believe in the wisdom of the separation of the races which prevails in the Southern States, and thinks that it is carried to an extreme which is not only short-sighted, expensive and troublesome, but which to an outsider, borders upon the ridiculous.

Then he added: "But Mr. Washington, accepting the situation as inevitable, for the time being at least, had adopted the theory of letting the race develop along characteristic lines."[44] During this visit Chesnutt and Washington developed a friendly relationship. Though Chesnutt publicly and privately disagreed with Washington, he respected Washington's sincerity. Neither questioned the other's objectives; each disagreed with the other's judgment.

With W. E. B. DuBois both men contributed in 1903 to a collection of essays presenting views of black writers on how to meet their needs.[45] Booker Washington called his essay "Industrial Education for the Negro." DuBois used a phrase that became famous, for it captured his belief that the Negro is "throwing money [and manhood] to the winds" by accepting industrial training instead of demanding higher education; DuBois' title was "The Talented Tenth."

Chesnutt's article is a powerful address on the fundamental contracts of the American state. Negroes had no need to present reasons for their natural rights; the Constitution foreclosed the question. The emphasis is apparent in his title, "The Disfranchisement of the Negro." He showed respect for Washington and for DuBois, but found both wanting. Neither had discovered the antidote for the poison of racial intransigence. Washington favored a restricted suffrage—which meant the loss of representation; and Washington advised Negroes to go slow in

---

43. *Cleveland Leader*, March 31, 1901.

44. Chesnutt, "A Visit to Tuskegee," MS. CC, Fisk, pp. 2, 4.

45. Washington *et al., The Negro Problem*.

215

seeking to enforce civil and political rights—which meant submission to usurpation.

Chesnutt spoke as plainly about the demands of DuBois:

The need of education of all kinds for both races is wofully [sic] apparent. But men and nations have been free without being learned and there have been educated slaves. Liberty has been known to languish where culture had reached a very high development. Nations do not first become rich and learned and then free, but the lesson of history has been that they first become free and then rich and learned. The process of education has been going on rapidly since the Civil War, and yet if we take superficial indications, the rights of the Negroes are at a lower ebb than at any time during the thirty-five years of their freedom, and the race prejudice more intense and uncompromising.

The leaders of the South had perceived the evils of slavery and its injury to whites and blacks and to the body politic at the time of the Revolution, yet they failed to abolish it. In 1776 their remedy was what it remained in 1903—"time, education, social and economic development." In some circles it had even become fashionable to question the Fifteenth Amendment. Chesnutt believed it "an act of the highest statesmanship, based upon the fundamental idea of this Republic, entirely justified by conditions."[46]

The article was published between *The Marrow of Tradition* and *The Colonel's Dream:* Chesnutt left no doubt that the Negro can solve his dilemmas only by insisting on equal treatment in every area.

Meanwhile Chesnutt's daughter Ethel graduated from Smith and accepted a job at Tuskegee. Eyestrain delayed Helen's completion of requirements, but she, too, thought of a position there.[47] Chesnutt and Washington found that their paths crossed, for Chesnutt traveled South, and Washington came to Cleveland.[48] For years they tried to thrash out disagreements. Washington showed himself as willing as Chesnutt to search common ground. "I do not mind in the least any man's differing from me in a high-toned, gentlemanly way as you always do; that kind of difference is one thing, low personal abuse is altogether another," he wrote in the spring of 1904.[49]

---

46. *Ibid.,* pp. 103, 110, 111.

47. Ethel Perry Chesnutt to Booker T. Washington, April 15, 1901, and Helen Chesnutt to Booker T. Washington, Jan. 13, 1901. Both in Booker T. Washington Papers, Library of Congress.

48. Booker T. Washington to Chesnutt, June 19, 1902, CC, Fisk.

49. Booker T. Washington to Chesnutt, May 31, 1904. CC, Fisk.

By then Washington had experienced "low, personal abuse." A month after Theodore Roosevelt's inauguration, he invited Washington to dine at the White House. Outraged white Southerners "fumed with dire imprecations."[50] Shortly after this, Washington wrote to Chesnutt:

Well, I suppose you have seen something of the storm that has been blowing down this way. I am not at all disturbed about it and in the end I believe that our race will be helped rather than hindered. Of course there are three or four political campaigns on just now and the incident is being exaggerated in its importance very largely on that account. The only thing that I am going to do is to keep still and saw wood.[51]

Chesnutt replied that he had seen something of the storm blowing down that way: "like you I think that everything of the sort will tend in the end toward the result which we seek." He added a distinguishing consideration:

I think, however, that the feeling manifested by Southern expressions concerning the little incident is very deep-seated. Underneath it all lies the fear of what they consider corruption of blood. But whatever they may call it, I think it would be vastly preferable to the sort of thing toward which they are tending under the present condition of things.[52]

Chesnutt was right that feelings about the incident were deep-seated. Francis J. Garrison of Houghton Mifflin wrote Chesnutt that "the outburst of the South over Booker Washington's dining at the White House shows how barbarous the whites of that section still are."[53] Washington's hope that objections would subside if he kept still and sawed wood till after elections proved unwarranted. When nearly two years had passed, Washington wrote Chesnutt again about the dinner. He said that he had accepted the invitation with his eyes open. For the first time he revealed that he had experienced a deeper concern at the time:

The invitation was in my hands for a day and during that period I had ample time to discuss the whole matter in all of its bearings with friends and to count the cost. Notwithstanding that I felt that in accepting this invitation I was not doing so as a personal matter but it was a recogni-

---

50. Quoted in Franklin, *From Slavery to Freedom*, p. 427.

51. Booker T. Washington to Chesnutt, Oct. 28, 1901. CC, Fisk.

52. Chesnutt to Booker T. Washington, Nov. 5, 1901. CC, Fisk.

53. Francis J. Garrison to Charles W. Chesnutt, Nov. 9, 1901. CC, Fisk. Garrison was the son of William Lloyd Garrison.

*tion of the race and no matter what personal condemnation it brought
upon my shoulders I had no right to refuse or even hesitate. I did my
duty in the face of the opposition of the entire Southern press and at
the risk of losing my life.*[54]

Chesnutt and Washington often discussed the suffrage. They never
agreed. Throughout their correspondence and the public expression of
their differences, they extended courtesies to one another. Chesnutt
made arrangements for Washington in Cleveland. He supplied Washington with information; he contributed money for Tuskegee.[55] Washington
employed Chesnutt's daughter Ethel. Later he employed Chesnutt's son
Edwin for an interval between Edwin's graduation from Harvard in 1905
and his finishing dental studies in 1915. For a summer Chesnutt's
daughter Helen was Mrs. Washington's guest at Tuskegee.[56] Chesnutt
and Washington remained polite. They were frank with each other, however; here and there they managed some humor, but as the years went
by and the disagreements continued, they sometimes grew testy.

Both thought and felt deeply about matters before them. Washington
told Chesnutt that Negroes must demand their constitutional rights, but
"after all the Negro will have to depend upon the influence which he
can bring to bear in his own immediate community for his ultimate defense and final rights." He added that "It is very difficult for any law
making body to give an individual influence or power which he does not
intrinsically possess." He was saying that no amount of legislation can
enforce an idea unsupported by the public. Washington said Senator
Blanche Bruce of Mississippi was swept out of office "not because he
was not a conservative, wise, and safe statesman but because he did not
have back of him an intelligent, property-holding, tax-paying con-
stituency." When all is said and done, rights depend upon local public
sentiment and upon knowledge, wealth, and character. Washington told
Chesnutt he would hope to talk the matter out, though he "would not
hope to come any way near converting you to my way of thinking."[57]

Chesnutt appreciated what Washington said about education and

---

54. Booker T. Washington to Chesnutt, July 7, 1903. Booker T. Washington Papers, Library of Congress.

55. Chesnutt to Booker T. Washington, Nov. 10, 1905. CC, Fisk. On one occasion
Washington stayed at Chesnutt's home on Lamont Avenue. Chesnutt to Booker T. Washington, March 12, 1906. CC, Fisk.

56. Chesnutt to W. E. B. DuBois, Nov. 21, 1910, CC, Fisk. Chesnutt explains his connections with Washington.

57. Booker T. Washington to Chesnutt, May 16, 1903. CC, Fisk.

property, but they weren't everything: "There is no good reason why we should not acquire them and exercise our constitutional rights at the same time, and acquire them all the more readily because of our equality of rights." Chesnutt had no confidence in the friendship of whites if such friendship usurped the place of rights: "If the white South will continue to ignore the Constitution and violate the laws," he wrote, "it must be with no consent of mine and with no word that can be twisted into the approval or condonation of their unjust and unlawful course."[58]

Washington thanked Chesnutt for writing freely and frankly. He agreed with much of what Chesnutt said about conditions of Negroes in the South. But this was a result of weakness; he repeated that no one could give the Negro strength unless he possessed it. The Negro would not always remain the weaker race. "With the same training," he wrote, "the Negro will show as good results as other races." But a white man on a plantation could still in the 1900s control 500 black votes. "No law passed by Congress or any state can prevent it, especially when there is ignorance mixed in with their poverty." Here Washington expressed insight into conditions reflected in operations of political machines.

Washington raised another consideration: "In the North you have Jim Crow work. In the South we have Jim Crow cars. In most sections of the North as much of a sensation would be created by a Negro going into a shoe factory or a printing office as if he went into a railroad car set aside for white people in the South." To show Chesnutt he was not interested solely in property, Washington sent a pamphlet he had written on lynching.[59]

Chesnutt answered this "confidential and private" letter about a month later. Meanwhile there had been some unpleasantness between Washington and Monroe Trotter, editor of the *Boston Guardian*. Trotter disapproved all that Washington said; he made this clear when Washington visited Boston. Chesnutt disagreed with Washington, but he thought Trotter went too far when he disrupted a meeting; he said so to Washington—and to Trotter.[60] Then Chesnutt wrote to Washington:

I wish to say that I differ from you most decidedly on the matter of a restricted franchise. It is an issue gotten up solely to disfranchise the Negroes, and with no serious intention of ever applying it to anyone else.

58. Chesnutt to Booker T. Washington, June 27, 1903. CC, Fisk.

59. Booker T. Washington to Chesnutt, July 7, 1903. Booker T. Washington Papers, Library of Congress. This letter does not appear in the Chesnutt papers at Fisk.

60. W. M. Trotter to Chesnutt, Jan. 1, 1902. CC, Fisk. This is a handwritten, signed letter. Trotter wrote: "I hope, Mr. Chesnutt, you have noticed what Mr. Booker T. Washing-

Chesnutt said that Washington's talk about protection of the ballot by educational and property tests meant that he was willing to throw himself upon the mercies of whites. As to a "sacred trust," Chesnutt wrote, "I doubt whether sacred is quite the word for a trust which was acquired by highway robbery of another class!" "I think," he answered to Washington's remarks, "that by recognizing and dwelling on these distinctions [weakness and strength] and suggesting different kinds of education and different degrees of political power . . . we are merely intensifying the class spirit." Chesnutt also thought that "What the black race has or has not been able to do in Africa should no more enter into the discussion of the Negro's rights as a citizen than what the Irish have not done in Ireland should be the basis of their citizenship here." Chesnutt characterized white Southerners:

They seem to me, as a class, barring a few honorable exceptions, an ignorant, narrow and childish people. . . . I make no pretense of any special love for them. I was brought up among them; I have a large share of their blood in my veins: I wish them well, and first of all I wish that they may learn to do justice. My love I keep for my friends and my friends are those who treat me fairly. I admire your Christ-like spirit in loving the Southern whites, but I confess I am not up to it.

Chesnutt thought that education would not accomplish what should be done. "Educate them all to a high degree and leave the same inequalities," he wrote, "and as old Ben Tillman is so fond of saying—he occasionally tells the truth by accident—you merely shift the ground of the problem; you do not alter its essential features." Chesnutt complimented Washington on his pamphlet on lynching, saying that the President's was not more forceful. As to the President's remarks, Chesnutt thought he "unduly magnifys [sic] the importance of the crime of rape." That crime, said Chesnutt, is not worse than it ever was, nor more common. It "only seemed so since the fashion grew up of burning Negroes for it, and making display headings in the newspapers upon the subject." He compared the crime of the white man raping the Negro woman with the crime of the black man raping the white woman: "It is

---

ton has been saying about the Negro and the Jim Crow car and I hope that it can no longer be truly thrown at us here that you are a warm personal friend to him."

Chesnutt's reply, a typed copy, evidently carries an incorrect date. See Chesnutt to W. M. Trotter, Esq., dated Dec. 28, 1901. CC, Fisk. Chesnutt sent his subscription and said he admired the *Guardian's* uncompromising stand: "I feel quite as deeply interested as any one can in maintaining the rights of the Negro, north, south, and everywhere; but I prefer, personally, to do it directly, rather than by attacking someone else."

the rape that is the crime and not the person who commits it."[61]

Repeatedly Chesnutt and Washington vied over their divergent views on suffrage. In late October Chesnutt wrote:

It is nothing less than an outrage that the very off-scourings of Europe, and even of Western Asia may pour into this Union almost by the millions annually and be endued with full citizenship after a year or two of residence, while native born Americans who have no interest elsewhere and probably never will have, must be lead around by the nose as members of a "child-race," and be told that they must meekly and patiently await the result of an evolution which may last through several thousand years before they can stand upon the same level of citizenship which any Sicilian or Syrian or Turk or any other sort of European proletary may enjoy in the State of Alabama.[62]

By 1904 Chesnutt's cup of despair overflowed. The bill to disfranchise black people in Maryland had gone through with no more commotion than would have a bill to repair a bridge. He said to Washington:"I have always admired your cheerful optimism and I sincerely hope it may stand the strain upon it. . . . But the present state of public opinion upon the race question is profoundly discouraging." Senator Ben Tillman of South Carolina had exhibited contemptuous disregard, but Governor J. K. Vardaman of Mississippi had gone far beyond that, and Bishop William M. Brown of Arkansas had desecrated the possibility of equal rights. President Charles Eliot of Harvard had attempted to justify the rigid caste system of the South—"which is the real thing holding the colored people down," and Chesnutt felt the foundations falling. He wondered "if we do not underestimate the power of race prejudice to obscure the finer feelings of humanity."[63]

The two men exchanged other thoughts, to the modification of the opinions of neither. Both became members of the Committee of Twelve, a group Washington founded to improve the position of the Negro. On one occasion when Chesnutt could not attend a meeting in New York, he wrote Washington that:

61. Quotations from Chesnutt to Booker T. Washington, Aug. 11, 1903. Booker T. Washington Papers, Library of Congress. This letter was signed and sent.

62. Chesnutt to Booker T. Washington, Oct. 31, 1903. Booker T. Washington Papers, Library of Congress.

63. Chesnutt to Booker T. Washington, March 5, 1904. Booker T. Washington Papers, Library of Congress.

no system which excludes the Negro or any other class from the use of the ballot and leaves this potent instrument in the hands of the people who are alien to him in sympathy can have any healthy effect in improving his condition.

Chesnutt could not see how any man with the interest of his people at heart could favor the new state constitutions of the Southern states—he called them "abominations":

I know that your heart is all right [he wrote], but I think your very wise head is wrong on that proposition, and I should regard it as a much more hopeful day for the Negro in this country when you cease to defend them [the new state constitutions].

Whatever the states did, "nothing is lost and everything gained" by insisting on equality.[64]

In 1906 another terrible riot occurred in Atlanta. "I notice a great deal has been said by colored people about the Atlanta matter," Chesnutt said. "And of course I have not failed to observe that those best qualified to speak, and whose utterances would carry most weight, have not been in a position to express themselves fully." Chesnutt said that "the value of equal citizenship is so great and so vital that it is worth whatever it may cost." He told Washington that "Slavery was as deeply entrenched as race prejudice yet it fell. And the sound of the trumpets, you will remember, shook down the walls of Jericho."[65]

Washington once mentioned the Atlanta riot. He said that every man who can do so should vote—but, he asked, how do you account for the Atlanta riot, the worst we have had in forty years? That occurred in practically the only Southern state where the Negro has not been disfranchised by constitutional amendment.[66]

Chesnutt's answer was in keeping with his thinking about the ballot:

I note what you say about the franchise in Georgia, and while the riot occurred in Georgia, it was not because the Negroes had exercised the Franchise or made any less progress or developed any less strength

---

64. Chesnutt to Booker T. Washington, Oct. 9, 1906. Booker T. Washington Papers, Library of Congress. On the Committee of Twelve, see W. E. B. DuBois, *The Autobiography of W. E. B. DuBois* (International Publishers Co., U.S.A., 1968), pp. 246-47.

65. Chesnutt to Booker T. Washington, Oct. 9, 1906. Booker T. Washington Papers, Library of Congress.

66. Booker T. Washington to Chesnutt, Oct. 17, 1906. Booker T. Washington Papers, Library of Congress.

than elsewhere but because of a wicked and indefensible effort to dis-franchise them.

Chesnutt agreed with Washington on one point: The Negro would enjoy his liberty only when a white party favorable to his rights had been developed in the South.[67]

Washington had won the friendship of the steel magnate Andrew Carnegie, who was to speak in Scotland on American conditions. Chesnutt wrote to Hugh M. Browne, secretary of the Committee of Twelve, about the projected remarks:

I do not at all agree with Mr. Carnegie or with Dr. Washington, whom he quotes, in holding it "the wiser course" to practically throw up the ballot. . . . Nothing in history goes to show that the rights of any class are safe in the hands of another. . . . I am unable to see how any self respecting man can, willingly and without protest, submit to the deprivation of so elementary and fundamental a right.[68]

Upon reading this, Washington wrote directly to Chesnutt. "I confess that after reading your letter I have almost reached the conclusion that it is impossible for me to ever get my thoughts regarding the franchise through the brains of any human being," he began. But in Chesnutt's case he tried. He protested that he agreed with Chesnutt on the importance of the ballot. If Chesnutt could find a line where he said the ballot was unimportant he would send a first-class Alabama possum for the Chesnutt Christmas dinner! But they differed on "methods of attaining to the permanent and practical use of the ballot." Some maintained that the ballot was a matter of first consideration, but the first considerations were earning daily bread and banking money. How often, he asked Chesnutt, do you vote? And how often do you earn your daily bread? How often do you go to school or attend church? "If the ballot were a matter of first consideration, one would vote every day in the year instead of spending his time in the laying of an economic foundation every day in the year." Chesnutt should think about Liberia: If the people there voted every day for a year they would have improved neither their economic condition nor their moral status "one iota." Washington thought "There is something deeper in human progress than the

---

67. Chesnutt to Booker T. Washington, Nov. 3, 1906. Booker T. Washington Papers, Library of Congress.

68. Chesnutt to Hugh M. Browne, Nov. 21, 1907. Booker T. Washington Papers, Library of Congress.

mere act of voting; it is the economic foundation which every race has got to have."[69]

The two were discussing aspects of twentieth-century conflict over relationships of the individual to the group: in areas of voting and of economics, how far can an individual exercise personal choice without impinging upon community needs? If he votes on substantive matters, will this meet his needs? Or is the cost too high in terms of group welfare? Washington was saying that an individual can be better off with no vote if it is a choice of that or eating, and that this applies whatever his race. Chesnutt was saying the matter is more complex. But an individual will be better off—he will be his own man, not the pawn of a collective entity that may exploit him—if he has his vote, even though he eats poorly. He thought the vote was even more important for Negroes.

Chesnutt replied that "As to the ballot, the importance of a thing is not to be measured by the number of times you do it. Birth. Death. Marriage."[70] It is not all of life to eat and put money in the bank. While both are necessary, "A free man can do both better than a mere serf, yoked to the mule, with no concern in life but his belly and his back." "You argue the question," he wrote, "as though the Negro must choose between voting and eating. He ought to do both and can do both better than either alone."

In October 1908 Chesnutt went to his typewriter again. He had read a gruesome story of a Mississippi lynching in the *Boston Transcript:* the victims were left hanging beside the railroad track where Washington would pass by them. The article contained statements ascribed to Governor J. K. Vardaman, who threatened more lynchings if Washington made more speeches in Mississippi. "I very much fear," Chesnutt wrote, "that the South does not mean to permit education or business or anything else to make of the Negro anything more than an agricultural serf."[71]

Washington immediately pointed out that the press distorted the picture. His presence was in no way connected with the lynchings: "I happened to be near the place when the lynching occurred." Though the lynchings were "inexcusable and barbaric in the highest degrees," "we must have such occurrences for a number of years." He added that

---

69. Washington to Chesnutt, Dec. 7, 1907. Booker T. Washington Papers, Library of Congress.

70. Chesnutt to Washington, Jan. 1, 1908. CC, pisk. This letter was not retained in the Washington Papers.

71. Chesnutt to Washington, Oct. 19, 1908. CC, Fisk.

"The lynching of the white lawyer in Tennessee yesterday, as bad as it is, will help matters." If Chesnutt could see what he had seen in Mississippi, if he could observe the accumulation of property, the building and the keeping of beautiful homes, the beginnings of business enterprises, the maintenance of schools, Chesnutt would realize the improvement in the condition of black people. He thought that Chesnutt "would be surprised at the large and growing number of strong and influential white people who are in favor of justice for the Negro and are not afraid to say so." Washington still believed that the loss of the ballot "cannot disturb [an] individual's influence." He had met hundreds of colored people who because of "their intelligence, their wealth, their high character in the larger and more fundamental sense exert ten times as much political influence as many ignorant and poverty-stricken white people in the state who do go through the performance of casting a ballot now and then."[72] Chesnutt remarked that there could be little hope for the Negro in the South except along those lines, "for from recent indications he is going to get very small aid or comfort through the Constitution or the Supreme Court or Congress."[73]

A little before this exchange, Chesnutt made a speech in the national capital where he was a guest of Mrs. Carrie W. Clifford, secretary for Women of the Niagara Movement, and honorary president of the Ohio Federation of Colored Women's Clubs. Chesnutt emphasized that rights must precede duties; he and Mrs. Clifford exchanged comments about their disagreement with Booker Washington. Washington does "emphasize the duties and says not a great deal about rights," Chesnutt observed. "That Mr. Washington is not indifferent to his rights may be gathered from the fact that when he makes a pilgrimage through a southern state, as he is doing in Mississippi at present, he hires a special car for himself and his party."[74]

Between substantive exchanges, the two men wrote about their families and what was going on.[75] When Washington published the *Life of Frederick Douglass* he sent Chesnutt a copy. Chesnutt thanked him, but commented tartly: "It's well written and readable, although the bibliogra-

72. Washington to Chesnutt, Oct. 22, 1908. CC, Fisk.

73. Chesnutt to Washington, Nov. 25, 1908. CC, Fisk.

74. Chesnutt to Mrs. Carrie Clifford, Oct. 15, 1908. CC, Fisk.

75. Chesnutt to Emmett J. Scott, March 25, 1909. Booker T. Washington Papers, Library of Congress; Chesnutt to Booker T. Washington, July 21, 1910. Booker T. Washington Papers, Library of Congress; Chesnutt to Booker T. Washington, Feb. 5, 1906. CC, Fisk.

phy did omit to mention my little volume upon the same subject in the Beacon series, doubtless an oversight."[76]

From this correspondence distinct positions emerge. Washington accepted a separation of the races while Chesnutt believed in integration at all levels. Washington accepted a postponement of rights and privileges until the Negro should be prepared to exercise them, but Chesnutt insisted all rights and privileges be accorded "now." Washington would entrust the management of Negro destinies to benevolent white people, but Chesnutt would trust only black people to control their affairs. Washington thought the vote was relatively unimportant; Chesnutt thought it was crucially important. To some extent both were elitists. Both thought the future of black people could be affected through politics. But Washington, the superb political operator, was ready to maneuver within the dominant white structure, while Chesnutt would have black leaders exert their own power through political channels. In most exchanges Washington remained optimistic, while Chesnutt remained dissatisfied and unyielding. But in 1908 it was Chesnutt who, disenchanted with President Roosevelt, mentioned to Washington that he hoped President Taft would use his office to benefit the Negro.[77]

The association between Booker Washington and Charles Chesnutt spanned four presidencies, a reform movement in Cleveland, and a progressive surge in the nation. It interlaced relationships each maintained with other figures. It proved a medium for defining positions. The two demanded opinions, explanations, and expansions of each other; neither dismissed the other's views. Though neither changed the opinions of the other, it was a relationship that sharpened each man's reasoning, exposing strengths and fallacies, sometimes even to himself. Each broadened the other's horizons.

Chesnutt and the Rowfant Club:
Americana in Miniature

As a topic for critical reviews, The Colonel's Dream was a sensation—but sales were small. In the spring of 1905 Chesnutt received a check from Houghton Mifflin covering the sales of the four other books during the six months just ended. The amount was $13.70.[78] It was plain that

---

76. Chesnutt to Booker T. Washington, Nov. 22, 1907. Booker T. Washington Papers, Library of Congress.

77. Chesnutt to Booker T. Washington, Nov. 25, 1908, Booker T. Washington Papers, Library of Congress.

78. Chesnutt to Houghton Mifflin & Company, March 6, 1905, CC, Fisk.

he must rely on other sources for a livelihood.[79] Whatever their literary standing, the popular influence of his books was less than he had hoped. There is evidence that he thought his books would one day sell.[80] But people were unwilling to buy them in sufficient quantities to allow him to devote himself to writing them.

Chesnutt was forty-seven. He had succeeded in many objectives: he had found a path to a substantial income; he had provided for his children advantages he had never enjoyed; he had traveled. Though he had made little money by writing, he had rubbed elbows with influential men, and he had become famous; he had "captured the few who know."[81] Among black leaders he was respected, and he had even achieved a personal social acceptance among white leaders of Cleveland. Though some thought him stuffy, and though others thought him anxious to let his language accomplishments be known, many consulted him.[82] Some included him in private events,[83] and others sought his opinion. A few black people found these successes annoying, but most of the growing black community regarded him as an example of achievement and wisdom and as a spokesman.[84] But every scrap of comment that Chesnutt

---

79. Chesnutt to Horace Traubel, Editor, *Conservator*, March 25, 1902. Chesnutt appreciated that his novels would reach only a limited audience. He wrote: "The writer who tries to treat these difficult themes in any other than a sensational way may not hope to number his readers by the hundreds of thousands, but he can find a large reward in the appreciation of discerning souls. This has not been denied me, and of it what you have said constitutes a very valuable part." Cited by permission of Mr. Charles L. Blockson, Norristown, Pennsylvania; Traubel's daughter gave this letter to Mr. Blockson.

80. Chesnutt to Carl Van Vechten, Feb. 23, 1926. Carl Van Vechten Papers, Collection of American Literature, Beinecke Rare Book and Manuscript Library, Yale University; by permission of Donald Gallup, Literary Trustee.

81. Hamilton Wright Mabie to Chesnutt, May 8, 1900. CC, Fisk.

82. Interview given by Rowena and Russell Jelliffe to Frances Richardson Keller, Feb. 27, 1972, Cleveland.

83. Among Chesnutt's white friends were Charles F. Thwing, president of Western Reserve University, and Rowena and Russell Jelliffe, directors of Karamu. See John B. Nicholson, preface, in Chesnutt's *Baxter's Procrustes* (Cleveland: The Rowfant Club of Cleveland, 1966), p. 55. Among Chesnutt's prominent personal friends Nicholson lists "Newton D. Baker, Ohio Governor Victor Donahey and family, Ambassador Myron T. Herrick, Huntington Howard and Ora Coltman, artists;...among Rowfanters especially, Archer Shaw, Paul and Julian Feiss, Peter Keisogloff, Willis Thornton," See H. Chesnutt, *Pioneer*, p. 268. A letter to E. J. Lilly mentions associates in the Rowfant Club: a former United States Senator, a former ambassador to France, three members decorated by France, and "half a dozen millionaires." Letter quoted by H. Chesnutt, dated Nov. 23, 1915.

84. Interview given by Russell W. Davis to Frances Richardson Keller, Sept. 30, 1971, Cleveland.

227

left shows he realized his most important project was in peril. He knew that "the unjust spirit of [racial] caste" prevailed.

He seized every opportunity to confront racial discrimination. He used his time, his energy, his talent, and his money. He sought a role in every activity that was taking place in Cleveland and in the nation, behind the scenes and in public view. He used every other appropriate avenue. From time to time individuals discriminated against him or his wife Susan.[85] Perhaps such acts embarrassed Chesnutt or offended him or inconvenienced him, but they seldom diverted him.

Chesnutt's association with the Cleveland Rowfant Club illustrates his attitude. The members maintained a decorous appreciation toward the literary arts and an exclusive posture toward the uninstructed. Their object was "Primarily, the critical study of books in their various capacities to please the mind of man; and secondarily, the publication from time to time of privately printed editions of books for its members."[86] To this, the "Code" appended a word: The Club would undertake "such features of entertainment as shall be considered expedient for the literary, artistic and social benefit of its members; and the acquisition and maintenance of property, either real or personal, by which these several objects may be more fully attained."[87]

Dues were an initiation fee of $50 and a yearly assessment, later a quarterly assessment, of $10. The members venerated traditions. The groundhog was a symbol, and Groundhog Day, or Candlemas, was reserved for the annual meeting. Each member provided a candlestick—some were elegant. At the member's death an extinguisher was placed over his candle, and the candlestick took a permanent position above the bookcases in the library.[88]

To achieve acceptance in this fellowship was a delicate matter. Someone had to die. But the difficulty of selecting replacements was assuaged by the automatic elimination of women and, until the name of Chesnutt came up in 1902, the understood elimination of Negroes and others considered unlikely to qualify as book-lovers. "Eligibility as mem-

85. Interview given Frances Richardson Keller by Mrs. Louise G. Evans, October 1, 1971, Cleveland. Mrs. Evans was a stepdaughter of Charles's brother Lewis. She stated that Susan Chesnutt was darker skinned than her husband. She said that Helen, Chesnutt's fair-skinned auburn-haired daughter, was able to travel with her father with no difficulty, while Charles and his wife Susan sometimes encountered problems.

86. "Questions and Answers about the Rowfant Club," a pamphlet. Rowfant Club Library, Cleveland, p. 3.

87. "The Rowfant Club in the Beginning" The Rowfant Club of Cleveland, pp. 10, 11.

88. "Questions and Answers about the Rowfant Club," p. 5.

bers, apart from other essentials," depended upon "the possession of qualities clearly in harmony with the aims and purposes of the Club." Two members must propose the name of a candidate in their own handwriting. The Council of Fellows balloted secretly after a candidate's name had been inscribed for two weeks, using white and black balls.[89] In the first encounter between Chesnutt and members of this *sanctum sanctorum* of literature, Chesnutt received at least two black balls, though he had friends willing to propose his name. Afterwards someone told him that "one or two members thought the time hadn't come" for opening doors to men of Negro descent, whatever their qualifications.[90] The Club returned the fee; according to regulation, prospective members paid in advance.

But Chesnutt's literary star was rising in 1902. Habitually he discovered subjects for stories in life experiences, so he wrote about a Cleveland Club and the activities of its members. In June 1904 the *Atlantic Monthly* published "Baxter's Procrustes," a delicious satire that went to the heart of book-loving, drawing distinctions among putterers, exhibitors, excluders, readers, and writers. Peace was declared when in 1910 Chesnutt became a member of the Rowfant Club, repeating in a letter that he guessed that "if they could stand it," he could.[91] Chesnutt's daughter thought the members "realized with very good grace that Chesnutt was making gentle fun of them."[92]

According to the Rowfant *Yearbook*, Chesnutt "entertained" many times. In 1912 he opened the presentations with "a brilliant paper: 'Who and Why Was Samuel Johnson.'" Ten presentations by Charles Chesnutt appear, the last in 1925. Few rated any description other than the *Yearbook* title, and no other talk rated "brilliant."[93] Whatever the credits, the Rowfant Club was a means of realizing a dream in the life of the man who once had hoped that "someday I may have a friend." Chesnutt enjoyed the fellowship of the Rowfant Club.

Unhappily there is more to the story. Chesnutt probably knew of Frank U. Quillin, who wrote in 1913 a book called *The Color Line in Ohio*. Quillin observed that men of the two races might meet as friends

89. *Code of Regulations of the Rowfant Club* (Cleveland, 1892), pp. 14, 15, 30, 31.

90. H. Chesnutt, *Pioneer*, p. 244.

91. Chesnutt to F. H. Goff, Dec. 10, 1910. CC, Fisk. Benjamin P. Bowland to Chesnutt, Dec. 8, 1910. CC, Fisk.

92. H. Chesnutt, *Pioneer*, p. 208.

93. *Yearbooks* of the Rowfant Club: 1913, p. 60; 1915, p. 41; 1916, p. 36; 1917, p. 37, 39; 1921, 1922, and 1925. Rowfant Club Library, Cleveland.

in business or in daily encounters, but never in social life. Quillin selected an incident in Cleveland to illustrate his point:

*There is a club of the leading literary men in the city, who have met for
years. In this club there is an author of large gifts, but who happens to
have almost an imperceptible amount of colored blood in his veins.
Some time ago it was proposed that the club have a banquet, to which
they would invite their wives. The idea was entered into with enthusiasm
until one of the members happened to think that it would be necessary
to have the wife of a colored member present. The whole thing was
then quietly dropped, the members of the club taking the following view
of the matter, as expressed by one of them: "Although I am a Southerner, I am broad-minded enough to admire Mr. A for his work. I like to
talk with him and shake his hand, but for my wife to meet his wife in
social equality is a very different thing. She would not agree to it, and I
could not blame her.*[94]

Chesnutt remained a member of the Rowfant Club until his death.
Long after that, in 1966, the Rowfant Club published a special edition—
the story "Baxter's Procrustes," with a biographical preface about Chesnutt by one of the members, John B. Nicholson.[95]

Family Portraits

While working out the conflicts of a writing career, Chesnutt led a full
family life. His brother Lewis married Carrie Perry, a sister of Chesnutt's
wife. Lewis and another brother, Jack, (Andrew Jackson Chesnutt, Jr.),
opened a photographic studio in Cleveland, and by the early 1900s they
did a good business.[96] In May 1904, while their youngest daughter, Dorothy, was finishing seventh grade, and while their son Edwin was a junior at Harvard,[97] the Charles Chesnutts moved to 1668 Lamont Avenue.[98] This was a beautiful house with a wide porch and forty windows

---

94. Frank U. Quillin, *The Color Line in Ohio* (Ann Arbor: George Wahr, 1913), pp. 157,
158.

95. Chesnutt, *Baxter's Procrustes* (Iowa City: The Prairies Press for the Rowfant Club,
1966).

96. Interview given Frances Richardson Keller by Mrs. Helen G. Cornwell, Oct. 1, 1971,
Cleveland. Mrs. Cornwell said that the Chesnutt brothers Lewis and Jack had done well in
social photography until the content of Charles Chesnutt's books became known. After
that they were obliged to do commercial photography, though they cherished no ill feeling
about the Chesnutt novels.

97. Chesnutt to Virgil P. Kline, March 19, 1905. CC, Fisk.

98. *Cleveland City Directory*, 1904, gives the address as 1668 Lamont Avenue; Later, in
1927, the *Cleveland Plain Dealer* mentioned Chesnutt's "big roomy house" at 9719 Lamont N.E., March 17, 1927. This seems to reflect a change in the numbering system.

and polished hardwood floors in the spacious rooms. An entrance hall was large enough to serve as a dance floor and to accommodate an orchestra at Christmas parties. There was a library for Charles. "It was an affluent house of the 1890s," said a friend. "Not shrieking of innovations, but furnished with good antique furniture."[99] The Chesnutts redecorated this home tastefully.[100]

Susan Chesnutt made a career of home and family. Somewhat straightlaced, and, like others steeped in Victorian tradition, a bit priggish—certainly of a managerial turn, Susan liked to supervise. Acquaintances remember her well-managed household and her well-trained maid. By middle life she had developed a dignified, rather imposing presence. She could be overbearing. There is a story that she disapproved a second marriage of Lewis Chesnutt, which took place five years after the death of his first wife, her sister. On one occasion the second wife's small daughter strayed into Susan's bedroom; Susan upbraided the child severely.[101]

Frequently Susan Chesnutt invited members of clubs to which the Chesnutts belonged, and members of her Emmanuel Church group. She entertained graciously. "One saw Mrs. Chesnutt as a hostess in her own home," a friend recalled. "One met her husband in a different way—in committee meetings, in a working relationship. She did not take part in community affairs with her husband."[102]

The house was seldom empty. Helen lived at home after she began to teach Latin in Cleveland Central High School. Taller than her father, troubled with eye problems so that she needed thick glasses, Helen was strong-minded. "not," said a lady who knew the family, "a gentle, tender kind of woman at all, but a very good disciplinarian." Clevelanders remember that "She was a whale of a good Latin teacher." A student recalled her as "a dedicated teacher who loved her students and who exerted a lot of influence over them." One of them, a thirteen-year-old boy named Langston Hughes, was writing his first plays and poems for the school Literary Magazine. He became Helen's lifelong friend. All

---

99. *Cleveland Plain Dealer,* March 17, 1927; interviews given Frances Richardson Keller by Russell and Rowene Jelliffe, February 27, 1972, and by Mrs. Helen G. Cornwell, October 1, 1971, both in Cleveland.

100. Letter quoted in H. Chesnutt, *Pioneer,* pp. 291-92.

101. Interview given Frances Richardson Keller by Mrs. Louise Evans, Oct. 1, 1971, Cleveland.

102. Interview given by Mrs. Rowena Jelliffe, Feb. 27, 1972, Cleveland.

who knew Helen speak of her abiding attachment to her father.[103]

After a year at Tuskegee, Chesnutt's daughter Ethel married Edwin C. Williams, the librarian of Case Western Reserve University.[104] For a time Ethel and her husband and baby lived in the Chesnutt home. Edwin Chesnutt, who was especially congenial with his mother, came and went. Susan and Charles felt concerned about Edwin's health, and often about his manner of living. After his son's graduation from Harvard, Chesnutt thought that Edwin's catarrhal problems would be alleviated by the climate of the Riviera; he sent Edwin abroad, supplying an allowance that permitted him to live in Europe for some time.[105] Chesnutt hoped that Edwin might think of a career where race would be less of an obstacle, for Edwin was darker skinned than his father. Chesnutt wrote to Virgil P. Kline, an attorney for Standard Oil, to inquire whether that company had openings. Chesnutt thought of "some civilized country where the color line does not run; this for reasons which we have talked over."[106] By September 1905 Chesnutt had made a contact in Cuba. But for some years Edwin hesitated. He studied shorthand; on and off he worked in his father's office. In 1910 he accepted a position at Tuskegee, but the following year he resigned.[107] Finally Edwin decided to study dentistry; in 1915 he graduated from Northwestern and passed the Illinois Dental Examination.

After Edwin began practice in Chicago, Susan visited him. A letter to Charles illustrates the concern both felt; it reveals tensions that affected Susan:

103. Interviews given by Mrs. Rowena Jelliffe, Feb. 27, 1972, and by Russell W. Davis, Sept. 30, 1971. Interview with Dorothy Chesnutt's husband, Dr. John Slade, on Feb. 26, 1972, in Cleveland. Dr. Slade was reluctant to cooperate. He did say, however, that Helen Chesnutt's hair was "a little bit red." Half a dozen others in Cleveland with whom the writer spoke confirmed these impressions. Helen Chesnutt took her M.A. at Columbia University in 1925, according to records in Smith College archives. See Langston Hughes to Chesnutt, Feb. 15, 1932, CC, Fisk. Helen Chesnutt was coauthor of a manual for teaching Latin: The Cleveland Plan for the Teaching of Languages with Special Reference to Latin (Chicago: John C. Winston Co., 1940). In November 1902, the Smith College Monthly published an article by Helen M. Chestnutt [sic], "The Problem of the South," pp. 116-21. It stresses the work at Tuskegee. Chesnutt to Charles W. C. Williams, March 26, 1926. CC, WRHS, Container 1, Folder 5.

104. Davis, Memorable Negroes in Cleveland's Past, p. 40.

105. H. Chesnutt, Pioneer, pp. 216, 222.

106. Chesnutt to Virgil P. Kline, March 19, 1905. CC, Fisk.

107. Chesnutt to John S. Durham, Sept. 5, 1905, CC, Fisk: Howard to Chesnutt, Aug. 19, 1905. CC, Fisk. Edwin's venture—and Ethel's—at Tuskagee were costly. Edwin's salary was $50 monthly.

I have been observing our son for two days and I think he is changing for the better. He secured a very nice suite of rooms for the sake of the reputation of the family and while he loves his friends he never forgets that his early training is better than theirs and I can assure you that he feels infinitely superior to any of them.[108]

Chesnutt's youngest daughter, Dorothy, like her mother of a somewhat darker complexion, lived at home and attended the College for Women of Western Reserve University; She became a probation officer of the juvenile court. In the 1920s Dorothy married John Slade, a veterinarian. For a while the Slades, too, lived at the Lamont Avenue house.[109] When Dorothy's husband entered medical school at Howard University, she taught English and French at Willson Junior High School. Her son was born in Cleveland in June 1925. Susan employed a nursemaid and took over his care.[110] So each of Chesnutt's grandsons— Charles Waddell Chesnutt Williams and John Chesnutt Slade—lived for a time in the Chesnutt home.

Chesnutt enjoyed these children. In later years he corresponded with his namesake, who studied law and who shared his grandfather's passion for racial justice.[111] For John Chesnutt Slade, his grandfather conceived stories that he sent to a publisher.[112] Though John Slade remembers the stories and recalls that his grandfather amused him with them,[113] and though correspondence with publishers attests their existence,[114] the manuscripts have disappeared.

Sometimes Chesnutt stayed home when his family went to a resort or traveled to Europe. He planned to write at those times, and he always needed to keep his business going to support the activities of his family. Once Susan took Dorothy to Atlantic City after an illness. Chesnutt wrote:

108. Susan [Chesnutt] to "Dear Dad," undated but marked 1923. CC, WRHS, Container 1, Folder 3.

109. Interview given Frances Richardson Keller by Dr. John Slade, Feb. 26, 1972, Cleveland.

110. H. Chesnutt, *Pioneer*, p. 295.

111. Charles W. C. Williams to Chesnutt, Jan. 24, 1931; Chesnutt to Charles W. C. Williams, Dec. 18, 1923; and March 26, 1926. CC, WRHS.

112. Chesnutt to Ferris Greenslet, Oct. 15, 1930. CC, WRHS, Container 1, Folder 5.

113. John C. Slade to Frances Richardson Keller, Nov. 17, 1971. Letter in the writer's papers.

114. See Chesnutt to Scribner's, Oct. 6, 1930. CC, WRHS, Container 1, Folder 5. See also note 112.

I have your letter of October 10. I cannot say it was unexpected. I quite appreciate that life is expensive, and I have no doubt that you have spent your money wisely and I hope you have gotten value for it. I certainly have given value for it, in good work.[115]

Chesnutt was successful in meeting these demands as well as demands he made of himself. At times the cost was high. In June 1910, five years after the publication of *The Colonel's Dream,* he suffered a slight stroke. He collapsed in his office. Upon his recovery some months later, his doctor insisted that he live less strenuously.[116]

From Cleveland Problems to National Affairs:
The Third Solution: Assimilation

Perhaps Chesnutt suffered the stroke at fifty-two because he put all but insupportable pressures upon himself. After the publication of *The Colonel's Dream* he added new activities. He felt an urgency about race, a compulsion to exert an influence over the trend of events. Many records attest his efforts. He opened a correspondence with Attorney-General William H. Moody on a case before the Supreme Court. Moody sent a copy of arguments and documents presented in *Clyatt v. United States,* "commonly called the Peonage Case."[117] Soon after that Chesnutt wrote President Roosevelt to support an appointment for an ex-Congressman from North Carolina, George H. White. By the "Redeemed" constitution, White's career "went down with the rape of his race's liberty." "His appointment," said Chesnutt, "would be received by the colored people of the nation as a recognition of their claim to some share in the administration of a government from which they are barred by the conditions which obtain in the Southern States." The President's secretary merely acknowledged receipt.[118]

The Committee of Twelve was conceived as a group of "prominent colored men" who would work on a national scale "for the advancement of the interests of the Negro Race."[119] Chesnutt believed it possible for men of different persuasions to work together. Though the

---

115. Quoted in H. Chesnutt, *Pioneer,* p. 264.

116. Ibid., p. 238.

117. W. H. Moody to Chesnutt, May 13, 1905. CC, Fisk.

118. Chesnutt to President Theodore Roosevelt, March 6, 1905, and Chesnutt to George White, March 6, 1905. CC, Fisk. William Loeb to Chesnutt, March 13, 1905. CC, Fisk.

119. The Committee of Twelve was organized July 28, 1904, in New York. Chesnutt took the place of W. E. B. DuBois, who resigned. See DuBois, *The Autobiography of W. E. B. DuBois,* pp. 246-47.

committee included men whose views varied widely, he noted that they all wished to promote good feeling "so far as that is possible without the sacrifice of vital principles."[120] Besides the instigator, Booker Washington, and Chesnutt, the other members were Hugh M. Browne, Charles E. Bentley, E. C. Morris, Charles W. Anderson, Archibald H. Grimke, George Clinton, Kelley Miller, J. W. E. Bowen, T. Thomas Fortune, and H. T. Kealing.[121] Through several years this Committee circulated "printed matter which tend[ed] to create public opinion in [their] favor and correct misinterpretation."[122] It prepared speeches for prominent persons in sympathy with Negro causes. It reprinted and circulated helpful addresses, and it worked for selected projects. The committee was a nationally conceived ancestor to other twentieth-century movements, as its 1908 statement testifies:
"Range of Inquiry" for the twelve members to keep on their desks:

1. Instances of success of our people along the several lines of progress enumerated by Mr. Carnegie in this address.

2. Instances of cooperative effort between whites and blacks in the south for the true development of the latter.
   For instance:
   East Bessemer Settlement, Alabama

3. Instances of efforts of the whites anywhere to help the Negro rise.

4. Instances of just criticism of the Negro both adverse and favorable.[123]

Though Chesnutt sought means to work for equality, these were years that confirmed an opinion for which he became notorious. Chesnutt took a stand that amalgamation was the only way to resolve race problems. In a letter to D. E. Tobias, author of a pamphlet on race prejudice, he cited two articles, "The White Man's Burden at Home," and "Le Préjugé des Races" (race prejudice). Chesnutt told Tobias that the two authors demonstrated beyond doubt "the unity of the human type."[124]

---

120.   Chesnutt to Hugh M. Browne, June 2, 1905. CC, Fisk.

121.   Hugh M. Browne to Chesnutt, May 20, 1905. CC, Fisk.

122.   Hugh M. Browne to Chesnutt, April 12, 1905. CC, Fisk.

123.   Hugh M. Browne to Chesnutt, May 14, 1908. CC, Fisk.

124.   Chesnutt to D. E. Tobias, Sept. 20, 1905. CC, Fisk.

Chesnutt took pains to show "the unity of the human type," for an old mythology proclaimed the innate inferiority of the Negro. The myth was the moral foundation for slavery and for the color-caste structure that supplanted slavery. Chesnutt thought it necessary to confront the myth as well as the conditions it perpetuated.

As early as 1900 Chesnutt had written articles for the *Boston Transcript*, expressing his views on race mixture. In 1903 he told his friend Charles F. Thwing, President of Western Reserve University, that the saddest spectacle in history is that of warring races upon the same territory, and that he hoped the American people could fuse out of the diverse races one free people.[125] In a letter to Representative E. D. Crumpacker, who told him that a Thomas Dixon book viewed any Negro inheritance as sure to corrupt "pure" blood, Chesnutt made a caustic answer:

There has always been a great deal of Southern claptrap about the disastrous results that would follow the intermingling of blood. Such intermingling as there has been, and there has been a great deal, has been done with the entire consent and cheerful cooperation of the white race, and I am unable to see any disastrous results that have followed so far.[126]

On March 19, 1904, the *Cleveland Gazette* reported a Chesnutt speech at All Souls Church: assimilation of the race by the whites was "the solution of the problem within 500 years, and . . . it is the only way out." The reporter added that Chesnutt thought there is room for only one race in the United States.

Three months later (June 1904) Chesnutt was at Harvard for Edwin's graduation; he had agreed to speak at that time for the Boston Literary and Historical Society. He prepared an address fifty-two pages long on "Race Prejudice: Its Causes, Results and Cures."[127] He took the position that differences in human types are due to "differences in climate, to the influence of different religions and forms of government, which . . . have reacted upon the mental and physical characteristics of the people." This is the position that environment plays the determining role:

We recall that a generation ago, the doctrine of the brotherhood of man was founded largely upon the Scriptures, which make us all the

125. Chesnutt to Dr. Charles F. Thwing, Sept. 29, 1902, CC. Fisk.

126. Chesnutt to D. E. Crumpacker, March 28, 1902. CC, Fisk.

127. Shortened to "Race Prejudice, Its Causes and Cures."

children of Adam, and through Adam the sons of God, and the illustrations which I have given you bear out, in the light of reason and science, the conclusion which our fathers reached by the eye of faith.

Though nature permits no crossing of lower forms of life, wherever races of men come together they mingle; this is the strongest proof of essential unity. Prejudice grew from an accumulation of differences; any one could create antagonism:

There was the contempt of the instructed for the ignorant, the contempt of the fair and comely for the black and homely [Chesnutt explained that cultural standards determine this], the contempt of the master for the slave; the scorn of the Christian for the heathen; the contempt of the native for the foreigner, or the citizen for the alien, of him who speaks a language fluently for him who speaks it brokenly or corruptly.

The remedy would be the removal of causes that gave rise to antagonisms. The customs of slavery produced some softening of differences. There has also been a tremendous quantity of mixed blood diffused within the Negro race, and this has produced a wide and gradual change of type. The physical type of the race has also improved because black people have been better fed and better clothed than under slavery. "People who can hold up their heads and feel that they are men and women and free citizens do not drag their dull way through life like fettered slaves. Men who read and think show it in their faces." "The same process which makes in two or three generations, out of stupid European peasants, leaders of men, is making out of the slaves of a generation ago, men and women who will...contribute their full share to the future greatness of the nation and of humanity."

Chesnutt thought that we could remove race prejudice only by getting rid of differences. He made a much-cited observation:

We have had preached to us of late a new doctrine—that of Race Integrity. We must so glory in our color that we must zealously guard it as a priceless heritage. Frankly, I take no stock in this attitude. It seems to me a modern invention of the white people to perpetuate the color line. It is they who preach it, and it is their racial integrity which they wish to preserve. They have never been unduly careful of the purity of the black race.

Every other people seeks to lose separate identity and to become American. By the third generation all are Americans, Chesnutt said. "Are we to help these white people build up walls between themselves and us, between our children and theirs? To fence in a gloomy back yard for our descendants to play in?" Chesnutt thought that "The whole policy of race separation is illogical and unjust and must sooner or later fall by its own weight"; "I not only believe that the admixture of the races will in time become an accomplished fact, but I believe that it will be a good thing for all concerned." Chesnutt saw an epoch in our nation's history when

all the people of this nation will join to preserve to all and to each of them for all future time that ideal of human liberty which the Fathers of the Republic set out in the Declaration of Independence, which declared that all men are created equal.[128]

The next day the *Boston Evening Transcript* quoted parts of the speech under large headlines: "Sure Negro and White Will Mix," and "Chesnutt Positive Races Will Remove Bar and Freely Intermarry."[129]

Three months later Chesnutt wrote to Robert Anderson, who had asked him to state what the Negro problem is:

I should say that it is a continuing problem which assumes some new stage every now and then, and will probably continue to vex us as long as the Negro in this country exists in the public consciousness as something distinct from the ordinary citizen, and whose rights, privileges and opportunities are to be measured by some different standard from that applied to the rest of the community.[130]

On October 9, 1906, Chesnutt had written to Booker Washington that it is impossible for two races to subsist side by side without intermingling.[131] A month later he remarked that "The American people will have to swallow the Negro in punishment for their sins. Doubtless the dose is a bitter one, but there is no other way out. It only remains for all of us to make the process as little painful as possible."[132]

In November 1906 Chesnutt spoke before the Cleveland Council of Sociology.[133] His topic was "Age of Problems." "More or less mixture of blood would seem to be inevitable where different races come in con-

---

128. "Race Prejudice, Its Causes and Cures," unpublished MS. CC, Fisk, p. 5. See also pp. 12, 41, 43, 44, 45, 51.

129. *Boston Evening Transcript*, June 26, 1905.

130. Chesnutt to Robert Anderson, Sept. 3, 1904. CC, Fisk.

131. Chesnutt to Booker T. Washington, Oct. 9, 1906. Booker T. Washington Papers, Library of Congress.

132. Chesnutt to Booker T. Washington, Nov. 3, 1906. Booker T. Washington Papers, Library of Congress.

133. Announcement signed M. A. Marks, Chairman, Nov. 12, 1906. CC, Fisk.

tact," he said, "and no system of social discouragement has ever proved sufficient to prevent it." By the census of 1890 there were one million half or more than half white, and of the remaining Negroes, at least half had a strain, more or less large, of white blood. "The Negro is a hard pill to swallow," he said. "The Chinese we have sought to keep out; the Negro is too big to throw up."

To Bishop William M. Brown of Arkansas, who insisted on Negro inferiority in his book *The Crucial Race Question*, Chesnutt sent a sharp challenge:

I do not know whether it ever occurred to you—it certainly has to me— that if the Creator had intended to prevent the intermixture of races, He might in His infinite wisdom have accomplished this purpose by a very simple method, as he had by the physiological laws which prevent the confusion of genera in the lower animals. I think it very fortunate for humanity that not all the ministers of God agree with you in your views in respect to the Negro. If so, his future fate in the country of his birth would be very sad and hopeless. [134]

The bishop made a lame gesture. He sent Chesnutt a letter from a Negro priest who also thought Negroes inferior. This impressed Chesnutt not at all. He had dealt with traitors before. [135]

Chesnutt had thus variously expressed what he increasingly believed— that only a slow evolutionary racial admixture would overcome caste obstructions. He expected no rapid changes, but he thought caste laws should be defeated. He had neither married a white person nor encouraged anyone close to him to do so. But he believed any law denying the right to marry as one pleased was an insult. When an anti-intermarriage bill came up in Ohio in 1913, Chesnutt worked to defeat it. He sought the assistance of Newton D. Baker, then Mayor of Cleveland. Chesnutt had some doubts about Baker's positions. This time, however, Baker made his opposition known in the Legislature. Chesnutt wrote to him:

Permit me to express the great pleasure your letter in reference to the anti-intermarriage bill has given me. I fear you thought my silence strange, after our interview. I find it a little difficult myself to account for,

---

134. Chesnutt to Bishop William M. Brown, Nov. 7, 1909, CC, Fisk.

135. Seward S. Willett to William M. Brown, Dec. 8, 1909. CC, Fisk. Chesnutt to Rev. J. E. Moorland, May 14, 1904, Moorland-Springarn Collection, Howard University, and Chesnutt to Rev. J. E. Moorland, July 22, 1904. Moorland-Springarn Collection, Howard University.

except that I am naturally of a somewhat dilatory habit of mind. . . . I have strained my emotions so much on this Race Problem that I was slightly disappointed and a little discouraged at what seemed to be your attitude at the time.[136]

The following year, 1914, a representative in Washington proposed Bill 1710 to forbid intermarriage in the District of Columbia. Representative William Gordon replied to a communication from Chesnutt that the bill "will receive my careful consideration."[137]

Dissatisfied with this noncommittal reply, Chesnutt wrote to his friend George A. Myers, proprietor of the Cleveland Hollenden Hotel barber shop. For years Myers had served as a one-man clearinghouse for racial affairs and as a liaison center between the black population of Cleveland and the Republican Party. Chesnutt sought his support in opposing the D.C. bill.[138] Chesnutt knew he could count on Myers, and he hoped that Myers could marshal enough opposition to table the bill. On this, as on other occasions, Chesnutt and Myers worked together successfully. The committee refused to report the bill.[139]

A few months later Chesnutt wrote Professor Paul Haworth:

In my opinion the only solution is the absolute and impartial treatment of the negro (applying of course the same standards applied to white men) in every walk and relation of life, without regard to race or color, even though it result, as in Brazil, in the fusion of the races.[140]

This was one of many comments that Chesnutt made in his remaining years. He had tried every other approach to racial proscription; he had laid his literary gifts at the feet of black people; he had involved himself in every supportive political and social action, yet a resolution eluded the nation. Chesnutt concluded that only one solution would eliminate racial caste from American life: assimilation. Toward the latter part of

---

136. Chesnutt to Newton D. Baker, April 3, 1913. CC, Fisk.

137. William Gordon to Chesnutt, April 9, 1914. CC, Fisk.

138. Chesnutt to George A. Myers, April 13, 1914. George A. Myers Papers, Collection 70, Box 16, Folder 5, Ohio Historical Society, Columbus.

139. Chesnutt to George A. Myers, April 22, 1908. George A. Myers Papers, Collection 70, Box 14, Folder 4, Ohio Historical Society, Columbus. On another matter see George A. Myers to R. J. Bulkley, June 19, 1911. CC, Fisk. Also Chesnutt to George A. Myers, Dec. 23, 1915, George A. Myers Papers, Collection 70, Box 16, Folder 7, Ohio Historical Society, Columbus; and George A. Myers to Chesnutt, Jan. 16, 1924. CC, WRHS.

140. Chesnutt to Paul L. Haworth, Sept. 2, 1914. CC, Fisk. Haworth was author of *America in Ferment* (1915).

the twenties (1927), the *Cleveland Plain Dealer* sent a reporter to talk with Chesnutt. The reporter quoted Chesnutt as having said at a Boston symposium:

The solution of the race problem is simplicity itself. Many states now penalize marriage between white and black. Let them simply ammend their laws to offer a bonus for interracial marriages. Require every white man to marry a black woman and every black man to marry a white woman. Then wed their children to other whites. Continue this for three generations and your problem will disappear.

Chesnutt told the reporter that he wrote this passage as a jest, but that in certain parts of the South it was bitterly denounced. Chesnutt may have intended his remarks as a joke but the *Plain Dealer* noted that he had added a word:

However, joking aside, that's exactly what is happening and will continue to happen. Whether the white folk like it or not, whether the colored folk like it or not, the colored race is being gradually absorbed.[141]

A year later someone asked Chesnutt whether he believed in intermarriage. He answered that "the social penalties are so great none but the brave or the reckless would dare it." "Personally," he added, "I believe that marriages are happier and more successful where people marry their own type. But experience has demonstrated that the races will mix, and if they are to continue to mix I believe it ought to be in a lawful way."[142] Chesnutt realized that to endorse amalgamation was one thing; to advocate it as a general remedy in early twentieth-century America was another. In a 1908 address in support of the Niagara Movement, Chesnutt had said:

If the difference of race were entirely eliminated, the problem would be at an end. But this we may as well dismiss from our consideration, as it is beside the question for the present.... We must consider the problem for our day with reference to other questions.[143]

Still Chesnutt's suggestion in the field of social relations was a little like Einstein's suggestion in the field of physics. Like the equation $E = MC^2$, it was a brilliant, alarming insight, simple, inclusive, illogical. It conjured

---

141. *Cleveland Plain Dealer*, July 17, 1927.

142. Chesnutt, "The Race Problem" (unpublished MS), February, 1928. CC, Fisk, p. 22. This is an address to "The Ohio State School."

143. Chesnutt, "The Niagara Movement" (unpublished MS). CC, Fisk, p. 22.

up visions of disaster. Yet in the end it might move the masses of mankind, as Einstein's insight moved the masses of matter. It might work.

Crescendo in Cleveland and in the Nation

All this time Chesnutt pressed his career of public service in Cleveland and national service to the Negro race. He also expressed to William H. Richards of the Bethel Literary and Historical Association his concern for underprivileged whites, and the belief that their liberties were bound up with those of the Negro. Chesnutt insisted that suffrage is fundamental to everyone's liberty. He wrote Richards that "the poor and unlettered need it [the vote] even more than the rich and the learned, for these can in a measure take care of themselves. It is the plain man's only bulwark against oppression."[144]

Chesnutt seemed gentle, but he could be cutting about pretensions of those who disfranchised the Southern Negro. In a 1906 address to the Cleveland Council of Sociology he referred to South Carolina Governor Benjamin R. Tillman, not by name, but unmistakably:

We are to have this "statesman" here to instruct our school teachers, I believe, sometime this winter. I have yet to learn whether he will appear with his pitchfork in his character as licensed mountebank, or as a teacher of the popular Southern brand of political morals and civic righteousness.

Chesnutt's disenchantment with President Roosevelt was apparent when he also referred to events that had occurred three months earlier in Brownsville, Texas. Three companies of a black regiment became involved in a riot. The citizens had shown displeasure with the black troops. Trouble ensued: a white citizen was killed, and two others were injured. A few days before Chesnutt spoke, President Roosevelt had based an executive action on an inspector's report that the black soldiers had murdered and maimed the citizens. With no hearing, no trial, and no further investigation, the President dishonorably discharged all the soldiers and disqualified them from all benefits.

Chesnutt pointed out that everyone will take advantage of the powerless. "Even the President of the United States," he said, "the apostle of the Square Deal, wishing to make an example, discharged without honor, a whole battalion of colored troops, under circumstances which the press of the country unanimously, so far as I have followed the comment, condemn as unjust and unfair."

---

144. On many occasions Chesnutt expressed belief that the freedom of white men is allied to the freedom of Negroes. Chesnutt to Professor Richards, Feb. 21, 1906. CC, Fisk.

In this powerful address, Chesnutt discussed equality. He gave a classic definition: Equality is "the right to share fairly and equitably in the use of the earth, which is our common mother, our common inheritance, our common grave."[145]

Outwardly Chesnutt appeared absorbed in business. At night in his library he explored literary ideas and attended to correspondence. "Life on Lamont Avenue had settled into a very pleasant pattern," his daughter wrote. "The Chesnutts were living for the most part busy and satisfying lives."[146] Yet Charles Chesnutt entered many lists. He conducted a restless search for means to exert influence in racial matters. Chesnutt felt anxious during these years; he often felt depressed, and he sometimes felt driven.

When Chesnutt could confront racial prejudice locally or nationally, he did so; he sought connections with groups. When he could recommend a deserving person of his race Chesnutt did that. When publishers wrote for opinions he gave them thoughtful replies. For example, after reading *The Brothers' War* by John C. Reed for Little, Brown and Company, he wrote them:

In spite of the legend on the cover, I do not think that 50 years hence, any one will write, and I feel quite sure that no one will publish a book devoted mainly to the justification of slavery, the glorification of the Ku Klux Klan, and a deification of Jefferson Davis and the gang of traitors who sought to destroy this Republic and perpetuate human slavery.[147]

Another time he learned that the Committee of Twelve intended to publish an "Address to the American People" prepared by a council of bishops. The address supported missionary undertakings in Africa. Chesnutt thought there was pressing business at home: "I am not able to see why Africa should be the scene of the great operations of the American Church."[148]

Many times and in many ways he expressed views on public questions—on bills before the Southern state legislatures or the Ohio legislature on bills before the Congress. Continuously he made his opinions known—in newspaper interviews, in letters, in articles, and in speeches.

---

145. Chesnutt, "The Age of Problems" (unpublished MS). CC, Fisk, p. 2. Delivered for the Cleveland Council of Sociology on November 12, 1906; see pp. 3, 4 § [sic].

146. H. Chesnutt, *Pioneer*, p. 227.

147. Chesnutt to Little, Brown & Co., n.d.. CC, Fisk.

148. See address delivered at Wilberforce University, "Race Ideals and Examples," June 16, 1913. MS, CC, Fisk.

Generous with his money and prodigal with his time, Chesnutt accepted offers to be heard. Most appearances pertained to racial topics, though some were literary. He accepted an invitation for a seventieth birthday dinner in New York for Mark Twain, whose publishers were bestowing an appropriate honor.[149]

In 1912 he sought membership in the Cleveland Chamber of Commerce. For many years thereafter he participated in its activities.[150] Willingly he served on boards of many Cleveland institutions. One of these became the Cleveland Urban League, the successor organization to the Negro Welfare Association; Chesnutt was an original board member. There is a story that Chesnutt disliked the use of Negroes as scabs, and that he successfully stood against this practice. The battle was fought at a meeting of the Negro Welfare Association Board. William R. Conners, Secretary of the organization, agreed to the use of Negro scabs when elevator operators of the Statler Hotel struck; he believed this would provide jobs for unemployed Negroes. But Chesnutt thought the opportunity a delusion; he pointed out that operators from other cities would arrive, with the result of bloodshed and no jobs. Chesnutt held his ground during hours of acrimonious disagreement. The next day elevator operators did pour into Cleveland.[151]

This stand was in harmony with an opinion Chesnutt championed before a Senate Committee in 1928. By that time certain union leaders were trying to persuade the committee to report out the Shipstead anti-injunction bill so that employers could not prevent strikes. The Cleveland Chamber of Commerce backed two Cleveland lawyers, Harry E. Davis and Charles Chesnutt, who went to Washington to speak at the hearing; Chesnutt pointed out such a bill would hurt black people because unions could and did discriminate, and because no one had power to prevent their doing so. "I make the charge baldly that the labor unions of the United States, broadly speaking, are unfriendly to colored labor, and I challenge them to prove the contrary," he said to the committee. He cited instances; one concerned a roadhouse proprietor near Cleveland who became dissatisfied with white help and employed Negro waiters. When the union protested, the owner got an injunction to preserve his business. Ironically, the union then attacked the issuance of

149. H. Chesnutt, *Pioneer*, pp. 213-15.

150. Charles E. Adams to Chestnutt [sic], April 9, 1912. CC, Fisk.

151. Interview given by Rowena and Russell Jelliffe, Directors of Karamu and friends of the Chesnutt family, February 27, 1972, at Cleveland. See William R. Conners to Chesnutt, Nov. 16 and Nov. 19; 1921. CC, WRHS.

the injunction as anti-Negro, though the union had always refused to admit blacks.[152]

On other occasions Chesnutt prevented harm. In 1915 F. P. Riddle of the Ohio Department of Agriculture arranged a tour for young people, the "Buckeye Corn Special Tour." Chesnutt got wind that as entertainment Riddle planned to show a pernicious anti-Negro movie, "The Birth of a Nation." Chesnutt wrote to Governor Frank B. Willis, calling attention to the Ohio Board of Censors' rejection of the film as unfit for exhibition. A gratifying answer came promptly. Governor Willis informed Riddle that he strongly disapproved of showing the film and that if it were shown he would cancel plans "to deliver an address to the Corn Boys" at their Philadelphia stop.[153]

Decades before the term became common, Chesnutt thought about integration as the only practical approach to the future. Yet in community activities he had to take account of problems arising from residential deprivation. As early as 1905 Chesnutt wrote an article for the Cleveland Journal advising a Social Settlement enterprise.[154] Chesnutt and others were thinking about ways of financing and operating a cultural center for the impoverished Central Avenue district. Chesnutt wanted an institution for both races that would develop democratic contacts.

People indicated interest, but no one proposed a plan. Later an impetus came from a prominent physician-philanthropist, an Oberlin graduate, Dr. Dudley Peter Allen. His acquaintance included members of the Men's Club of the Second Presbyterian Church as well as Charles Chesnutt and other Cleveland Negroes. At this time two Oberlin graduates had registered for Master's degrees at the University of Chicago. The young students, Rowena Woodham and Russell Jelliffe, came to know Graham Taylor, a professor of social economics who founded Chicago Commons, and Jane Addams, who founded Hull House. By the end of their Chicago year the two students had decided to marry and to seek an opportunity in Cleveland.

As he looked back over fifty Cleveland years, Russell Jelliffe recalled: "We read the constitution to discover what unfulfilled promises were there." Speaking of the project they developed, Rowena Jelliffe remem-

---

152. Russell H. Davis described this occasion to the writer, September 30, 1971. See transcript of Chesnutt's remarks in Senate Hearings, 70th Cong., 1928, pp. 606-609.

153. Chesnutt to Gov. Frank B. Willis, Nov. 25, 1915; Frank B. Willis to Chesnutt, Nov. 24 [sic], 1915. CC, Fisk. Evidently the typist made an error in the date.

154. W. O. Matthews (per A.D.) to Chesnutt, Dec. 4, 1905. CC, Fisk. Chesnutt was dissatisfied with segregation in the Young Men's Christian Association and the Phyllis Wheatley Home.

bered that "Charles Chesnutt was in at the beginning." She described his appearance in 1915 when she had met him. He was in his middle fifties. "He looked like a ruddy Englishman," she said. "He had a shock of white hair. He was about 5 feet 9 inches tall and weighed perhaps 155 pounds—not heavy-set at all. He was fair-skinned and he had very striking blue eyes. He was tastefully dressed. He was not foppish or over-fastidious, but he always dressed carefully. He gave the impression of a gentle, inquiring turn of mind."[155]

In 1914 Chesnutt wrote to A. T. Hills of the Men's Club, suggesting a plan for a Central Avenue undertaking.[156] By 1915 the area had become more appropriately known as the "Roaring Third"—a popular designation for about forty blocks that lie east of Central Avenue between 14th Street and 55th Street. For a time newcomers found themselves within sight of the wealthy and within walking distance of lavish Euclid Avenue residences. In 1915 some old families still lived there, but many were moving away. Great houses were being demolished or converted to social agencies. Contingents of Negroes and Europeans were scrambling for shelter in the already stuffed buildings that remained, as the whole spectrum of urban ills descended upon them. At the heart of the district, at 33rd Street and Central Avenue, a notorious "den of iniquity" called the "Z Club" emitted the sounds of Starlight Boyd; customers could hear him, and they could listen to tirades damning the white man. Three blocks from that spot, on the corner of Prospect Avenue and East 30th Street, stood the staid Second Presbyterian Church. There the Men's Club still counted most of the business leaders of Cleveland. Unquestionably these gentlemen and their families found the "Roaring Third" an anomaly when they attended services and club meetings. Successive waves of indigent newcomers were overflowing the area, threatening to submerge the Second Presbyterian Church.

One day Dr. Allen brought the matter to the attention of the Men's Club" the Roaring Third was "practically under the eaves of this church," and the Men's Club had a responsibility "to help those people."[157] After discussion, the gentlemen commissioned Dr. Charles Briggs and A. T. Hills to do something. With Dr. Allen's approval they approached the Jelliffes.

One reason the Jelliffes had wanted to come to Cleveland was that it was an outgrowth of the Connecticut Western Reserve territory. Western

---

155. Interview, Rowena and Russell Jelliffe, February 27, 1972, Cleveland.

156. Chesnutt to A. T. Hills, Feb. 18, 1914. CC, Fisk.

157. Quoted in H. Chesnutt, Pioneer, p. 260.

Reserve migrants were by and large those persons who brought progressive ideas from the Atlantic Coast, the Jelliffes thought. Cleveland was built on diversified industries; it was a growing community, and it possessed wealth. Clevelanders had elected a line of progressive mayors—Tom L. Johnson, Newton D. Baker, Harold Burton. This was a plus for the tally sheet, though later the Jelliffes became disenchanted with Newton D. Baker, who, said Russell Jelliffe, "was prone to give lip-service to projects—but to do nothing." Rowena Jelliffe recalled an occasion when a brilliant Harvard graduate, a black man, presented a letter of introduction to Baker. Baker let the young man sit in his office for an hour and a half, but he never saw him. Instead he sent his visitor, Charles W. White, to call on another black attorney, then something of an ambulance chaser, who was in no position to help. This brush-off offended the young man. Despite Baker's indifference, Charles White became—and remained till his death in 1972—a distinguished jurist of wide reputation.

The Jelliffes had pondered the questions "what is the means of people coming together and living together to mutual advantage?" and "what will hold people together?" There must be a meeting place, not a place for herding people, but a place where each person could sense respect, where individual and group activities could take place. The creative arts, especially theater and dance, would provide fields for mutual endeavors. After some years, the Jelliffes found a name *Karamu*, the Swahili word for *place of joyful meeting*. They amended the concept to mean a place of joyful contact with and for the whole community—a place to expand a neighborhood of human interests.

The Jelliffes never accepted the term "Settlement House." Like Chesnutt they disapproved the segregation of the "Settlement Houses"; it was an outcome all three wanted to avoid. In other years Chesnutt contributed money to the Jane Hunter Home, which became the Phyllis Wheatley Home. This institution was segregated, however, and he thought it a mistake to separate young black girls from other girls. He believed that community institutions should build integration and acceptance. Though problems were manifold, he became deeply interested in the Karamu idea.

At their first meeting, Chesnutt accompanied the Jelliffes on a tour of the "Roaring Third." He knew it well, for he had explored the district and observed the people.[158] After this tour and after intensive study, the Jelliffes wrote a report. It documented what Chesnutt had observed—that

---

158. Ibid., pp. 260-61.

247

this district where most of the 15,000 Cleveland blacks resided was home to people of other nationalities, races, and religions, and that almost all the newcomers were poor. The cultural life the district could offer consisted of 7 pool rooms, 22 saloons, 24 cigar and news stands, 5 cheap theaters, several dance halls, and an indeterminate number of small "game houses" scattered among private dwellings.[159] The "game houses" were houses of prostitution or houses that preyed upon children and young people.

Apart from its immediate function, this 1915 report was a study of a community in ethnic and racial transition; the common denominator was poverty, a hopeless future the common specter. One-tenth of the 5,540 school children were in trouble with truant officers. In the three remaining playgrounds discrimination existed, not only against black people but against Jews and other minorities. The Jelliffes and Chesnutt were looking upon the problems of every city in the United States. Inhabitants must struggle so desperately to survive that exclusiveness and segregation inevitably resulted.

The Jelliffes intended to banish those horrors. They encountered every difficulty. But they incorporated and purchased with $4,184 of the Men's Club money a two-story house and adjacent cottage beside Grant Park, one of the remaining playgrounds. By December 19, 1915, they had opened the doors. Despite suspicions, 1,300 boys and girls became members in six months. More were boys than girls, and more were white than black. The Jelliffes immediately needed additional facilities, and Chesnutt used his time and influence to get help from schools. His assistance was important, particularly in making arrangements permitting use of the Longwood School on 35th Street. "Chesnutt took pride in his black ancestry," said Rowena Jelliffe, as she spoke of those early struggles. "His respect for every effort coming out of the black world and for every reaching for equality showed this. He wanted to help us for he believed in practical equality. He could help because his opinion was respected by the Men's Club and by University people."

Though he was less active in later years, Chesnutt remained interested in Karamu; his daughter Dorothy did volunteer work there for some time. But the Men's Club soon had done with the impulse that prompted their attention. At the end of the first year they withdrew, and they moved their house of worship to a more serene location. "They were embarrassed by the Jelliffes," commented Russell Jelliffe. "And we were embarrassed by them—by their conservatism and their lack of com-

---

159. Selby, *Beyond Civil Rights*, p. 19.

prehension of societal growth. We knew from the beginning that we would have to break away." The Jelliffes found other support, and over the years they raised an endowment fund. Despite financial hazards, the Jelliffes believe that in their fifty years as directors of Karamu they built a neighborhood of excellence, where there could be "genuine communication," a "genuine respect," and an "affection that transcended race and class."[160]

Chesnutt and W. E. B. DuBois
Strike an Entente Cordiale

Relations between Chesnutt and W. E. B. DuBois were cordial. The two were often in agreement, though chance and distance prevented frequent meetings and though in the end they would travel distinctive routes to racial peace. They felt a common purpose; they took account of one another's positions; on many activities they supplemented one another's thinking. As early as 1903 they discussed articles each would contribute to a collection of essays, *The Negro Problem*. "Speak out in no uncertain tones," DuBois counseled. "We've got to stop Mr. Washington's heresies." DuBois inquired whether Chesnutt was ready to put some time and money into a national Negro journal. DuBois was; he "would like to hear of helpers."[161]

Both were preparing articles. Chesnutt described his "firm stand for manhood suffrage and the enforcement of the constitutional amendments." He had emphasized the Constitution; he considered disfranchisement constitutions of the Southern states invalid. Chesnutt suspected it was the DuBois book *The Souls of Black Folk* that ought to get credit for a peonage investigation in Alabama.[162]

Chesnutt commented on the suggestion about a national Negro journal. There were a good many "colored" papers; Chesnutt noted their difficulties: "The question of support would be the vital one for such a journal." Chesnutt remarked that "what the Negro needs more than anything else is a medium through which he can present his case to thinking white people, who after all are the arbiters of our destiny." Editing was a second vital consideration. Perhaps this influenced DuBois. Chesnutt wrote: "To do it [the editing] properly would require all the

---

160. Interview, Rowena and Russell Jelliffe, Feb. 27, 1972, Cleveland, at their home; see Playhouse Settlement to Chesnutt, July 17, 1924. CC, WRHS, Folder 4.

161. W. E. B. DuBois to Chesnutt, May 5, 1903. CC, Fisk.

162. Herbert Aptheker, ed., *The Correspondence of W. E. B. DuBois: Selections, 1877-1934*, vol. I (Amherst: University of Massachusetts Press, 1973), p. 56.

time of a good man—he ought to be as good a man as yourself."[163]

Not a month later Chesnutt mentioned the DuBois position in a letter to Booker Washington. The three men had written their essays; they were thinking and corresponding about their views. Chesnutt's emphasis had been distinct; he thought that neither the vocational education of Washington nor the higher education of DuBois would purchase equality. He held that the suffrage should be the vehicle. He tried to show Washington how the Washington position could redound to the disadvantage of black people: "Those who would discourage the higher education of the Negro use your words for that purpose," he told Washington. But Chesnutt also thought that because of his connection with Atlanta University it was hard for DuBois to discuss Negro rights without stressing higher education. Education was not the pivotal issue. "Neither sort of education has anything directly to do with the civil and political rights of the Negro—these would be just as vital and fundamental if there were not a single school of any kind in the Southern states."[164]

From time to time Chesnutt and DuBois corresponded. In every letter DuBois showed respect for Chesnutt; in every reply Chesnutt showed respect for DuBois. At the time DuBois moved to Atlanta he had begun to lay plans for an Encyclopedia Africana "which shall contain the history and conditions of the Negro race in the world." This epochal venture was to commemorate "the Fiftieth Anniversary of the Emancipation of the Slaves and the Ter-centenary of the landing of the Negro in America." He invited Chesnutt to act on the editorial board; he wanted "the best scholars of all races."[165] Chesnutt was "very willing to act on the editorial board, and to do any work for which I can find time or would be thought qualified."[166]

The next day DuBois wrote again to solicit Chesnutt's presence at the 1909 Meeting of the Niagara Movement. It was to be held at Isle City; DuBois wanted a hundred people there.[167] But Chesnutt answered that Mrs. Chesnutt had not made up her mind about vacation plans. If she decided on Atlantic City, he could attend some meetings.[168]

---

163. Chesnutt to W. E. B. DuBois, July, 1903. CC, Fisk. (The day of the month is illegible.)

164. Chesnutt to Booker T. Washington, Aug. 11, 1903. CC, Fisk.

165. W. E. B. DuBois to Chesnutt, July 9, 1909. CC, Fisk. DuBois first planned volume one for 1913, and hoped for the whole by 1919.

166. Chesnutt to DuBois, July 16, 1909. CC, Fisk.

167. DuBois to Chesnutt, July 10, 1909. CC, Fisk.

168. Chesnutt to DuBois, July 16, 1909. CC, Fisk.

He had attended meetings the year before in Oberlin, where he had been a speaker. He titled his address "The Niagara Movement." It was fitting that there should be a meeting to create a healthy public opinion on the rights of the Negro at Oberlin. The Niagara Movement took its name from the place where it was organized; "I trust," Chesnutt said, "It will grow in size and influence until it parallels the great cataract whose name it bears, and that it may sweep over this country with resistless force." Several years ago, he said, DuBois had

conceived the idea ... of a movement which, bringing together a few leading minds for counsel and a multitude of willing hands for support, should combine in an effort to stem this tide of prejudice which in our pessimistic moments seems to be sweeping everything before it. ... It means that they must meet and fight all the surviving instincts of savagery which at times seem to mock our civilization, and which are so deeply rooted in human nature that in moments of passion or prejudice they burst the shell of civilization and leave havoc and desolation in their wake.[169]

Chesnutt said that the Niagara Movement was formed to answer questions: "What can be done to close the gap which separates the white people and the Negro people of the United States? What can the Negro do?"

He can resist in all proper ways aggression against his lawful rights. ... A man who will tamely submit to oppression will never inspire respect in the oppressor or generous sympathy in the looker-on.

He spoke about rights and duties:

The Niagara Movement is designed to promote among colored people the sense of self-respect which will urge them to seek these rights in whatever forum touches them, and among white people a sense of justice, humanity and of fair play which will willingly concede these rights. Once gained the Negro will not be found lacking in the performance of the duties which grow out of them.[170]

Chesnutt supported the Niagara Movement as he had supported the Committee of Twelve and Tuskegee.[171] He felt concern that Washington

---

169. Chesnutt, "The Niagara Movement" (unpublished MS), 1908. CC, Fisk. pp. 1, 2.

170. Ibid., pp. 7, 8. See Chesnutt to W. E. B. DuBois, Nov. 21, 1910. CC, Fisk, pp. 3, 5.

171. Chesnutt served on the central committee or board of all. For the NAACP, which succeeded the Niagara Movement, he served on the General Committee. Mary White Ovington to Chesnutt, Dec. 15, 1911. CC, Fisk.

and DuBois should differ more than they agreed. On occasion Chesnutt attempted to achieve some accommodation. About a year after DuBois had invited Chesnutt to the Niagara meeting, he asked Chesnutt to sign a protest. Washington was in England, and DuBois found it outrageous that Washington was giving the impression that conditions were improving in the United States. Chesnutt thought it would be in poor taste for him to sign "what in effect is in the nature of an impugnment of Mr. Washington's veracity, or at least which it would be only human in him to look upon in the light of a personal attack." He explained to DuBois that his son was in Washington's office at Tuskegee, that one daughter had taught there, and that another had been a visitor for several weeks. As a member of the Committee of Twelve, Chesnutt had just signed Washington's appeal for an increase of the Tuskegee endowment. In more than five pages Chesnutt discussed issues.

"Mr. Washington is a professional optimist, avowedly so," he began. Chesnutt imagined the English took his statements with a grain of salt. Chesnutt quoted the Washington interview in the *London Morning Post* to which DuBois had taken exception. Washington had said that "The Negro problem in the United States will right itself in time," and that when America came to "a more accurate understanding of the difficulties which the masses of the working people in other parts of the world have to struggle against, it will have gone far toward solving the race problem." Chesnutt could see nothing wrong there. Chesnutt cited Washington's remark that the "worst happenings get talked about." "You have recently published a newspaper letter in which the same statement is made [a propos of colored soldiers in the West]," Chesnutt told DuBois.

Chesnutt wondered whether the protest was not "at least equally as pessimistic as Mr. Washington's interview was optimistic." The protest spoke of "Mr. Washington's suffering daily insult and humiliation." "I have no idea that Mr. Washington feels himself daily insulted and humiliated," Chesnutt wrote. "Whether he ought to is a question. As a fact, I imagine he thinks that he is daily honored and uplifted." Chesnutt could offer no explanation, although he guessed Washington wanted to cut a good figure. The DuBois protest would be signed by gentlemen who could not have attained their positions without the sense of justice of white people, "however imperfect that sense of justice may be in some other respects." Chesnutt believed that the Negro in the South would get his rights only when there would be a party of southern white people friendly to his aspirations. If Washington encouraged such feelings "he will have done a good work even though he should fall short in other respects."[172] Chesnutt earnestly believed that only a united front would wring concessions from white America; in his relations with Washington and DuBois he showed that he yearned for working understandings. About one month after he had commented on the Washington interview, Chesnutt sent DuBois a new story for *Crisis*, "The Doll." "I have read your novel, *The Silver Fleece*," said Chesnutt. "It is well conceived and beautifully worked out, and is another example of your wonderful versatility." Then Chesnutt commented again about the white image: "It will probably be said that you haven't described a single decent white man in the book—God knows they are bad enough in these parts, but you show them no mercy." Chesnutt commended "the high standard of quality and interest of *Crisis*." In two years DuBois had materialized his idea for a national Negro magazine as well as Chesnutt's idea that it be well financed and that as good a man as DuBois should edit it.[173]

Not a month later Chesnutt received a note of thanks for his contribution of $50 to the National Association for the Advancement of Colored People, which succeeded the Niagara Movement. Because the Secretary, Mary White Ovington, had gone to Chicago, DuBois wrote the letter himself.[174]

On and off they corresponded—not as Chesnutt had corresponded with Washington to express differences of opinion, perhaps to alter attitudes, but to share information, to supplement and to encourage one another, to express respect. For many years Chesnutt sent substantial contributions to the NAACP. In 1915 when the first volume of the *African Encyclopedia* appeared, he told DuBois that he had learned much about Africa, and he expressed admiration.[175]

Later in 1915 Chesnutt contributed an article on woman suffrage to *Crisis*. Not until August 1920 did Congress acknowledge the injustice of limiting suffrage to males. In attitudes toward women Chesnutt showed some values arising from a double standard, but this was limited to thoughts about writing. In later years he regretted that "virtue has gone

---

172. Chesnutt to W. E. B. DuBois, Nov. 21, 1910. CC, Fisk, pp. 5, 6.

173. Chesnutt to W. E. B. DuBois, Dec. 20, 1911. CC, Fisk.

174. Mary White Ovington to Chesnutt, Dec. 15, 1911. CC, Fisk. Chesnutt to Oswald Garrison Villard, April 19, 1916. CC, Fisk. Many letters between Chesnutt and Walter White and Chesnutt and James Weldon Johnson exist. The White letters, WRHS and the Library of Congress; the Johnson letters, the Beineke Library, Yale University, and the Library of Congress. ' See Chesnutt to Charles T. Hallinan, April 7, 1914, CC, Fisk; New York Office NAACP to Chesnutt, March 13, 1924, CC, WRHS, Folder 4; Mary White Ovington to Chesnutt, May 5, 1917. CC, Fisk.

175. Chesnutt to W. E. B. DuBois, June 5, 1915. CC, Fisk.

out of fashion in fiction," and he lamented that heroines of the 1920s were "unchaste." Once he noted that "Claude McKay's *Home to Harlem* is very well written, but I don't recall a decent woman character in the book."[176] He singled women out for such strictures, applying them less rigidly to judgments about male characters; but Chesnutt felt no double standard when it came to civil rights.

Should women vote? Despite Victorian predispositions Chesnutt took an unequivocal stand in his 1915 *Crisis* article: "I believe that all persons of full age and sound mind should have a voice in the making of the laws by which they are governed, or in the selection of those who make those laws."[177] Chesnutt remarked that many women have interests outside the family.[178] He repeated about women what he had said in other cases: "Experience has shown that the rights and interests of no class are safe so long as they are entirely in the hands of another class."[179] So far as women constitute a class, their rights cannot safely be left in the hands of men. He thought women's rights needed protection and that women needed to be guarded against oppression, that the ballot was the most effective weapon, that women should secure it and use it to protect their rights. Unlike some sentimentalists, Chesnutt expected no sudden improvement in the conduct of affairs after bestowing the vote on women. The contrary could happen, because of lack of experience, for "women are certainly no wiser or more logical than men."

Chesnutt would no more tolerate color discrimination against women than against men. He disagreed with his contemporary, Senator Benjamin R. Tillman of South Carolina. Tillman wrote to the woman editor of the *Maryland Suffrage News*. DuBois reprinted the letter in *Crisis* in his woman suffrage series, perhaps to show the workings of democ-

---

176. Chesnutt, "The Negro in Present Day Fiction" (unpublished MS), address delivered at Oberlin, n.d., but c. late 1920s, p. 18. Chesnutt begins this passage with "The heart of any romantic novel is the heroine."
In another undated manuscript, "The Negro in Literature," p. 24 (CC, Fisk), Chesnutt was beginning to think of women in a less romanticized fashion.

177. Chesnutt, "Women's Rights," *Crisis* 10 (August, 1915), 182-83.

178. Chesnutt, "Address to Nurses" (unpublished MS), CC, Fisk: "So the women have gone to work, partly from necessity, partly because their own self respect will not permit them to be mere barnacles on society" (p. 2).

179. Chesnutt, "Women's Rights," *Crisis*, 10 (August, 1915), 182-83. See Chesnutt, "To the Public" (unpublished MS), 1920, CC, Fisk, p. 3. Eleven years later, Chesnutt recommended the election of a woman candidate for city council. Chesnutt to Mayo Fesler, October 16, 1931. CC, WRHS, Container 1, Folder 6.

racy.[180] Tillman was unable to conceive of a crusade "to force woman suffrage on the South":

A moment's thought will show you that if women were given the ballot, the Negro women would vote as well as white women. Experience has taught us that Negro women are much more aggressive in asserting the "rights of that race" than the Negro men are. In other words, they have always urged the Negro men on in the conflicts we have had in the past between the two races for supremacy. We found it hard enough to maintain good government under such conditions without adding to our perplexities by giving the ballot to women.

Tillman bared his thinking further. "With a 'free vote and fair count,' which we have never been willing to give the Negroes and never will, in my judgment," he saw a new "Negro domination." He preferred that South Carolina remain "redeemed," as in 1877, "by its own true sons by the aid of the shot gun and pistol, as well as by the superior intelligence of the white managers, who cheated the Negroes mercilessly, because it was necessary." He told the editor of the *Maryland Suffrage News* that he was "enclosing two or three speeches on the race question, in which I boldly told the Republicans to their teeth on the floor of the Senate, that we 'shot the Negroes,' 'cheated them' and 'stuffed the ballot boxes' "[181]

The next year DuBois wrote Chesnutt to obtain his signature for an album for Joel Spingarn, an honored white colleague.[182] So it went, the two men developing cordial, mutually appreciative attitudes. In 1924 Chesnutt sent a story, "The Marked Tree." DuBois published it in installments.[183] Regularly DuBois ran contests; he invited Chesnutt to judge them, and Chesnutt wrote thoughtful critiques.[184] Still later, DuBois invited the Chesnutts to the wedding of his daughter Yolande and the poet Countee Cullen. DuBois thought of establishing a literature prize in Chesnutt's name. Finally in 1927 DuBois was one of those who proposed Charles Chesnutt for the Spingarn award.[185]

---

180. "B. R. Tillman to the Editor of the Maryland Suffrage News," *Crisis*, January, 1915.

181. Ibid.

182. W. E. B. DuBois to Chesnutt, Sept. 16, 1924. CC, WRHS.

183. Chesnutt, "The Marked Tree," Part I, *Crisis*, 29 (December, 1924), 59-64; Part II, *Crisis*, 29 (January, 1925), 110-13. Chesnutt to W. E. B. DuBois, Sept. 16, 1924. CC, WRHS, Folder 4.

184. Herbert Aptheker, ed., *Correspondence of W. E. B. DuBois*, pp. 316-17, 343.

185. W. E. B. DuBois to John Hope, June 7, 1928, telegram sent to Morehouse College,

Sometimes the two agreed on goals or programs, but for different reasons. Both insisted on the vote—DuBois stressing that it would open opportunities such as higher education, but Chesnutt stressing a minimum protection of civil rights. They agreed on no temporizing with Southern injustice. DuBois seems first to have thought that scientific knowledge would lead to egalitarian laws and practice, then finally to have despaired and espoused communism. Chesnutt also despaired; but he came to believe there was no solution save the eventual submergence of racial characteristics through assimilation. DuBois had been a founder of the American Negro Academy, an organization committed to cultivating the "uniquely Negro" heritage of American blacks; despite a DuBois-inspired invitation, Chesnutt probably never joined because he foresaw amalgamation.[186] A sophisticated scholar and world traveler, DuBois approached the situation of the black people of the United States from the perspectives of world history and the Pan-African Movement of which he was a founder. Chesnutt developed an evolutionary view, and his knowledge of African history broadened as he grew older; but he approached American problems from the perspective of having lived in the United States as a black man who appeared white. The agreement of the two men was much less than complete; yet their respect for each other and their pride in each other's accomplishments were unstinting.

Atlanta, Library of Congress. W. E. B. DuBois to Chesnutt, Jan. 4, 1927. CC, Fisk. Chesnutt to DuBois, n.d., CC, Fisk, confirms the wedding invitation.

Arthur B. Springarn to Chesnutt, Feb. 29, 1928. CC, Fisk. When a testimonial was arranged to honor W. E. B. DuBois by purchasing and renovating his birthplace and presenting it to him, Chesnutt contributed $100.

186. Chesnutt to John Wesley Cromwell, Secretary, American Negro Academy, March 29, 1899. John Wesley Cromwell Papers; in possession of Adelaide Cromwell Gulliver, Boston University, Boston, Massachusetts.

AN AMERICAN CRUSADE

8

CODA TO THE
STORY OF A LIFE

Over Here

Chesnutt expressed his fears for a world in which "whole peoples stand ready to spring at one another's throats."[1] In 1914 rival nations did dissipate the accommodations that permitted commerce. Few wanted war; yet millions of men found themselves hurled at one another.

The war surprised Clevelanders. It seemed distant, almost irrelevant. Despite some forebodings, voters reelected Newton D. Baker mayor. Sharing the expectation that life would go on as it had gone on, he approved an Immigration Bureau for newcomers still pouring into Cleveland;[2] the city opened a bathhouse for them. Since the zoo also needed larger facilities, the city moved the animals to Brookside Park. The next year some women planned a Missionary Union for foreign conversions, although the Ohio National Guard opened a civilian Military Training School.[3] Others planned a Shakespearean Garden.[4]

In 1914 the Chesnutts purchased an automobile.[5] There were so many cars that the state set a speed limit of eight miles per hour for congested districts and fifteen miles per hour for residential sections. Soon a city ordinance required taillights for four-wheeled vehicles, the lawmakers thinking it prudent to include baby carriages.[6] These mea-

---

1. Chesnutt: "The Niagara Movement" (unpublished MS), 1908. CC, Fisk.

2. Rose, *Cleveland*, p. 721.

3. Avery, *A History of Cleveland and Its Environs*, vol. 2, pp. 486, 482, 621, 665.

4. Rose, *Cleveland*, p. 726.

5. H. Chesnutt, *Pioneer*, p. 263.

6. Rose, *Cleveland*, p. 721.

sures went out of date faster than the council could pass them. The automobile changed the locations of family living and the content of family thought. The Chesnutts bought dusters and gloves against the dusty roads and maps to follow them,[7] but they had enjoyed their car only a few months when an accident occurred. One dreary February afternoon Chesnutt took his family and a young guest for a drive. His car skidded on a wet hill, then crashed, killing the girl and injuring Susan. No one had anticipated such a tragedy.[8]

But whatever the private and public consequences, industrialists lunged into spirals of activity. Some were now war-oriented. Reflecting the achievements and aspirations of the people, the faces of the city grew more streamlined and geometric or else more convoluted and swollen. Officials condemned rows of elegant brick residences to make way for a gas company building. In the Public Square, workers replaced a lily fountain with a statue of Tom L. Johnson. Thenceforth there were Clevelanders who gathered about the figure for open-air protest meetings.[9]

The ancient Cuyahoga, once a clear, clean, winding river, had become a carrier for coal and iron products and a refuse receiver for factories and furnaces as quantities of dirty oil seeped over its banks. Clevelanders visited springs in outlying parks, for by 1915 the unfiltered water was so disagreeable that thousands preferred to carry fresh spring water to their homes. Policemen had to keep order at the sources.

Planners thought about a union terminal project to connect a system of local travel with a terminal and management complex. As reports of European atrocities increased, the struggle over the lakefront property broadened. The Pennsylvania Railroad, the New York Central Railroad, the state, the city, and other interests grappled for every inch.[10]

Despite preoccupations, it proved impossible to ignore the war. As nations vied for American good will, as Cleveland industries joined in supplying the combatants, people turned toward news from Europe. Industrialists and naval officers urged the defense of American shipping.

Chesnutt realized that military performance was important to restructuring the black image. While he was pouring his energies into writing *The Marrow of Tradition* in 1901, he had accepted the chairmanship of

---

7. H. Chesnutt, *Pioneer*, p. 273.

8. Ibid., p. 264. *Cleveland Gazette*, Feb. 27, 1915; James W. Russell to Chesnutt, March 11, 1915. CC, Fisk.

9. Rose, *Cleveland*, p. 729 and p. 726.

10. Ibid., pp. 727-30.

the Committee on Colored Troops for the 35th Encampment of the Grand Army of the Republic, a national commemorative assembly. That was a demanding job. He thought that Americans little appreciated the service Negro soldiers had rendered from the beginning of the Republic; he knew there was resistance, especially in the South, to allowing black people to possess military knowledge and to gain military prestige.

Once in 1916 he was discussing this with Harry E. Davis, another light-skinned Negro attorney. Davis had been a lieutenant of the Cleveland Company of the Ninth Battalion, Ohio National Guard. The Davis and Chesnutt families had long been friends who paid social calls at one another's homes, and who shared community interests. Davis told Chesnutt about his younger, light-skinned brother Russell H. Davis, who was attempting to enter a war-born program at Western Reserve. The University established a plan by which men could take courses for credit with military training. The authorities called the enterprise S.A.T.C., Student Army Training Corps. With Perry Jackson, another young man of some African lineage, later a well-known judge, Russell Davis, applied for admission. Though the dean suggested they would be more comfortable at Wilberforce, he told the young men they could register for classes. But he must exclude them from the army training program.

Chesnutt saw discrimination, and he telephoned his friend Charles F. Thwing, president of Western Reserve. "You take the boys in!" he said to President Thwing. Chesnutt pointed out that there had been many Negroes in the United States Army, if only because the Army had no knowledge of their origins. No regulation separated the races; this had been done by custom, and it was unconstitutional. Harry Davis suggested that Chesnutt see Newton D. Baker, who had been appointed Wilson's Secretary of War, for this was a national policy matter.[11]

Though no records show that Chesnutt conferred with Baker, Thwing and Chesnutt and Harry Davis arranged a conference in Washington with military personnel. Russell Davis remembers that Chesnutt told the Southern army officer that there were many men of some African lineage in the regular forces. The officer demurred. Chesnutt then said, "Well, what am I?"

"You are a white man," the officer replied. When Chesnutt informed him of the truth, the officer backtracked. Russell Davis recalls that he said, "Well, after we get old, we do look alike."

By the time this conference had taken place, four other young Afro-Americans had applied for the S.A.T.C. program at Western Reserve.

---

11. Chesnutt to Newton D. Baker, March 7, 1916. CC, Fisk, a letter of congratulation. Baker replied March 8, 1916. CC, Fisk.

The Southern officer took a chance. "I'll tell you what I'll do," he said. "I'll tell them I'm enlisting you; you enlisted and I'm taking you and housing you and you're living together and I'll leave the ruling up to them."

"The officer did just that and didn't ask," said Russell Davis. Two days later the officer received a telegram: "With reference to segregation your policy o.k."[12]

While the outcome was questionable, what they got was preferable to a refusal or segregation; the presence of the young men would affirm their right to enter any program.

As demands for preparedness increased, there was talk of raising the colored battalion of the Ohio National Guard to regiment size. In July 1916 Chesnutt apprised Baker of Adjutant General Hough's remark that "if the National Government would sanction it, he would give the colored men a regiment right away,... because the existing organization... deserves the increase."[13] Baker would only refer the suggestion to the Militia Bureau. He told Chesnutt that he hoped plans pursuant to new legislation would harmonize with the request, and that he "strongly favored opening up the military service as far as possible to colored men."[14]

In spring 1917 Chesnutt learned that the promulgators of *The Birth of a Nation* were undeterred by the disapproval of the Ohio Board of Censors. They had only waited for a new administration. When the movie passed, they scheduled it. Determined as ever to prevent such an attack, Chesnutt wrote to Munson R. Havens, secretary of the Cleveland Chamber of Commerce. Chesnutt analyzed the intent: the picture exploited the alleged misconduct of colored Union soldiers during Reconstruction; the villain, a would-be Negro rapist, was a captain in the Union Army. The picture glorified "that organization of traitors known as the Ku-Klux-Klan." As art, the movie was "a superb and impressive thing, and all the more vicious for that reason." To present it would be unwise "when all citizens should stand together to support the honor of the nation." Chesnutt pointed out that the purpose was to make money by stirring up race prejudice and race hatred." He summarized the truth about the performance of black men in military service:

---

12. Interview given by Russell H. Davis to Frances Richardson Keller, September 30, 1971, Cleveland.

13. Chesnutt to Newton D. Baker, July 24, 1916. CC, Fisk.

14. Newton D. Baker to Chesnutt, July 31, 1916. CC, Fisk.

There are already four colored regiments in the regular army with a military history in past wars of which they and the nation may well be proud. There are several complete regiments of colored militia, and battalions in several other states, and similar units proposed in other places.

Chesnutt asked the Chamber of Commerce to prevent the showing. Havens responded that he could only present the letter to the Chamber,[15] but he changed his mind after a committee of black men called on him. In a second letter of the same date he told Chesnutt he had telephoned the mayor's secretary and added a personal protest.[16] Cleveland banned *The Birth of a Nation*.

When the United States entered the war, Chesnutt thought, "we might have kept out of it, by some sacrifice of war profits . . . and some loss of self-respect and the respect of other nations." But political conditions relevant to the way Americans would live were at stake.[17]

When Chesnutt learned of the shoddy treatment of Negro soldiers in Southern training camps, he did what he could.[18] It was little enough. In other ways he supported the war effort—through planting a victory garden, through assisting in Liberty Bond sales, through participating in rallies. When churches were responding to the call for sweaters and trench candles for soldiers, Chesnutt spoke to the congregation of Cory Church. There the wonderful black preacher Hezipybah O'Connell damned society for segregation policies, recognizing at the same time that those policies would weld black people together. After Chesnutt's speech Pastor O'Connell raised his celebrated baritone voice to lead the singing of the war ditty "Over There."[19]

When the first company of Negro soldiers left Cleveland, Chesnutt addressed the recruits. We might have kept out, he said, "but we were confronted by a situation in which the freer and more democratic nations of Europe were in a death grip with an arrogant autocracy which was threatening to conquer and reduce them to vassalage." It might not

---

15. Chesnutt to Munson Havens, April 3, 1917. CC, Fisk.

16. Munson Havens to Chesnutt, April 4, 1917. CC, Fisk. There is a second letter from Havens to Chesnutt dated April 4, 1917. CC, Fisk.

17. Chesnutt, "Address to Colored Soldiers Leaving Cleveland" (unpublished MS), 1917. CC, Fisk.

18. Chesnutt to Capt. William R. Green, Nov. 24, 1917. Quoted in H. Chesnutt, *Pioneer*, pp. 275-76.

19. Interview given by Rowena and Russell Jelliffe to Frances Richardson Keller, Feb. 27, 1972, Cleveland.

have been our concern if the German people had been willing to live under such a government. "But when they attempted to force it on the whole world, with threats directed even to America," it was clear that democracy depended on the destruction of that menace.

"Any man who suggests a doubt as to the fighting qualities of the Negro brands himself as ignorant of history," Chesnutt said. The soldiers were going into war as "colored troops." "There are some of us," he said, "who would like to see you fighting in the regiments with white men, side by side. It would be a better example of the democracy for which we are fighting." But there were compensations: "any gallant deeds they may perform will be credited to them . . . and [credit] can not be stolen by some white man." Chesnutt noticed that the Germans criticized the French and the English for bringing black men to Europe to fight white men. He scoffed that such a criticism could come from

men who torpedo peaceful merchant vessels and leave their crews to drown, men who have left Belgium like a sucked orange, who have bombed peaceful civilian populations, and slaughtered women and children, and who have preached and practiced the doctrine of ruthless frightfulness.

Chesnutt thought the reason for the objection was that black men were such fearless fighters that the Germans were afraid to face them.[20]

Chesnutt never accepted a less-than-equal status, but he would fight for improvement. When the government refused to train black officers in regular programs, he worked for an officer training program for black men. Emmett J. Scott, Special Assistant to the Secretary of War,[21] and Colonel Joel E. Spingarn insisted on black officers, even though they were denied equal status. For this Scott and Spingarn drew wide criticism among Negroes; but Chesnutt defended them. Years later he wrote to Spingarn: "It was not the ideal thing, of course, but it was the best that could be done."[22]

It angered Chesnutt that flagrant discrimination existed in all services from the beginning to the end of the war, and that there was no hesitation in exploiting the brave black soldiers of American forces overseas.

---

20. Chesnutt, "Address to Colored Soldiers," p. 3. See also pp. 11-12.

21. Emmett J. Scott was secretary to Booker Washington, who died in 1915; Scott then became special adviser to the Secretary of War.

22. Franklin, *From Slavery to Freedom,* pp. 449-50. Chesnutt to J. E. Spingarn, Jan. 15, 1931. CC, WRHS, Container 1, Folder 6.

To Idlewild in Michigan

Movements from farm to city, from East to West and from South to North accompanied the advance of industry in the 1920s. There was a backlog of demand—for women's garments, for automobiles, for machines and tools, for home furnishings, for an ever-increasing flow of oil and electricity. There was a nostalgia for a normalcy that never was, at the same time that there was a yearning for a consumer heaven. People felt dislocated and anxious as the cost of living soared. But the stock market also rose, and lists of subscribers to brokers' services lengthened. Installment buying became routine; the centers of social gravity shifted away from the home and the church and the family.

New words came into the language; through them symbols of self and society spoke for a groping generation. Flappers appeared. They bobbed their hair. They danced the Charleston. They smoked. They rode in rumble seats and played in speakeasies. Hemlines went up, waistlines went down, and Louis Armstrong and Duke Ellington and Paul Whiteman made jazz the rage. In Harlem the black intellectuals embarked on a quest, bringing forth a "renaissance" of the literary spirit.[23]

Though he felt uncomfortable with the trappings of the twenties, Charles Chesnutt took notice of the changing social climate. He remained active and interested in the facets of American life in which he had taken part. In 1923 the *Cleveland Topics* printed an editorial approving the separation of students at Harvard; Chesnutt expressed disappointment to editor Charles T. Henderson:

If this utterance had emanated from a Florida "Cracker" or a Georgia "red neck," or even an Alabama senator, I should not have been surprised; but from a man brought up in Cleveland, educated in its public schools where he went to school with colored children, and with a mother such as yours, who was widely known as a generous and broadminded woman, who to my personal knowledge has eaten in public with colored people, it came as a surprise, to say the least.

I really cannot understand the basis of your emotional turmoil.[24]

Ill health plagued Chesnutt from time to time. He often needed to rest. He had to remember his doctor's admonition, delivered after he

---

23. See Frances Richardson Keller, "The Harlem Literary Renaissance," *North American Review*, June, 1968.

24. Chesnutt to Charles T. Henderson, April 20, 1923. Quoted in H. Chesnutt, *Pioneer*, pp. 293-94. Chesnutt to Roscoe C. Bruce, Feb. 23, 1923. CC, WRHS, Container 1, Folder 3. Chesnutt evidently wrote earlier to Roscoe Conkling Bruce about the Harvard policy.

suffered the stroke in 1910, that he must live less strenuously. In 1920 appendicitis flared up; peritonitis set in so that he was again "laid up for several months." From that time he was never quite free of digestive difficulties.[25]

But he had been fortunate in 1918 to find a competent partner. She was Helen C. Moore, a white woman, an excellent stenographer and office manager, to whom Chesnutt could entrust his business. In the 1920s a court stenographer earned $18 a day, but by the 30s the rate had gone up to $10 an hour. As time went on, Chesnutt changed his office location again, and he changed the name of the firm to Chesnutt & Moore—though he kept the custom of serving tea at four to staff and callers.[26] When his hearing became impaired in the latter part of the anxious decade, he gave up the reporting in which for so long he had set so high a standard. Because of Helen Moore's competence, Chesnutt could depend on a good income through the twenties. He invested in real estate and in the stock market.[27] He and his family were able to travel to Europe and to the American West; he and they spent summers at Idlewild in Michigan.

Idlewild was a resort located about 350 miles north and west of Cleveland and only a little distance from Baldwin, Michigan. It comprised an area surrounding a beach and a clubhouse on an island and including three clear deep lakes. Vacationers drove over the sandy roads and through the tall, sweet-scented pines, where lightning storms could crack the thunder out but where waxen Indian pipes and huckleberries and pink clusters of trailing arbutus grew. Idlewild was a gathering place of well-to-do families; most summer inhabitants were Negroes from Chicago, Detroit, and Cleveland, who sought the clear sparkling mornings and the bracing air of the northern Michigan midsummer nights.

Susan discovered Idlewild. After they had rented a cottage for a season, the Chesnutts began to think about buying a place. But they decided to build. People of all ages loved Idlewild for the excellent fishing,

25.   Chesnutt to H. C. Tyson, Nov. 22, 1922. CC, WRHS.

26.   H. Chesnutt, Pioneer, pp. 297-98.

27.   Helen C. Moore to Chesnutt, Aug. 29, 1921. CC, WRHS, Container 1, Folder 4. See Chesnutt to Carl Van Vechten, March 25, 1931, Collection of American Literature, Beineke Rare Book and Manuscript Library, Yale University, by permission of Donald Gallup, Literary Trustee; Chesnutt to Joseph Banton, April 22, 1924. CC, WRHS, Container 1, Folder 4. In the letter to Banton, Chesnutt enclosed a check for $700 for the purchase of lots in Idlewild, Michigan. Chesnutt invested in other real estate, as indicated in Chesnutt to Marie Henderson, March 20, 1924, CC, WRHS, Container 1, Folder 4, and several other letters between Chesnutt and Marie Henderson. See The Mutual Mortgage Company to Chesnutt, Jan. 1, 1922. CC, WRHS.

boating, and swimming, the fine food at the island clubhouse, the lazy days, the log fires for summer evenings, the dancing over the water's edge.

Until the end of his life Chesnutt loved this place. Once he wrote to a young girl about it. Anne Joyce Cassidy, the only daughter of a friend, became ill. He told Anne that he had gone through an operation for appendicitis: "You must not be discouraged or downhearted," he wrote. "I was an old man and I got over it, and you are—you must be by this time—a young woman." Chesnutt remembered how Anne had come to his office and danced for him when she was small.

Last summer [he wrote] I spent my vacation at a summer resort, and every night I would go up to the Clubhouse where there was a good band and dancing floor, and dance the whole program through to the Home Waltz. I danced only with the young and good looking girls, and if you had been there and had favored me I suspect you would have been the leader of the bunch.

I hope you will get nicely over your illness and be in a position to enjoy the good things to which your youth entitles you.[28]

But Chesnutt's "dear little friend Anne" never saw Idlewild; a few days after he wrote to her, she died.

On Haiti and Dependence

Predictably, Chesnutt had a feeling for the repercusions of American acts abroad on the fortunes of black people. He grew more knowledgeable. He disapproved of United States domination of Cuba after the Spanish War;[29] he began to inform himself about African peoples[30] and about South American nations, particularly Brazil; he expressed fears of world conflict years before the outbreak of hostilities in Europe.[31]

When the war was over, Chesnutt saw no justification for American intervention in Haiti; he worked to terminate it. In February 1922 when United States troops occupied Haiti he signed a brief written by Ernest Angell.[32] Angell, a lawyer formerly associated with Squire, Sanders, and

---

28. Chesnutt to Anne Joyce Cassidy, May 12, 1923. CC, WRHS, Container 1, Folder 3.

29. Chesnutt's attitude changed as his knowledge broadened. He disapproved all Latin American domination by the United States.

30. Chesnutt to Thomas Jesse Jones, Oct. 5, 1923. CC, WRHS, Container 1, Folder 3.

31. Chesnutt, "The Niagara Movement," a speech delivered in 1908 at Oberlin.

32. Walter L. Flory to Chesnutt, Feb. 28, 1922. CC, WRHS, Container 1, Folder 2.

Dempsey of Cleveland, was now acting as attorney for Santo Domingo. The brief was to go out over the signature of Moorfield Storey, former President of the American Bar Association. They intended to marshal support for the King Resolution for United States withdrawal. Walter L. Flory, a Cleveland lawyer, quoted Angell's letter about the brief: "Mr. Storey has signed it, as have Frankfurter and Chafee of the Harvard Law School, Adelbert Moor of Buffalo and some others here in New York."[33]

Chesnutt signed the brief "very willingly indeed, my only regret being that my name cannot add greater weight."[34] He secured the signature of Judge F. A. Henry, former judge of the Court of Appeals of Ohio; he spoke to others but found some unwilling because "they think it would be disloyal to suggest that the United States Government could do anything wrong." But Chesnutt believed that "The United States ought to be able to help the Haitians out of the rut without entirely depriving them of their hard-earned and long maintained independence."[35]

Angell needed Chesnutt's support. Senator Pomerene, of the Senate Committee investigating the Haitian question, was the political opponent of Senator Frank B. Willis of Ohio; Willis could count on the black vote as Pomerene could not. Angell was perfectly willing to use this.[36]

Chesnutt was eager to cooperate. A group was to present the brief to Secretary of State Charles Evans Hughes on April 27, 1922. There would be a delegation representing substantial conservative organizations. So Angell asked Chesnutt to approach Senator Willis and to bring pressures of the black community to bear:

You could demand that [Willis] support the three resolutions . . . for withdrawal of our forces from Haiti and Santo Domingo, for opposition to any loan to Haiti at the present time (the present proposed loan would subject Haitian finances and indirectly the Haitian Government to complete control by the United States for the next thirty or forty years) and finally, provide the practical means for the withdrawal of the American forces, the restitution of a genuine native re-constituted Haitian Government.[37]

---

33. Walter L. Flory to Chesnutt, Feb. 28, 1922. CC, WRHS, Container 1, Folder 2.

34. Chesnutt to Ernest Angell, March 18, 1922. CC, WRHS, Container 1, Folder 2.

35. Ibid.

36. Ernest Angell to Chesnutt, March 20, 1922. CC, WRHS, Container 1, Folder 2.

37. Ernest Angell to Chestnutt [sic], March 18, 1922. CC, WRHS, Container 1, Folder 2.

Chesnutt did bring pressures to bear on Willis, and he persuaded George P. Hinton, president of the Caterers' Association, and Harry C. Smith, editor of the *Cleveland Gazette,* to do so.[38] But the effort was insufficient to prevent the exploitation of the Haitian peasantry and the many years of United States control over Haitian assets that Angell had feared.[39]

Reflections

During the twenties Chesnutt corresponded with old friends, and he mused, sometimes, on well-remembered events. Some letters he sent and received are unexplained. But they are no longer altogether mysterious. In 1924 he was in touch with J. D. Wetmore, an attorney of New York City.[40]

It would seem that the two felt an intimacy not apparent in any other correspondence. Wetmore visited in the Chesnutt home; Chesnutt visited Wetmore's home in New York. Wetmore sometimes wrote in a jocular tone suggesting long familiarity; sometimes he described devastating family and racial problems.[41] It appears that Wetmore lived as a white man. He married a white woman and practiced law in the white community. He had a beautiful daughter who learned of her Negro heritage at eighteen when her parents became estranged. The unfolding of these events suggests some of the Chesnutt stories. An observer must wonder whether J. D. Wetmore was a member of Chesnutt's family of whom he kept track for many years. About a year after the stock market crash, Wetmore committed suicide. Chesnutt sent a letter to be forwarded to the widow.[42]

Chesnutt never ceased to support the organizations he approved. He made efforts to put the Dyer Anti-Lynching Bill through Congress;[43] he was one of the first and most faithful adherents of the *Journal of Negro History,* for he believed this journal would be a testament of creative

---

38.   Chesnutt to George P. Hinton and Chesnutt to Harry C. Smith, both dated May 6, 1922. CC, WRHS.

39.   Chesnutt to Rev. Bailey, May 6, 1922; Frank B. Willis to Chesnutt, May 8, 1922; H. C. Bailey to Frank B. Willis, May 17, 1922. All in CC, WRHS, Container 1, Folder 2.

40.   J. D. Wetmore to Chesnutt, Dec. 2, 1924. CC, WRHS.

41.   J. D. Wetmore to Chesnutt, Aug. 29, 1924. CC, WRHS, Container 1, Folder 4.

42.   Chesnutt to Herman N. Schwartz, Aug. 1, 1930. CC, WRHS.

43.   Harry C. Gahn to Chesnutt, March 3, 1921, and T. E. Burton to Chesnutt, March 3, 1921. CC, WRHS.

thought and of achievement.[44] He was generous with contributions to every worthy black cause; there are many letters in several collections which either solicit or appreciate his interest. Many mention substantial contributions.

Chesnutt corresponded with figures new on his horizon. He wrote to and received letters from men and women he never met and from others he met only after mutual efforts. John R. Lynch, the dynamic black congressman of Mississippi, regretted "that I did not have the extreme pleasure of meeting you in person on the occasion of your recent visit."[45]

Chesnutt corresponded with Benjamin G. Brawley, historian of the Negro in literature and art. Chesnutt congratulated Brawley, for Brawley's work gave evidence of "a tremendous amount of erudition and research," and of "the very high quality of your intellect." But he said:

There are some conclusions in "The Social History of the American Negro" which I perhaps would not have arrived at, but it is a real historical document, absolutely without rancor (where so much could be excused), and with no more bias than should naturally be expected from a friendly advocate.[46]

Chesnutt and Brawley probably never got together, nor did Chesnutt meet Clarence Darrow, though both hoped for a meeting. Chesnutt once made a point of calling on Carl Van Vechten; through the later years of the twenties they corresponded.[47]

Chesnutt still had dealings with business interests; he sold serial rights to *The House Behind the Cedars* to the *Chicago Defender;* he sold movie rights to the Micheaux film corporation, a black business enterprise.[48] Micheaux wanted to film Rena's story, but they would educate the faithful Frank and finally marry Rena to him.[49] Chesnutt sent their

---

44. Carter G. Woodson to Chesnutt, Feb. 26, 1923. CC, WRHS. This is one of several letters that attest Chesnutt's connections with the *Journal of Negro History.*

45. John R. Lynch to Chesnutt, Sept. 2, 1918. CC, Fisk.

46. Chesnutt to Benjamin G. Brawley, March 24, 1922. Moorland-Spingarn Collection, Howard University, Washington, D.C. Benjamin Brawley to Chesnutt, Aug. 26, 1921. CC, WRHS.

47. Chesnutt to Van Vechten, Nov. 19, 1926, and Jan. 12, 1927, and Feb. 23, 1926. Collection of American Literature, Beineke Rare Book and Manuscript Library, Yale University, by permission of Donald Gallup, Literary Executor.

48. Chesnutt to Mr. Pratt of Houghton Mifflin & Company, Sept. 19, 1921. CC, WRHS.

49. Oscar Micheaux to Chesnutt, Jan. 18, 1921. CC, WRHS.

portion of the small amounts he received from Micheaux to Houghton Mifflin.[50]

But Chesnutt felt the sadness of growing older when Houghton Mifflin wrote in August 1924 that unless he wanted to buy the plates for *The Wife of His Youth* and *The House Behind the Cedars*, they would be glad to hear that he had "no objection to our disposing of them with others of our books which we are sending to the melting pot."[51] Chesnutt replied:

I have your unwelcome letter of April 28th, with reference to killing beyond hope of resuscitation my two books, THE WIFE OF HIS YOUTH, and THE HOUSE BEHIND THE CEDARS. I appreciate your attitude in the matter, but the books have had a rather long life, I imagine, for novels of minor importance, by a writer who has neglected to keep himself in the public eye.[52]

For how much would they sell the plates? Houghton Mifflin replied that Chesnutt could have them for $100: "We presume you are aware that these are very heavy, though they would not occupy any very great amount of space," they wrote.[53]

Despite his deteriorating health the later years of the twenties brought Chesnutt involvement in society as well as personal concerns. Late in 1927 he and Susan took Helen to the hospital for a ruptured appendix. Peritonitis followed; many months passed before Helen was well. Upon learning of the death of the daughter of Dr. and Mrs. Emmett J. Scott, Chesnutt wrote a feeling letter:

We only learned some little time after the event of the death of your beautiful and talented daughter, Clarissa, and we were just about to write to you when our minds were sidetracked by what came near being the same thing in our family.[54]

---

50. Chesnutt to Houghton Mifflin & Company, Jan. 24, 1921. CC, WRHS.

51. Houghton Mifflin & Company to Chesnutt, April 28, 1924. Houghton Library, Harvard University. Cited from the Reserve Collection by special permission of Houghton Mifflin & Company.

52. Chesnutt to Houghton Mifflin & Company, May 23, 1924. Houghton Library, Harvard University. Cited from the Reserve Collection by special permission of Houghton Mifflin & Company.

53. Houghton Mifflin & Company to Chesnutt. Houghton Library, Harvard University. Cited from the Reserve Collection by special permission of Houghton Mifflin & Company.

54. Chesnutt to Emmett Scott, Nov. 22, 1927. CC, Fisk.

Threescore and Ten

The year 1928 was a high point in Chesnutt's life and career. He marked the fiftieth anniversary of his wedding on June 6, and on June 20 his seventieth birthday. Charles and Susan had intended to celebrate their half-century of marriage "in the conventional way," but Helen's forced absence from home prevented this. But he observed that "fifty years is a long time for two people to live together," and that he was sure his wife was "a woman of great patience and endurance to have put up with me so long."[55] To another friend, who sent roses, Chesnutt wrote:

I can imagine marriages where fifty years would seem like an eternity, but except when I look at my children and see my gray hairs in the mirror, it doesn't seem any time at all, and Mrs. Chesnutt admits that she hasn't found it very tiresome; and we are both willing to hang on a while longer yet.[56]

But two days after the marriage anniversary, news of a crowning event came from a particular friend, the executive secretary of the National Association for the Advancement of Colored People; James Weldon Johnson wired that in Los Angeles, on July 3, 1928, the Spingarn Award Committee of the NAACP would confer on Charles Chesnutt the highest recognition his peers could bestow.[57] Though Chesnutt was growing more frail and though he tired easily, his spirit was jubilant; he and Susan happily planned the trip to the Coast.[58]

Telephone calls and letters of congratulation poured into the Lamont Avenue residence. There were many articles. H. C. Smith, editor of the Cleveland *Gazette*, thought it "most encouraging" that Chesnutt's achievements were recognized by "his own people." He couldn't resist a "P.S.": "Don't you think our portrait of you was much better than the *Plain Dealer's?*"[59] Alain Locke, editor of *The New Negro,* wrote: "Please accept my heartiest congratulations upon the Spingarn award. It should long ago [have] been given you. The medal gains lagging prestige in this year's award."[60] The novelist Jesse Fauset was pleased with the for-

---

55. Chesnutt to Frieda Fliedner, June 8, 1928. CC, Fisk.

56. Chesnutt to Alta M. Bien, June 8, 1928. CC, Fisk.

57. James Weldon Johnson to Chesnutt, June 8, 1928. CC, Fisk, a telegram.

58. Despite health problems, Chesnutt wrote that his health was reasonably good, though he was growing old. Chesnutt to Mrs. F. C. Jones, June 14, 1928. CC, Fisk.

59. H. C. Smith to Chesnutt, June 19, 1928. CC, Fisk.

60. Alain Locke to Chesnutt, June 16, 1928. CC, Fisk.

mal recognition of Chesnutt's services to American literature.[61] Carl Van Vechten wrote to Chesnutt, and he telegraphed the award committee: "It is my contention that the Spingarn Medal committee has covered itself with glory!"[62] David Gibson, a Cleveland business man, wrote his "Dear old friend":

I know of no one who has accomplished more in a specific condition than yourself—not only by precept but example.

You have lived, reared and educated a fine family, done your work not only to this last specific end, but added to a broader human understanding that will permit future generations to do like wise with more ease and happiness.[63]

Chesnutt enjoyed the accolades and the trip to the Coast. When he returned, he worked on a novel, *The Quarry;* before the year was out he had sent it to Knopf, the publisher.[64]

Despite his failing health, despite the crash that climaxed the anxious decade, Chesnutt went to his office. He wrote, and he took part in public affairs. But he felt pressures, and he sustained losses. R. B. Pettit of the Union Trust Company told Chesnutt he was obliged to require additional collateral or an immediate payment of $1,000 on Chesnutt's loan of $18,500.[65] Helen Moore, Chesnutt's good friend and office associate, who managed everything now, wrote a little good news: a street car ride was "two cents on the Euclid Line," and Miller's Restaurant served coffee for five cents.[66]

At election time Chesnutt told Walter White that colored people owed the Hoover administration nothing; it had made entirely insufficient efforts.[67] Chesnutt had changed some political positions. In 1930 he had been unable to vote for a Democrat for senator because he would have had to change his affiliation. "While it [the Republican Party] is a rotten party," he told the candidate Robert Bulkley, "I have not been able to

61. Jesse Fauset to Chesnutt, Sept. 3, 1928. CC, Fisk.

62. Carl Van Vechten to Chesnutt, June 30, 1928. CC, Fisk. Chesnutt to Carl Van Vechten, Sept. 6, 1928. Collection of American Literature, Beineke Rare Book and Manuscript Library, Yale University, by permission of Donald Gallup, Literary Executor.

63. David Gibson to Chesnutt, Aug. 27, 1928. CC, Fisk.

64. Chesnutt to James Weldon Johnson, Dec. 28, 1928. CC, Fisk.

65. R. B. Pettit to Chesnutt, May 5, 1930. CC, WRHS, Container 1, Folder 5.

66. Helen C. Moore to Chesnutt, Aug. 15, 1930. CC, WRHS, Container 1, Folder 5.

67. Chesnutt to Walter White, Sept. 6, 1930. CC, WRHS, Container 1, Folder 5.

convince myself that the Democratic Party is any less putrid." But he was sure many black voters would support Bulkley, and he would vote for him.[68]

In that election month of November 1930, the *Clevelander* published a Chesnutt article, "The Negro in Cleveland." It bore a misleading out-of-context caption: ". . . race problem . . . not acute." But everything in the article reflected dissatisfaction. Chesnutt noted that most desirable neighborhoods were resistant to Negroes, that "Negroes as a class live on a low economic plane," that "many unions, including most of the railroad unions, exclude Negroes. . . . The reaction to the barrier of segregation which confronts the Negro almost everywhere has resulted, in Cleveland, as elsewhere, in the effort to supply among his own people many of the opportunities which he is denied. . . . The greatest handicap which the Negro in Cleveland, as elsewhere, has to meet is his color, which he cannot change, and the consequences of which he cannot escape."

[Negroes] still have a long and hard road to travel to reach that democratic equality upon the theory of which our government and our social system are founded, not to desire and seek which would make them unworthy of contempt.[69]

Chesnutt Measures a Man

Who has not seen cities that, possessing earth and air and waters, cacophonously seek the skies? Chesnutt drove over the asphalt pavement spanning the old valley and stretching across the banks of the crooked Cuyahoga.

Above a forest of smokestacks, water towers, and drawbridges laced at the sides with metal triangles and poised in uneasy dominance rose an ancient eastern tan-brick structure; here and there were spires of European origin, begrimed, benighted, fixed among blackened buildings, yet bearing a strained relation to clumps of workers' houses—dingy outcrops that looked as if they had been turned into the ground.

Chesnutt considered all that he saw, and he wrote to his friend in the cold December of 1930 that "Cleveland conditions are reflected in almost every city of the country" and that "many of the same conditions

---

68. Chesnutt to Robert Bulkley, Aug. 25, 1930. CC, WRHS, Container 1, Folder 5. Helen Moore had written Chesnutt on August 15, 1930 (CC, WRHS, Container 1, Folder 5), saying she hoped they would get some of Bulkley's campaign work and that "he's a fine man besides being one of our best customers."

69. Chesnutt, "The Negro in Cleveland," *The Clevelander*, November, 1930, p. 2.

exist in other parts of the world."[70] Serbs, Slovenians, Italians, Poles, English, Orientals, Turks, Hungarians, Irish, Negroes—this was where they lived. Chesnutt saw a river the color of all the rest, its serpentine course almost indistinguishable from air and smoke and humans and structures. As he drove north, he caught no glimpse of the great gray lake he knew was paces away from the moving cars.

Though he was unable to escape the hard realities of the thirties,[71] in either a personal or a social sense, Chesnutt experienced satisfactions; he heard from his grandson, Charles W. C. Williams, that he would become a great-grandfather. He expressed his feelings for Susan's devotion during his illnesses to W. P. Dabney: "A more loyal and devoted wife no man ever had, and I've got my job cut out for the rest of my life to make her feel how much I appreciate her devotion."[72]

He had passed threescore and ten. Chesnutt went about slowly and carefully, and he often felt less well than he could wish. But he worked on his writing and he stopped by the office. Hearing was somewhat difficult, but he could see and read, and he could think well.

Nine months before he died, Chesnutt received a letter from Walter White, executive secretary of the NAACP. White asked his help on a matter of importance to black people and to the American nation: Had Chesnutt noted that among those mentioned as a successor to Mr. Justice Oliver Wendell Holmes on the Supreme Court of the United States was "your fellow townsman and friend, Newton D. Baker"? The NAACP was in a position to bring pressure to bear upon the appointment; White told Chesnutt that "naturally, we are checking up very carefully on the record of every person mentioned." Because of "an intimate acquaintanceship with him," would Chesnutt give a detailed picture of Baker's attitude on the race question? White would hold Chesnutt's reply in confidence. "Among the other things we ought to watch in Baker's record is that he does believe in residential segregation and, if I remember correctly, signed a pamphlet as a member of the 'Shaker Heights Protective Association.'" White wanted an opinion "as detailed and as full as you feel it ought to be."[73]

70. Chesnutt to Sidney B. Thompson, Dec. 5, 1930. CC, WRHS, Container 1, Folder 5.

71. Chesnutt to Carl Van Vechten, March 25, 1931. Collection of American Literature, Beineke Rare Book and Manuscript Library, Yale University, by permission of Donald Gallup, Literary Executor.

72. Chesnutt to W. P. Dabney, Oct. 13, 1931. CC, WRHS, Container 1, Folder 6.

73. Walter White to Chesnutt, Feb. 2, 1932. CC, WRHS, Container 1, Folder 6.

A week and a day later Chesnutt sent a thoughtful three-page reply, which was a factor in preventing the name of Newton D. Baker from coming to further consideration.

Chesnutt apologized for the delay; he had been ill, but also it was difficult to reply. Chesnutt realized the importance of what he would say. Beyond question he most wanted to give wise counsel on an appointment to the Supreme Court. He said that Baker was an excellent lawyer and a fine gentleman. His relations with Baker had always been cordial. "But Mr. Baker is a Southerner, with all that the word even at its best implies."

In saying this, I am not unmindful of the fact that the late Justice White was a Southerner, to say nothing of Justice Harlan, both of whom, especially the latter, never to my knowledge let the matter of race becloud their judgment or color their decisions.

Chesnutt had often discussed the race problem with Baker, but had only recently felt critical. "He is a clever advocate," Chesnutt thought. While Baker would not "consciously seek to make the worse appear the better part," Chesnutt perceived that Baker could "make whatever side he takes on a controverted subject seem right."

Chesnutt told White that Baker admitted signing the agreement of the Shaker Heights Protection Association. Baker's reason was that practically all he would leave to his wife and children would be his residence, and that the value would go down by half if he were to have a colored neighbor. This was "probably true enough, I am sorry to say." Chesnutt had insisted that the owner's agreement was an evasion which the Supreme Court could not tolerate—but Baker had "frankly disagreed with me and said he thought they would sustain it." Chesnutt would leave it to White "whether or not Mr. Baker would be a sound man to pass on a case involving such a question."

Chesnutt recalled another discussion. Baker had said about a Chicago mayoralty race that William Thompson used the ignorance of thirty or forty thousand Negro voters to defeat his opponent Deneen, the better man. Chesnutt's friend, the late George A. Myers, took the matter up with Baker, and suggested that Thompson would have been elected without the black vote, and that there had been no need to mislead black voters. Chesnutt said that several letters went back and forth between Baker and Myers. They would be interesting.

Moreover, Chesnutt had recently talked with Baker about a solution to the race question, and Chesnutt had suggested the amalgamation of the races.

276

Mr. Baker said that was absurd, unthinkable, and he said it in a tone of voice and with a flash of the eye, which seemed to class it as akin to incest or sexual perversion. Of course, he probably reflected the opinion of ninety-nine white people out of a hundred, but in the event of a general law forbidding the intermarriage of the races, which is always possible, I again leave to you whether it would be safe to have the question decided by a judge with such a preconceived opinion.

But Chesnutt repeated that it had been difficult to write about Baker, "a man to whom I am indebted for many business favors."[74] As always Chesnutt had placed the interest of his race above any other consideration. This was the last far-reaching act of his public life.

Perspectives

Chesnutt never recovered from the illness he mentioned to Walter White; it was an illness brought on by arteriosclerosis complicated by hypertension.[75] But on and off he read, he wrote, he saw his family. He even looked in at his office until a few days before his death. One day he came home feeling exhausted and saying that he would go to bed. A week later at 5:30 on the afternoon of November 15, 1932, he died in the city where he was born, and where for a half a century he lived vibrantly.[76]

Charles Waddell Chesnutt was an ambitious man in a worldly sense. He wanted to live pleasantly, he appreciated fine surroundings, he liked luxuries. He desired social acceptance in the world as it was—and he got it. At twenty-three he set down his reasons for leaving Fayetteville: "It is not altogether the money," he wrote. "It is a mixture of motives. I want fame, I want money, and I want to raise my children in a different rank of life from that I sprang from."[77] Yet in achieving these ends, Chesnutt never deprived or misused others. While he was overcoming the limitations of his rural beginnings and growing to national stature, he helped those whose lives touched his life.

---

74. Chesnutt to Walter White, Feb. 10, 1932. CC, WRHS.

75. In addition to "Arteriosclerosis" and "Hypertension," the certificate of death (dated 11-17, 1932) mentions "hypertrophied prostate," and, as "contributory causes of importance not related to principal causes," "herpes zoster" and "toxemia." State of Ohio, Department of Health, Division of Vital Statistics, Cleveland.

76. The certificate of death states that Chesnutt's last day of work was November 1, 1932. Remarks of Rev. Andrew S. Gill, Pastor of Emmanuel Episcopal Church, at Chesnutt's funeral are held at the Cleveland Public Library.

77. Chesnutt, Journal 2, March 26, 1881. CC, Fisk.

What can be said of a man who preserved carefully every scrap of paper on which he ever wrote a word, who kept copies of every letter he sent—and sometimes copies of several drafts of letters—who kept a vast store of letters and communications people sent to him, who kept every word written about him that he could lay hands on, and who did all this from the time he was sixteen until he died at seventy-four? Such a man was ambitious in a personal sense. He wanted posterity to remember him; he made plans about it in his early twenties. He even thought about the person who might write his biography. It occurred to him before he had done the work of his life that he would seem "conceited" to that prospective biographer—unless, happily, he drew a sensitive, understanding person "of excellent taste and literary judgment." It is amusing that this attempt to woo posterity proved effective; at the least Chesnutt can lure historians, who have never been resistant to records or indifferent to flattering views of their taste and literary judgment. Chesnutt strove to achieve a place in history. Beyond doubt he merits a place: he was an artistic innovator and an articulate, tireless proponent of the not-so-new "new" militancy; he defined a third posture toward racial injustice, by his activities suggesting outlines of a legal and educational program.

Some have speculated why Chesnutt stopped writing novels. He was a good writer, praised by critics, a creator who combined stories with social history to pioneer a distinctive genre of American literature. The truth is that he was still attempting novels and still writing fine short fiction almost until he died. But he had run into a conflict insoluble in fiction. Long before, he had realized that his novels would fail to produce the results he wanted. He desired those results more than he desired to write novels. He was less interested in literature as art than in literature as a means of attaining social justice. Nevertheless, he merits literary recognition as a superlative writer of short fiction.

Few have realized what an excellent expository protagonist for the black race Chesnutt became. He wrote a biography, letters, and many reviews, speeches, articles, and essays, all fearlessly conceived and skillfully executed, and he did this at the highest tide of American racial antagonism. His expository writings remain models for a militant age. Insisting on the immediate rights of all persons, he mounted formidable campaigns against tyranny. they are examples fit to stand for people of all times. Even though Chesnutt continued these attacks to the end of his days, and even though he came to consider confrontation imperative, we cannot measure his stature by his writings. Chesnutt's writing was of secondary importance to him. What was of first importance was achieving a society where standards of humanity would prevail over standards of color. This was his project.

To accomplish it he used every resource. He made appearances in Cleveland. He undertook lecture tours, speaking to students, church groups, clubs, and civic and political organizations in other parts of the country. He tried to exert influence on institutions, on Congressmen, on the President. He appeared before congressional committees, he worked behind the scenes, he cooperated with people of both races. He gave encouragement to other writers and to politicians of merit in his eyes; he applied pressures to the laggards. He prevented several racial attacks. He joined and worked for organizations geared toward the achievement of racial justice. He served on many boards. He sought accommodations among black leaders so that they would work together effectively. He contributed his time, his talent, and his energy; to more than a dozen black organizations he regularly contributed substantial amounts of money; for many years they depended upon him. He tried to do in his public life what he could not do in his novels, where he concerned himself with the emotional situations of his characters and his readers.

Chesnutt's life was tragic, for he found no way to accomplish what he wanted to do. He saw defeat and he knew despair. His life was triumphant, for he never gave up; he lived creatively, considerately, outgoingly, knowledgeably, yet believingly. Almost alone, he lived toward his vision of brotherhood.

AN AMERICAN
CRUSADE

EPILOGUE

$\mathcal{T}$he struggle for racial justice continues and the community in which Charles Chesnutt lived has recognized his efforts toward human understanding: The citizens of Cleveland have named a street and a school for him. Recently they inscribed his name in the Cleveland Hall of Fame of the Western Reserve Historical Society.

AN AMERICAN
CRUSADE

BIBLIOGRAPHICAL NOTE

harles Waddell Chesnutt preserved an enormous amount of written material from the time he was sixteen until he died at seventy-four in 1932.

His daughter Helen wrote the first biography, a collection of journal entries and letters to and from her father, to which she added comments and recollections. When Helen Chesnutt published her book in 1952, she made a presentation of her father's papers and effects to Fisk University; but many letters that appear in her book were not included in the gift to Fisk.

Some substantial differences exist between the letters reproduced in Helen Chesnutt's biography and the letters signed and sent by Chesnutt that are held in other collections. This is noticeable in letters sent to Booker T. Washington (held in the Library of Congress), and it is conspicuous in letters sent to George Cable (held at Tulane University). Journal entries reproduced in Ms. Chesnutt's book differ occasionally from the handwritten journals she gave to Fisk. The effect of the letter variations and the journal omissions is often to obscure the meaning or to change the mood to something milder.

These differences could result from deliberate editing, or they could result from error and oversight, or from both. In her acknowledgments Helen Chesnutt stated that many papers were "yellowed, faded and very brittle," and that copying them "took several years and many typists worked at it." Some discrepancies can be so explained. Others could have occurred because Chesnutt often revised letters before sending them; there would sometimes be two or three handwritten versions of the same letter in the Fisk Collection. It is not unlikely that in the final draft Chesnutt included some sentences and phrases and made other changes that do not appear in the copies he kept. Most of the discrepancies, however, are occasioned by the omission of a word or phrase or by the rearrangement or rewording of sentences.

After Helen Chesnutt died in 1969, the Rowfant Club of Cleveland made an important presentation of a smaller collection of Chesnutt papers to the Western Reserve Historical Society. Many Chesnutt letters can be located in recipient collections. These include the James Weldon Johnson Collection at the Beineke Rare Book and Manuscript Library of Yale University; the Century Collection at the New York Public Library; the Walter Hines Page Collection and the Houghton Mifflin Collection at the Houghton Library at Harvard; the Booker T. Washington papers at the University of Maryland; the Hamilton Wright Mabie Papers, the Carter G. Woodson Collection, and the National Association of Colored People Papers at the Library of Congress; the John Bruce Collection at the Schomburg Library; the Benjamin G. Brawley Papers, the Jesse E. Moorland Papers, and the Joel E. Spingarn Papers at Howard University; the George A. Myers Papers at the Ohio Historical Society, Columbus; the George Washington Cable Papers at Tulane University; the John P. Green Papers at the Western Reserve Historical Society. the W. E. B. DuBois Papers at the University of Massachusetts. Some letters and memorabilia are held in private collections: Charles L. Blockson owns letters Chesnutt wrote to Horace Trauble; Mrs. Helen G. Cornwell owns pictures and books given to her by the Chesnutt family.

In all collections I have preferred letters sent and signed by Chesnutt and his correspondents to any other versions. I have used the handwritten journals instead of the edited journal entries in Helen Chesnutt's biography. Still, Ms. Chesnutt provides the only information on many details of her father's life, and in some instances the only records. I have therefore used her material, but cautiously, when it seemed in keeping with the thrust of the most reliable evidence. This is a matter of judgment rendered difficult because selection has occurred in most collections; some letters and copies of letters between correspondents appear in one collection and do not appear in the initiating or receiving collection, while other letters appear in both collections.

Several persons living in Cleveland at the time of the preparation of this biography knew Chesnutt; most of those contacted willingly supplied recollections and information. I am indebted to Ellen Holland Keller, instructor in English Literature at Western Reserve University. Ms. Keller interviewed members of legal firms with which Chesnutt was associated and the proprietor of the bookstore Chesnutt frequented. She visited places where Chesnutt lived and worked, supplying impressions and details; she provided valuable guidance to source materials. In the course of several visits to Cleveland, I talked with members of Chesnutt's family: they were Ms. Helen G. Cornwell, stepdaughter of Chesnutt's cousin John P. Green; Ms. Louise Evans, stepdaughter of Chesnutt's brother Lewis; Dr. John Slade, Chesnutt's son-in-law, who married his daughter Dorothy.

I was fortunate to interview other persons whose public and private lives were associated with that of Chesnutt. I am grateful to Rowena and Russell Jelliffe, Directors of Karamu; their careful and generous efforts to supply material broadened this study. Russell W. Davis, a long-time friend and associate of Chesnutt and his family, enriched the work immeasurably by providing his remembrances and by permitting me to review and use materials from his private library.

Other individuals supplied valuable information and materials: James Garcia of International Business Machines interviewed Richard Gillespie, Public Relations Officer of the *Wall Street Journal*, at the offices of Dow Jones & Company in New York. W. L. Andrews of the Department of English Literature of the University of North Carolina supplied genealogical materials. M. Sauzedde, mayor of Thiers, France, a village which is a sister city of Fayetteville, North Carolina, provided an important source book, John A. Oates's *The Story of Fayetteville and the Upper Cape Fear;* it was then out of print and difficult to obtain in the United States.

The Cleveland Public Library, the Howard University Library, the Fayetteville Public Library, the Schomburg Library, and the Library of Fayetteville State University called my attention to materials in their possession. I am particularly appreciative of the skillful assistance of Mrs. Virginia Hawley, Curator of Collections of the Western Reserve Historical Society; her knowledgeable guidance led to the discovery of articles and other items, some in other collections under her care, and some in distant places. I appreciate the patient assistance and the gracious hospitality offered me by the staff of the Fisk University Library during the two summer periods I spent in Nashville.

Chesnutt published many articles and stories in magazines; many of these are available at the Library of the University of Chicago. Stories published in the early years of Chesnutt's career in *Puck* and *Tid-Bits* can be located in the New York Public Library; this library possesses complete holdings of newspapers published during the six months of Chesnutt's residency there, including the *New York Mail and Express* for which Chesnutt wrote financial reviews. The scrapbooks that Chesnutt kept contain newspaper clippings of reviews of his writings; these and manuscripts of published and unpublished works are items of the Chesnutt Collection held at Fisk University.

Records of Cumberland County, North Carolina, may be studied in the Archives at Raleigh. The *Cleveland City Directory* and issues of

Branson's *North Carolina Business Directory* held at the University of Chicago proved informative. Chesnutt himself preserved pamphlets and programs that are in the Fisk or Western Reserve Historical Society collections. Boston, Washington, and Cleveland newspaper articles are preserved in those cities and in university libraries, as well as in Historical Society collections in Cleveland and in Columbus, Ohio.

It is regrettable that certain works Chesnutt sent to publishers and mentioned in letters have disappeared. Nowhere was it possible to locate the book of children's stories Chesnutt sent to Houghton Mifflin, the "book" *Aunt Hagar's Children,* which went to Small Maynard and Company, the "Valentines," which Chesnutt told the Arthur D. Clark Company he would send soon, or the story "The Sisters," which the *Pittsburgh Courier* wanted to serialize.* Since Chesnutt kept everything it is puzzling that these manuscripts have disappeared. Hopefully further efforts may uncover them.

*Letters documenting these titles are: Houghton Mifflin to Charles W. Chesnutt, 1928?, Houghton Library, Harvard University; *Pittsburgh Courier* to Charles W. Chesnutt, March 10, 1924, CC, WRHS, Container 1, Folder 4; Arthur D. Clark Company to Charles W. Chesnutt, Aug. 22, 1922, CC, WRHS, Container 1, Folder 2; Charles W. Chesnutt to Baer, Sept. 1, 1922, CC, WRHS, Container 1, Folder 2; and Small Maynard & Co. to Charles W. Chesnutt, Aug. 8, 1919, CC, WRHS, Container 1, Folder 1.

INDEX

Adams, Cyrus Field, 213
Adams, Henry, 201
Adams, Oscar Fay, 158
Addams, Jane, 245
African Encyclopedia, 253
African Methodist Episcopal Zion
  Church, 37, 40
Aldrich, Thomas Baily, 118, 150
Allen, Dr. Dudley Peter, 245–46
Allen, James Lane, 154, 158
American Missionary Society, 36
American Negro Academy, 256
Anderson, Charles W., 213, 235
Anderson, Robert, 238
Angell, Ernest, 267–68
Appomattox Court House, 33
Aristotle, 63
Atlanta Constitution, 158
Atlanta University, 163
Atlantic Monthly
  Chesnutt's reaction to, 156
  Chesnutt's stories published by,
    118, 141, 143, 153, 155, 229
  editors of, 148, 150
  Howells's article published by,
    164
Ayler, Mr., 50

Baird, General, 32
Baker, Newton D., 208
  appointed Secretary of War,
    261
  considered as possible Supreme
    Court Judge, 275–76
  mayor of Cleveland, 239, 247
  reelection of, 259
Baker, Ray Stannard, 192
Banks, Nancy, 165
Barber (character in *The Marrow
  of Tradition*), 189, 191
Bash, Julia, 119
"The Beacon Biographies," 159–60

Beime, F. J., 93
Bentley, Charles E., 235
Berbeist, Roger, 92
Bethel Literary and Historical
  Association, 242
The Birth of a Nation, 262–63
Black Code, 34–35, 39
Blaine, Senator James G., 67, 106
Blyden, Dr. Edward, 127
Board of Negro Ministers, 143
Boardman, Samuel W., 209
Bone, Robert, 200
Book Buyer, 158
Bookman, 158
Boston Guardian, 157, 219
Boston Literary and Historical
  Society, 236
Boston Transcript
  Chesnutt published in, 157, 236
  Chesnutt's reaction to, 224
  editors of, 166, 187, 210
  review of Chesnutt, 163, 238
"The Bouquet," 151, 164
Bowen, J. W. E., 235
Brawley, Benjamin G., 270
Briggs, Dr. Charles, 246
Brown, Roy M., 196
Brown, Sterling, 197–98
Brown, William M., 221, 239
Brown, William Wells, 81
Browne, Hugh M., 223, 235
Bruce, Senator Blanche, 66, 218
Bruce, J. E., 211
Bryant, David, 36
Bryant, Rowena, 184
Bulkley, Robert, 273
Burton, Harold, 247
Burton, Theodore E., 212
A Business Career, 150–52

Cable, George Washington
  correspondence with Chesnutt,

113–14, 287
friendship with Chesnutt, 120–35
opinion of Chesnutt, 185–86
stories written by, 168
Cade, Waddle, 179, *See also* Census Records
Cade, William, 19, 181
Cain, Susan, 37
Cape Fear River, 25, 44, 174
Carnegie, Andrew, 223
Carolina Observer, 27
Carteret, Major, 188–91
Case Western Reserve University, 232
Casino Roller Rink, 105
Cassidy, Anne Joyce, 267
"A Cause Celebre," 94
Census Records, 174–82
Centennial History of Cleveland, 147
Century
    Chesnutt's essay rejected by, 131
    Chesnutt's reaction to, 122
    editors of, 119–20, 155, 185
    controversy caused by, 134–35
Chamberlin, Joseph Edgar, 166–67, 187, 210
Charles Orr School, 10
Charlotte, North Carolina, 47, 59
Chesnutt & Moore, 266
Chesnutt, Andrew Jackson (brother), 19, 230. *See also* Census Records
Chesnutt, Andrew Jackson (father), 19, 25–30, 35, 55, 58. *See also* Census Records
Chesnutt, Dallas (uncle), 19, 107
Chesnutt, Dorothy (daughter), 139, 230–33, 248
Chesnutt, Edwin (son), 8 (photo),

106, 218, 230–32
Chesnutt, Ethel (daughter), 8 (photo), 19, 79, 216–18, 232
Chesnutt, Helen (daughter), 8 (photo), 19, 79, 216–18, 231, 271–72, 287
Chesnutt, Lewis (brother), 3 (photo), 19, 52–55, 230–31, *See also* Census Records
Chesnutt, Lilly (sister), 19, 48, 115
Chesnutt, Mary Ochiltree (cousin, stepmother), 19, 48, 57
Chesnutt, Susan Perry (wife), 15 (photo), 19, 63, 79, 106–7, 118, 140, 162, 231–32, 272, 275
Chicago Defender, 270
Chicago Ledger, 116
Childs, Nick, 119
Christian Union, 64–65
Civil Rights Act of 1875, 42–43
Clarendon Bridge, 33
Clews, Henry W., 92
Cleveland, Ohio, 25, 100–35, 147
Cleveland Council of Sociology, 238, 242
Cleveland Chamber of Commerce, 244
Cleveland City Directory, 113
Clevelander, 274
Cleveland Gazette, 143, 236, 269
Cleveland, Grover, 106, 147
Cleveland Hall of Fame, 283
Cleveland Journal, 245
Cleveland Leader, 110, 215
Cleveland, Moses, 106
Cleveland Plain Dealer, 105, 241, 272
Cleveland Social Circle, 119, 153
Cleveland Topics, 265
Cleveland Urban League, 244
Cleveland Voice, 117
Clifford, Carrie W., 225

Clinton, George, 235
The Colonel's Dream, 92
  plot of, outlined, 194–96
  publication of, 207, 216, 234
  review of, 226
Colored American, 211
"A Complete Race Amalgamation
  Likely to Occur," 168
Conjure stories, 53, 108, 152–55
The Conjure Woman, 155–58,
  199, 203
"The Conjurer's Revenge," 118
Conners, William R., 244
Crisis, 253–54
The Critic, 163, 211
Crumpacker, Edgar D., 212, 236
Cuba, 232, 267
Cumberland County, 30, 174
Cuyahoga River, 101, 260, 274

Dabney, W. P., 275
Daily Record, 191
Darrow, Clarence, 213, 270
"Dave's Neckliss," 141
Davis, Elder, 19–20, 72–73
Davis, Harry E., 244, 261
Davis, Jefferson, 243
Davis, Russell H., 261
De Forest, John William, 202
de Ropp, Baron, 92
Democrats, 39, 80, 142
Deneen, Charles S., 213
Detroit Free Press, 116
Dictionary of American Authors,
  158
Dixon, Molly, 153
Dixon, Reverend Thomas, 202,
  213, 236
"The Doll," 253
Doubleday, Page & Company,
  159, 187
Douglass, Frederick, 79, 160–61, 225

Dow, Jones, and Company, 91, 97
"The Dr.'s Wife," 116
Du Bois, W. E. B., 163, 215–17,
  249–56
"The Dumb Witness," 151
Dunbar, Paul Lawrence, 203

Edmonds, Helen G., 190–91
Edmonds, Richard Hathaway, 202
Edwards, Harry Stillwell, 134, 202
Edwards, Johnathan, 41
1867 Constitution of North
  Carolina, 38
Elam, William C., 93
Eliot, Charles, 221
Emmanuel Church 118, 140, 231
England, 146
Europe, 144–46

Fact Stranger than Fiction, 184
Family Fiction, 117, 134
Fauset, Jesse, 272
Faust, 78
Fayetteville, North Carolina, 25–44
Fayetteville Colored Normal
  School, 19, 61, 78, 84–85
Fayetteville Hotel, 63
Fayetteville National Bank, 19, 85
The Fayetteville Observer, 85, 111
Fayetteville State University, 37
Fetters, William, 194–95
Field, Cyrus W., 91
The First Glass, 49
Flora Stone Mather College for
  Women, 118
Flory, Walter C., 268
A Fool's Errand, 70, 192, 197
"The Forgotten Man," 149
Fortune, T. Thomas, 148, 214,
  235
Forum, 131, 149–50
Fowler, Frank, 174, 183

297

299

ABOUT THE AUTHOR

*F*rances Richardson Keller received her Bachelor of Arts degree at Sarah Lawrence College, an M.A. at the University of Toledo, and her Ph.D. at the University of Chicago (in 1973). For the last four years she has taught American History, Black History, and Women's History at San Jose State University. Before that time she taught at Chicago City College, at the University of Illinois, Chicago Circle, and at the Northwest Campus of the University of Indiana.

Her preoccupation with history began long before that, however, as she recollects here: "No one can say with precision when an informal education begins. But I recall sitting on the ledge at the bottom of the doors opening onto a balcony off the upstairs library of my family's old red brick home on Dayan Street in Lowville, New York. I must have been eight or nine, for my feet just touched the floor. I had eagerly read every word of a little brown American history book. Yet a feeling of great disappointment came over me; I realized I could take no part in those adventures, for they were in our past. They seemed alive—but finished."

The rest of Dr. Keller's life has, by her own admission, been a successful if turbulent quest to involve herself in those historical events that were her present. Her journey from Lowville, in time and space and human dimensions, took her to the campus of the University of Chicago in the mid-1960s, where a general social unrest and an acute racial dissatisfaction were daily fare. In her studies she learned the dreams and despairs of black and white Americans concerned with slavery and its consequences, while daily she faced decisions involving racial difficulties affecting her life and the lives of her children. She came to see that the perils of poverty, like those of ethnic and racial disadvantage, were expectable precipitations out of the past; and with that vision came a per-

303

sonal urgency about the resolution of issues thus forcefully brought to her attention.

"In my explorations I had come upon the story of Charles Waddell Chesnutt, an American of Afro-American descent who made a decision to eschew compromise and to pursue a commitment to human justice." Dr. Keller's book attests her growing understanding that our history is crucial in forming our identities as persons and as a people, as well as her efforts to take her part in the compelling adventure of our present.

Brigham Young University Press, a member of the
American Association of University Presses, shares fully
the AAUP dedication to excellence in university press
publishing.

At BYU Press we focus mainly—but not solely—on
Western regional studies and early childhood education.

Authors with manuscripts in these and related areas
may submit queries to Managing Editor, BYU Press,
218 UPB, Brigham Young University, Provo, UT 84602,
USA.